D1064151

The Developing Economies and Japan

4

The Developing Economies and Japan

Lessons in Growth

Saburo Okita

UNIVERSITY OF TOKYO PRESS

The publication of this book was assisted by a grant from The Japan Foundation.

UTP 3033-47123-5149
ISBN 0-86008-271-7
Printed in Japan

Second Printing, 1981

Contents

Preface vii

Part I Developing Countries in the World Economy

Current Thinking about Development 5

An Integrated Approach to Food, Nutrition, and Economic Growth 13

Doubling Rice Production in Asia 23

Dynamic Division of Labor and the International Order 47

Transfer of Resources to Developing Countries 59

Part II The Japanese Example

Developing Economies and the Japanese Experience 93

Causes of Rapid Growth in Postwar Japan and Their Implications for Newly Developing Economies 105

Relationship between Population and Development: The Japanese Experience 149

The Experience of Economic Planning in Japan 195

Part III Japan's Relations with the Developing World

North-South Dialogue 229

Economic Relations between Japan and Latin America 239

Comparison of Two High-Growth Economies: Japan and Brazil 243

The Japan-ASEAN Relationship: Conflict and Interdependence 253

Index 279

Preface

As the 1980s begin, the world's political and economic state is one of uncertainty. Although many held high hopes that the 1970s would be a decade of progress toward a world of peace and prosperity, and indeed some auspicious events and trends can be pointed out, a number of new problems also appeared which have grave implications in every corner of the world.

The question of energy resources and their development is one that affects both developing and developed nations, and promises to change their interrelations. The problems of food resources, of population growth, of trade balance, of currency exchange rates—all these issues are relevant to every nation, but are of crucial importance in the developing nations, which are also involved in their own struggles to survive and stay afloat in an increasingly uncertain world environment.

The essays collected in this volume are addressed to the question of economic development—how it can be invited and encouraged, and how it can occur without threatening national integrity and traditions.

For some years, both on behalf of the Japanese government and as a private individual working in economic research at the national and the international level, I have been involved with the problems of economic development and economic planning. In the course of my work, I have traveled widely and talked with a great many people—government officials, economists, bankers, farmers, scholars—about the problems of growth and development.

As an economist, I have studied these problems in a general way, and have often been asked to talk or write about economic development and how it can best be fostered in those nations which are struggling to reach a minimal level of prosperity for all of their people. In addition, because I am from Japan, I have often been asked how the experience of economic growth in Japan is relevant to the rest of the developing world.

Japan occupies a unique position as a sort of pivot between the developing and developed economies. As an industrialized and economically advanced coutry, it has obligations and ties to the rest of the developed world. At the same time, however, as an Asian nation and one whose growth is a relatively recent phenomenon, Japan is in a position to share its historical experience and its expertise with those nations, in Asia, Africa, and Latin America, who are traveling down the same path toward industrialization and growth.

The Japanese economy, of course, is facing severe problems of its own as these words are written: its dependence on imported oil for energy has made it especially vulnerable in the current worldwide energy crisis. But at the same time its historical experience as a developing nation would seem to have some relevance to the Third World; and indeed many of those nations are looking to Japan for whatever it can offer in the way of advice and aid.

The essays collected herein were written for the most part during the past six or seven years. Many were written to be delivered as speeches or papers at international conferences on economic development; others were written at the invitation of private or governmental bodies in individual countries. My purpose in publishing them in this form is to gather together in one place a record of my own experiences in economic planning and the knowledge that I have gained from my associations with people all over the world. If my work can contribute in any way to progress along the road to peace and prosperity for all the world's people, I will be well satisfied.

April 1980 SABURO OKITA

The Developing Economies and Japan

PART I
Developing Countries in the World Economy

Current Thinking about Development

At a recent meeting of the United Nations Committee for Development Planning (CDP) concerning a world development strategy, one thing that came out was that there are divergent issues in developing countries. Although there are common organizations such as the Group of 77, which emerged from the first UNCTAD meeting in 1964 on the basis of solidarity among developing countries, we must also recognize the diversity of stages of development and the nature of the economic issues being confronted. I have suggested, therefore, that there should be different strategies for different groups of countries rather than just a single strategy for the entire developing world. Broadly speaking, we need to consider four groups of developing countries.

One of the groups is made up of the oil-exporting countries with surplus current accounts. (This does not include all oil-exporting countries: in OPEC as a whole the surplus has declined sharply from some $60 billion in 1974 to somewhere around $18 billion in 1978, and many of the OPEC countries have turned into deficit countries rather than surplus countries.) Their problem is how to utilize surplus capital more effectively for development. They need technical advice and know-how imports because in internal development they are still very much underdeveloped.

The second group is the rapidly industrializing countries. This group—called "newly industrializing countries" (NICs) by OECD—includes 11 countries: South Korea, Taiwan, Hong Kong, and Singapore in Asia; Mexico and Brazil in Latin America;

This chapter is the text of a speech delivered at the United Nations Centre for Regional Development, Nagoya, to the Seminar on Rural-Urban Transformation and Regional Development Planning, November 1978. Reprinted with the permission of the United Nations Centre for Regional Development.

and Spain, Portugal, Greece, Turkey, and Yugoslavia in Europe. The common feature of these countries is the very rapid process of industrial growth and rapid expansion of the export of manufactured products. They are taking advantage of an abundant labor supply and relatively low wages compared to the industrial countries, and they have developed a comparative advantage in the world market for labor-intensive products such as textiles and many other manufactured goods. Some of them are already moving into more sophisticated industrial products such as electronics, machinery, shipbuilding, and steel and have started exporting these products. For this group the necessity is not soft loans or grants but rather commercial or near-commercial loans. They also need access to markets for their manufactured products in the developed countries and access to capital markets as well.

The third group of countries is made up of those which depend upon primary product exports. We can call these the intermediate developing countries. Most of them are countries with per-capita GDP over $200. For these countries the necessary measures are commodity agreements, the establishment of common funds, and the stabilization of export earnings (STABEX) and the resulting incomes. Some of the third group countries are moving into the second category of rapidly industrializing countries. The Philippines, Thailand, Malaysia, and possibly Indonesia are developing in this direction.

The fourth group is the poor countries. By World Bank figures these are the countries with less than $200 per-capita GDP. For these poor countries the so-called basic human needs approach may be the important concept. There have been many reports prepared on this topic. I remember in working on the Pearson Report* that emphasis was placed on giving aid to those countries which could attain viable economic growth, with aid given according to certain performance criteria such as success in accelerating export expansion, which then enables countries to acquire necessary foreign exchange to buy necessary imports. Another criterion was the rate of domestic savings for financing development. The idea was that support to these countries would aid them in attaining viable economic growth so as to enable them to gradu-

* Lester B. Pearson: *Partners in Development: Report of the Commission on International Development* (New York: Praeger, 1969).

ate from the aid recipient stage and perhaps even to eventually become aid givers. If countries can graduate from the recipient stage one after another, then the world will see better conditions and the aid-receiving countries will decline in number. This is also desirable from a political point of view in that the continual dependence of poor countries on aid is somewhat demoralizing.

This concept is what we may call the efficiency principle of assistance and has been criticized by development experts and developing countries, particularly because such an approach may aggravate discrepancies between poor developing countries and more fortunate developing countries, with the gap widening and the more fortunate ones closing the gap with the developed or industrialized countries. The Sussex Group, in particular Richard Jolly and others, were critical of this Pearson Report approach, and eventually the International Labor Organization (ILO) advocated the so-called basic human needs approach.

There have been many criticisms of the basic needs approach as well. Some Latin American countries are critical of it because they are already in the middle- and higher-income category and they may be disqualified as recipients if the basic-needs criterion is strictly applied. They are also suspicious about outside intervention into domestic policy, especially with regard to the very touchy aspects of distribution of income within the country. Furthermore, some countries are suspicious about rich countries' giving aid for basic needs in lieu of supporting industrial growth which may eventually compete with the industrialized countries.

Although there are such criticisms of the basic needs approach, many countries view it as a necessity, at least in their own domestic policy, in order to maintain political stability and to attain social justice. Many countries have become more and more interested in this approach.

At the same time, in many countries cultivable land is limited, and the so-called "population explosion" the past three or four decades has resulted also in a labor force "explosion" which will have to be absorbed into some type of employment. In the European countries, industrialization was able to absorb surplus labor or outlets were created for surplus labor through the discovery of new land. Overall population growth has been about one-half the rate of current economic growth in the developed countries. In Japan also, which began industrializing somewhat earlier than other Asian countries, the non-agricultural sector was able to absorb the surplus labor from agriculture, and for several decades before World War II the agricultural population was constant. Around 1880 Japan had about 80 percent of its labor force in agriculture; about 30 million people, including family dependents, lived in rural areas. By 1940 the nation's population had increased to somewhat over 70 million. While the percentage of the labor force engaged in agriculture declined to about 40 percent, the rural population remained about 30 million. There was not much migration out of the country.

In other Asian countries, however, the rapidly increasing labor force—sometimes growing as much as 3 percent annually—will have to be absorbed domestically, and the non-agricultural sectors, such as industry and services, are not growing rapidly enough to absorb new entrants into the labor force. Agriculture will have to absorb at least part of the increasing number of workers. This is a very different picture from the historical experience of Japan or the European countries. Even here, however, there are differences among the developing countries of Africa, Latin America, and Asia. In most of Latin America and Africa there still are very large areas to cultivate, and the absolute population is relatively small compared to Asia. Thus this surplus labor and labor absorption problem is most crucial in Asia.

Some time ago, J. K. Galbraith wrote that there should be different diagnoses for different continents concerning the most essential supplies for development: in Africa it should be textbooks, in Latin America land reform, and in Asia machinery. I do not agree with his last remarks concerning Asia. Machinery may apply to the industrialization of some Asian countries, but for countries with an increasing labor force where agriculture is still predominant, the creation of employment opportunities is the most basic and essential necessity.

How to solve this labor absorption problem is a very crucial question. In several of the Asian developing countries the introduction of so-called high-yielding varieties of rice and other crops has resulted in higher output and yield, but it has not necessarily resulted in the spreading of employment among the labor force. Machinery is more obedient and more quiet than human workers, and the substitution of machinery for labor has sometimes taken place in areas which have had improved yields and production of agricultural products. So the question is how to introduce measures which increase output in agriculture as well as increasing labor opportunities in rural districts. This is a crucial problem which many of the Asian countries are now facing.

I have suggested that high-yielding varieties, introduced through irrigation in order to allow for double-cropping in large parts of South and Southeast Asia, might bring about increased employment as well as greater output in rice production.* The main idea is to introduce various irrigation schemes, particularly for rice paddies. There is a regular relationship between the percentage of paddy fields with irrigation/drainage and per-hectare yield of rice. In the case of Japan, 98 percent of paddy rice fields have controlled water supply and drainage, and yield per hectare is around 6 tons. In South Korea and Taiwan, water control systems are at 70 to 80 percent, and their yield is around 4 to 5 tons. (South Korea has recently exceeded the Japanese level of 6 tons; however, it is not yet clear whether this level can be maintained.) In most of South and Southeast Asia, irrigation and drainage control is only at about 30 to 35 percent, and a very large part of even this irrigation is inadequate. Adequately irrigated areas comprise only around 3 or 4 percent of total paddy fields. The yield of rice is about 2 tons per hectare, or one-third that of Japan. Since irrigation is a rather expensive investment, I felt that as an international scheme of development assistance, irrigation would be a suitable project.

Professor Shigeru Ishikawa has produced a paper on labor absorption in Asian agriculture, and one of his findings was that human labor applied to paddy production in Japan was reportedly nearly 525 man-days per hectare.[1] This was about three times higher than most of South and Southeast Asia, the same multiple as the yield. This may indicate that there is some room for introducing very labor-intensive types of agriculture with improved yields per

* "Doubling Rice Production in Asia" (Okita and Takase), reprinted in this volume beginning on p. 23.

[1] Asian and Pacific Development Institute, Bangkok, 1978.

hectare; that is, without lowering living standards, there may be ways of absorbing substantial numbers of people into agriculture. This is probably the key factor in the agrarian countries of Asia.

Another area of concern is how to absorb more labor into the urban areas in productive, not consumptive, employment opportunities. Sometimes labor must be absorbed by consumptive measures, but in countries which are poor and where average incomes are low, if additional employment does not produce additional output, then the average income level may go down. So the creation of productive employment in both rural and urban areas is a crucial issue in this part of the world.

In many countries, labor-intensive industrialization has been emphasized, but sometimes a dilemma is faced when labor-intensive products are not competitive in the world market. This may also be true in some cases in agriculture: rice production in Asia may be more expensive than in Australia, for example, with its plentiful land and capability for mechanization, or in North America with its large-scale mechanized production; but if sufficient rice is not produced in Asia, it will have to be imported. Importing rice will not aid in labor absorption and it will raise the problem of how to finance such imports or how to earn foreign exchange.

Some industries face a similar dilemma. But unlike the case of agriculture, there is room for selecting a type of manufacturing which is by nature labor-intensive. Part of the problem of the dynamic international division of labor is that the labor-surplus countries are moving toward labor-intensive industries and are exporting part of their products to more developed countries with higher wages. The most typical case is the export of textiles from newly developing countries. Here the problem is import restrictions set by the richer countries. It is a very undesirable development when richer countries start restricting imports of products in which the developing countries have a comparative advantage, but throughout the world this trend is increasing, and developing countries will have to work out measures to solve this difficulty. One is to widen the scope of cooperation among developing countries, mutually utilizing their markets by organizing a kind of common market. Another is to expand domestic production and domestic consumption. Furthermore, there will have to be some positive measures to offset the working of the market forces—in some cases to protect domestic production from outside competition in order to maintain employment.

So labor absorption in both urban and agricultural activities requires a very deliberate search for policy measures and policy planning. Policy formulation will have to be based on a bottom-up approach rather than on a top-down approach because there are many areas in which the experience of the developed countries cannot be applied to the developing countries of today. Also, many policies applicable to Latin America may not be applicable to Asia where the population density per hectare of cultivated area is significantly higher. In Japan before World War II no one talked about labor productivity; instead they stressed per-hectare productivity because there was always the pressure of labor on land and productivity meant increasing the yield of land rather than the saving of labor. Only when industrialization proceeded after the war was the labor productivity concept introduced in connection with economizing or saving labor for agricultural production.

Neither, according to the agricultural economist Professor Seiichi Tohata, did Japan have the concept of full employment before World War II. Instead the emphasis was on the concept of *total* employment, which meant that in both the rural and urban sectors everyone somehow held some job but all were working for very low incomes. This concept of total employment may have some relevance for the many Asian countries today which are under the very heavy pressure of a large labor force.

These are some of the issues I wanted to mention here, and in concluding I would like to introduce some calculations from a global point of view in relation to this basic needs approach. In a recent article Paul Streeton and S. J. Burki estimated the total amount of capital necessary to make up the shortfall in basic needs.[2] Their calculations were based on estimates of shortages in food, water, sewage disposal, housing, health, and education to meet basic needs. The result was something like a $12 billion annual investment spread over 20 years from 1980 to the year 2000. Including recurrent costs, the combined figure equals a $25 to 30 billion annual shortfall in meeting basic human needs. This is less than 10 percent of the annual $400 billion world military ex-

[2] Paul Streeton and S. J. Burki: "Basic Needs; Some Issues," *World Development* 6:3, March 1978.

penditure. Although meeting basic minimum needs should be accomplished primarily through the efforts of the countries themselves, the elimination of absolute poverty from the entire world is a joint responsibility of both the developed and developing countries. If people of the world would pay more attention to this aspect and look at the figures which show that relatively small expenditures could meet the shortfalls for basic needs, then people might have second thoughts about the possibility of eliminating poverty from the world. It is not an impossible undertaking if more international cooperation is combined with the efforts being made by individual countries themselves.

An Integrated Approach to Food, Nutrition, Population, and Economic Growth

I am not very sure if I should have accepted the invitation to lecture at this time, when world food policy has come to a crossroad of a very fundamental nature. However, I venture to present some ideas in the hope that they will serve, at least in a small way, to clarify the major world issues we are facing today.

The most fundamental issue now, it seems to me, is whether we should anticipate a "surplus" or a "shortage" in the future world food supply. I am aware, of course, that the key issues in this session of the FAO Conference are, one, international agricultural adjustment, and two, world food security policy. These two issues, however, contain some contradictory elements. In case we assume, basically, a surplus of food in the future world market, adjustments based on the rational international division of labor deserve added attention. On the other hand, if we assume, basically, a food shortage in the world—that is, the second alternative—food security policy should receive priority.

When I read the McDougall memoranda this time I was deeply impressed by his foresight and his humanistic motivation in looking at world food problems some 30 to 40 years ago. His major concern was, as I interpret it, to bring the food and nutrition problems together and, by pursuing a policy of better nutrition for the poor and undernourished people, to find a solution to the problem of a world surplus of food, with an expanding demand for these commodities. At the same time, if governments followed freer trade policies and reduced protection for domestic agriculture, cheaper

This chapter is the text of the 1973 McDougall Memorial Lecture of the United Nations Food and Agriculture Organization. It is reprinted with the permission of the FAO.

food would become available and it would be easier for low-income people to purchase better food and improve their nutritional standards.

During the 40 years since the McDougall memorandum of 1935, the world food situation has under gone substantial changes. Better nutrition for poorer people in rich countries has been accomplished to a considerable degree, together with a more equitable distribution of income, and the consumption of food, in particular high-quality food such as meat and dairy products, has greatly increased. The trouble is, however, that such a process of improvement of nutrition seldom has gone beyond national boundaries, and a sharp contrast between the nutritional levels in rich and poor countries has persisted. International trade in agricultural commodities has partially been liberalized, but we are still far from having free trade for those commodities. Moreover, as a result of the worldwide food shortage of the very recent past, advocates of greater protection for agriculture have been encouraged to strengthen their position on the grounds of national security.

The world is now facing the dual problem of adjusting domestic agriculture for better efficiency and of increasing domestic production, sometimes regardless of cost, in preparation for a possible food supply shortage in global terms. From McDougall's time until very recently, excluding the wartime shortages, the world food market has generally experienced a surplus. Though there was a basic shortage of food in poor countries from the nutritional point of view, this could not appear as effective demand because of the lack of purchasing power of these countries.

Food and Nutrition in Japan

Let me describe some aspects of the postwar experience with food and nutrition problems in Japan. Food imports have been greatly increased in the course of the last two decades thanks to the ready availability of food in the world market and Japan's increased earnings of foreign exchange by expanding export trade, particularly of industrial products. Although the domestic production of rice (which is the main staple cereal for the Japanese) has been maintained at self-sufficiency level, production of wheat, barley, soybeans, etc., was substantially reduced and replaced by imports.[1] Imports of animal food grains such as maize and sorghum expanded from almost nil in the mid-1950s to nearly 10 million tons in 1972. This was necessary to meet a sharply increasing domestic demand for meat, eggs, milk, and other high-quality food products.

Because of the uninterrupted supply of foodstuffs from abroad until very recently, few Japanese felt insecurity in depending heavily on imports. Now, after experiencing a worldwide food shortage, many people have started arguing for higher self-sufficiency in food supply. However, experts are pointing out that, in order to attain self-sufficiency in food at the present level of consumption, nearly twice as much land would have to be added to the presently cultivated area in Japan, and this is physically impossible even if cost aspects are disregarded.

Agriculture in Japan has thus undergone a very far-reaching change in the course of the last two decades. The labor force in agriculture declined from 35.9 percent of the total in 1950 to 14.3 percent in 1971. Agriculture's share in the net domestic product declined from 19.8 percent to 4.7 percent during the same period. Adjustment of agriculture to such a rapid and extensive change was a tremendous task. Rapid expansion of manufacturing industries and services, increase in the share of non-farm income of farm households, improvement of transport systems connecting rural areas to urban centers, and other factors external to agriculture aided in the process of adjustment to a large extent. With the rising per-capita national income, from U.S. $250 in 1956 to $1,518 in 1970 ($1,740 and $2,284 in 1971 and 1972 respectively), the nutritional standards of the people have steadily improved. Intake of animal protein increased from 22.6 grams per person per day in 1956 to 34.2 grams in 1970. Intake of fat and oil increased from 21.8 grams to 46.5 grams during the same period. Incidence of diseases such as tuberculosis and beriberi, as well as infant mortality, declined sharply as nutritional standards improved. According to Toshio Ohiso, Director of the National Institute of Nutrition, malnutrition practically disappeared in the late 1950s

[1] Wheat production declined from 1,531,000 tons in 1960 to 440,000 tons in 1971, and barley production was reduced from 1,206,000 tons to 364,000 tons during the same period.

when per-capita national income rose to around $300. Dr. Ohiso also states:

> The Japanese nutritional experience has potential value for other countries. It illustrates a high level of nutritional state and national health attainable with a largely vegetarian diet, high in carbohydrate, low in fat, and using fish and animal food as complementary sources of protein. This is significant for developing countries that must select specific goals for adequate national nutrition and for advanced countries that have the freedom to change their diets.[2]

According to a recent announcement of Japan's Ministry of Welfare, average life expectancy reached 70.49 for males and 75.92 for females in 1972; those are about 25 years longer than the life expectancies of Japanese 40 years ago. Also instrumental in the remarkable improvement in health and nutritional conditions in postwar Japan were vigorous promotional efforts for dissemination and demonstration of nutritional requirements, especially during the earlier postwar years when the food and nutritional situation was at a critical stage. The government passed a Dietitians Law and a Nutrition Improvement Law, and measures such as training dietitians, employing dietitians for mass-feeding program, initiating a national school lunch program, conducting a national nutrition survey every year, setting a recommended national nutritional standard, promoting so-called "Kitchen Car" activities for demonstration purposes, etc., were adopted. In addition, promotional activities for better nutrition have been conducted in tandem with the dissemination of knowledge about family planning and contraception, and this has been effective as it reduces psychological obstacles for housewives to participate in such activities.

Food and Nutrition in the Developing World

I am afraid I have dwelt too long on Japan's recent experiences.

[2] "Diet and Nutritional Status of Japan," *American Journal of Clinical Nutrition*, July 1968.

It was not because I wanted to boast about our accomplishment but because I am searching for some hints for the solution of world-wide problems by an integrated approach to nutrition, health, population, food, and income.

We find very often in developing countries a vicious circle of malnutrition and poverty. Food is like fuel for engines. Without a sufficient amount and adequate quality of fuel, engines will not work. Moreover, in the case of the human body there is a minimum requirement of calories just for keeping the body alive. Intake of calories over and above such a minimum can only be converted into work. If food is insufficient people cannot work efficiently. Moreover, insufficient food in terms of both quantity and quality during childhood affects the health conditions of the next generation. Malnutrition makes the human body susceptible to many kinds of disease, thus reducing the efficiency of work by individuals and by their society.

There is also a vicious circle of high birth-rate and poverty. If mothers suffer from malnutrition, infant mortality is high. Mothers want to bear a large number of children to insure against early death of their babies. If a society is very poor there will not be a sufficient number of hospitals or clinics. Communication and transportation will be inferior. Little electricity will be supplied to villages and the darkness of night will halt or hamper many social and economic activities. Illiteracy will stay high because of the malnutrition of children and financial difficulties in maintaining schools. Most people will stay in agriculture, in which the incentive for having a small family is not as strong as in cities. Thus, in a society where income is very low, the "infrastructure" for the implementation of an effective population policy does not exist.

When the average income keeps on rising and reaches a certain level, there seems to be a threshold where the birth rate starts a sharp decline. In view of the records of demographic changes in East Asian countries including Japan, this threshold is likely to be in the range of per-capita national income of $200 to $300. In the case of Latin American countries this threshold level seems to be higher than in East Asia. In China, judging from what I saw and heard in Peking when I visited there in April 1972, the birth rate seems to be declining sharply although their per-capita national income is estimated by foreign observers at around U.S. $100.

We observe in China that efforts to limit the family size are being made through various policy instruments. I venture to guess that for the effective lowering of the birth rate, a combination of the following four factors is important: first, determined effort by the government in implementing population policy: second, the spread of primary education; third, an adequate level of nutrition; and fourth, an adequate level of income.

Next year will be the United Nations Population Year, and the World Population Conference is to be held in Bucharest, in August. I hope very much that the Conference will take an integrated approach, especially in close cooperation with the FAO, to population problems. Personally, I have a strong sense of urgency about introducing effective measures to reduce the rate of increase in world population. As has been pointed out by several FAO studies in the past, there will be little hope for improved nutrition and food intake for many of the developing countries if the population keeps on increasing at the current rate. Here the time element is very crucial: if human society fails to introduce effective measures in controlling the growth of population, possibly during this decade, the question of food and population may become an almost insoluble problem.

Although there may be short-term fluctuations between surplus and shortage in world food supply, it seems to me that the long-term trend is toward shortage. If that is the case, we will have to build our food policy on that basis, as I mentioned in the earlier part of this lecture. Vigorous effort to increase food production as well as to reduce birth rates will be required. In addition, measures to prevent wasteful consumption of foodstuffs, better ways to preserve and store food, rational distribution of food based on nutritional requirements, and so forth will become necessary.

Working toward a Solution

Let me illustrate some of the policy measures to be derived from the above considerations.

First of all there must be adequate arrangements for providing emergency food resources. Dr. Boerma of FAO has already made a concrete proposal in this regard and I hope, personally at least, that his proposal will receive worldwide support. In view of the depletion of world food stocks, especially the diminishing surplus food stocks of the United States, there must be some arrangement, internationally agreed on, to prepare for possible food shortages in the future. This is of vital importance for food-deficient countries which depend on external supply for their survival. It is particularly important for low-income countries because the margin of subsistence is very thin in those countries and they are affected most adversely by world food shortages. Because of the limited availability of foreign exchange in these countries, they simply cannot buy high-priced foods.

Introduction of an effective food ration system will be necessary especially for low-income, food-deficient countries. This rationing system should be based on nutritional requirements and should prevent waste of food in upper-income groups at the expense of malnutrition in lower-income groups. A similar idea may have to be introduced internationally. In rich countries, intake of excess calories, protein, and fats is observable, and such excess intake often causes diseases. In future, rich countries may have to introduce policy measures for preventing wasteful consumption of foodstuffs.

Strategy for development assistance should also be reviewed on the basis of the above considerations. As I stated earlier, at least in the case of Japan, a per-capita national income of about $300 was the level at which malnutrition was practically eliminated. If a strict rationing system is introduced, this may be realized even at somewhat lower levels of income. The purpose of development assistance may have to be geared to the elimination of serious malnutrition all over the world by guaranteeing minimum nutritional and health standards for all people. This may require modifications in the underlying philosophy of the Pearson Commission report, for which I myself was partially responsible as one of the Commission members. The report, published as *Partners in Development* in 1969, emphasized the efficiency principle of aid in the sense that the aid-recipient countries should make the best use of aid for attaining higher rates of economic growth, larger domestic savings, and expanded export trade. The report emphasized the importance of self-help efforts of aid-recipient countries and expected those countries, in due course, to "graduate" one by one from the status of aid recipient.

Although the above idea is valid in substance, it may not be a sufficient condition for eliminating mass poverty from the entire world. If the efficiency principle of aid is applied too strictly and the developing countries with better economic performance in utilizing aid are given priority, there will be a widening gap in the level of incomes among developing countries. In the case of Japan, and possibly in many other countries, there is a system of equalization subsidy to local governments. This system guarantees that poorer local governments will automatically receive subsidies from the central government in order to meet the minimum requirements for local administration such as primary and secondary education, health measures, social security, etc. Extension of a similar idea transcending national boundaries may someday become a reality, although this seems rather remote given the prevailing attitude of the national governments today.

If the world cannot expect in the near future a large-scale food aid program based on the global welfare concept, the countries will have to find alternative possibilities. One such possibility is an adjustment of the industrial structure in both developing and developed countries. Because of rising wages, highly industrialized countries are losing their comparative advantages in many branches of industry—in particular, those in labor-intensive industries such as textiles. Moreover, social disincentives for physical production are increasing as people tend to consume more services than goods, and work discipline generally weakens as a society approaches affluence. On the other hand, in many of the developing countries, the supply of labor is still abundant and wages are still low. People are more work-oriented and the work efficiency is improving as general education spreads among people. Such a tendency will enable presently poor countries to start expanding their exports of manufactured goods in exchange for food imports. Several delegations attending the recent GATT Ministerial Conference held in Tokyo recommended a policy of increased exports of manufactured goods from developing countries and demanded the opening of the domestic market of developed countries for such exports. This will require structural adjustments of industries in developed countries but it will help to reduce rates of domestic inflation by substituting cheaper imported goods for high-cost domestic products. More important is that such a policy will enable developing countries to purchase necessary food from abroad.

Coming back to the nutritional aspects, in low-income countries efforts must be made to increase the intake of protein from cheaper sources such as pulses and fish. The soybean has been, and still is, a major component of the Japanese diet, as was dramatized by the recent "soybean shock" felt by the Japanese people when the United States government announced a temporary embargo on soybean exports. Higher priority must be given to pulses as an important source of protein. Another relatively inexpensive source of protein is fish meat. Mr. T. Hisamune, President of the Japan Marine Fishery Resources Research Centre, who gave an opening address at the Eighth Session of the FAO Committee on Fisheries last April, emphasized the importance of coastal and inland water fishery as an important method of obtaining animal protein in low-income countries. This type of fishery is usually operated by small-sized or family-based management. Until recently Japanese fishery was broadly based on such small-scale fishing, and in view of the widespread underutilization of fishery resources in coastal or inland water grounds, and of the serious shortage of animal protein in many of the developing countries, due attention should be paid to the potentiality of developing this type of fishing.

Lastly, there are the population problems. Most of the industrialized countries are gradually approaching zero population growth due to the steady decline in their birth rates. It would be desirable, however, to accelerate this process and reach a static population as early as possible in those countries in view of the high per-capita consumption of energy and other natural resources and the effect of this consumption on the environment. Developing countries are also expected to reduce the rate of population increase, although they will reach zero growth at a somewhat later stage than the developed countries in view of their present high rate of population growth. The question is how to shorten the transition period from a stage of high birth and high death rates to that of low birth and low death rates. Here an integrated attack on the problem will be needed, as mentioned earlier in this lecture.

The world food system is at a critical point. Shortages of food will be more serious than surpluses. If there is a danger of shortage, rather than surplus, apart from short-term fluctuations, we must realize that what we are doing now will have a far-reaching effect on future generations. We should be aware of the possible consequences of the conduct of our current generation on posterity.

Doubling Rice Production in Asia

Today, in the developing countries, which have about 70 percent of the world's population, there are acute food shortages. At the same time, the developed countries are suffering from a serious recession and lack of demand, and government policies are directed towards stimulating demand by providing increases in budgets for public works, encouraging housing construction and inducing private consumption.

According to a report of the Worldwatch Institute, "The Politics and Responsibilities of the North American Breadbasket," written by Lester Brown, there is a long-term trend for food deficits to increase in Asia, Africa, and other areas, as indicated in Table 1. The major source of supply of food grains is North America, and other continents are increasingly dependent on the supply from North America.

A recent study by the U.S. National Academy of Sciences on the long-range prospects of U.S. food production[1] indicates that

Table 1. The Changing Pattern of World Grain Trade

(million tons)

Year	North America	Oceania	Latin America	Africa	West Europe	East Europe & USSR	Asia	Total
1959/60	+ 39	+ 6	0	− 2	− 25	0	− 17	+ 1
1969/70	+ 56	+ 12	+ 4	− 5	− 30	0	− 37	0
1975/76	+ 94	+ 8	− 3	− 10	− 17	− 27	− 47	− 2

Source: Lester Brown: "The Politics and Responsibilities of the North American Breadbasket."

This paper was written, with Dr. Kunio Takase of the Overseas Economic Cooperation Fund (OECF) in 1976, when the author was President of OECF.

[1] U.S. National Academy of Sciences: "Agricultural Production Efficiency" (Washington, D.C., 1975).

there may be limits to future increases in the capacity of U.S. agriculture to produce surpluses which can be supplied to the rest of the world. As Table 1 shows, Asia is the continent suffering from the greatest deficit, and the deficit is increasing substantially over time. It is an absolute necessity to increase food production in Asia to cope with the increase of the population and to curb the heavy dependency on imports, particularly those from North America.

The main purpose of this Program is to achieve a long-term, stable, and self-sufficient supply of rice in Asia, but at the same time, it is intended as an anti-recession measure by stimulating export demand in the developed nations. Since Asia has 70 percent of the world's developing-country population and since it suffers from the most serious food shortage, the Program focuses on increasing food production in Asia.

The scope of the Program is, however, limited to rice production for a number of reasons. Rice is the staple food of Asians and the most suitable crop for monsoon Asia, in addition to which there is an advantage in that the yield can be improved comparatively easily. Rice is tasty, easy to digest, and a good energy source, which suggests that in the future there may well be large-scale increases in its consumption outside Asia, as it comes to be recognized as an excellent food for all mankind. The cost per calorie is lower than that of bread and other comparable foods. Of course, we do not deny the importance of other food crops to be multicropped with rice, favorably affecting the utilization of land and the maintenance of soil fertility, as well as improving farmers' incomes.

Because of its low economic return and long gestation period, its instability, and administrative difficulties, agricultural development was not given high investment priority until 1973, when an unprecedented food crisis threatened and the significance of eradicating rural poverty was fully recognized. Recently, the share of the agricultural sector in financing by international organizations has sharply increased. The World Bank increased agriculture's share from 12 percent in the period 1964–68 to 20 percent in 1968–73 and 32 percent in 1975. For the Asian Development Bank, there was an increase from 12 percent in the 1968–73 period to 25 percent in 1974. In the case of the Overseas Economic Cooperation Fund (OECF), there was also a rapid expansion, from 6 percent in the 1961–73 period to 15 percent in 1974. At the World

Food Conference held in Rome in November 1974, it was decided to cooperate in emergency food assistance and stockpiling and to create a World Food Council, a Food Information Center, and the International Fund for Agricultural Development.

The Program intends not to duplicate but to complement these efforts, and emphasizes what we can do to make a major contribution towards attaining common goals. The experience of Japanese agriculture, which is typical of Asian agriculture with abundant monsoon rainfall and small-scale family farming, may contribute to modernizing agriculture in Asian developing countries, particularly in the following four features:

(1) A high level of irrigation[2] engineering at the farm level which has been refined through more than one thousand years of history;

(2) Integrated agricultural techniques including varieties, fertilizers, chemicals and farm machinery suitable to rice production in monsoon Asia;

(3) The initiative of farmers as well as education and training systems; and

(4) The support of the government including land reform policy, rice price supports, and various subsidy programs.

Side by side with efforts to increase food production, efforts must be made to lower the rate of population growth. In Japan the birth rate was reduced by half in thirty years, from 36 per thousand in 1920 to 18 per thousand in 1950. In South Korea, Taiwan, Hong Kong, and Singapore it was reduced by half in about fifteen years. Adequate food supply improves nutrition and helps lower the brith rate. Reduction of the birth rate in Asia by half in 25 years may be a desirable target.

Parallel with the promotion of food production, industrialization is necessary in order to raise per-capita income and provide employment opportunities for the rapidly increasing labor force. Industries can also support food production by providing agricultural inputs such as fertilizers, insecticide, pumps, implements, and farm machinery. Harmonious balance between food production and industrial development is essential in order to strengthen the national economy of each country as a whole.

[2] The word "irrigation" used in this paper includes all functions related to effective water control required for rice production, not only irrigation but also drainage and flood control.

Limitations of the Green Revolution

As of 1975, the total harvested area of paddy in sixteen Asian countries or areas (excluding China and Japan)[3] was approximately 80 million hectares. Of this, 65 percent depends on rainfall, 33 percent is inadequately irrigated, and only 2 percent is adequately irrigated.[4] As can be seen in Figure 1, paddy production, in the fifteen years from 1960 to 1975, rose about 43 percent, from 114 million tons to 163 million tons. However, since the total population of the sixteen countries grew by 42 percent during the same period, from 790 million to 1.13 billion, per-capita paddy production hardly increased; it rose only from 143 to 145

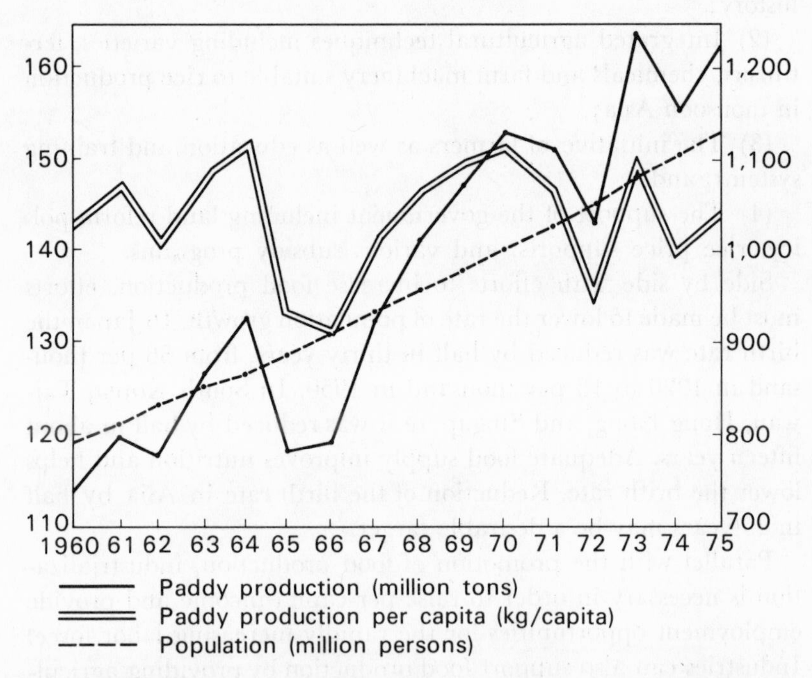

Fig. 1. Paddy production and population in 16 Asian countries (1960–75).

[3] These countries or areas were Afghanistan, Bangladesh, Burma, Taiwan, India, Indonesia, Cambodia, South Korea, Laos, West Malaysia, Nepal, Pakistan, the Philippines, Sri Lanka, Thailand, and South Vietnam.

[4] "Inadequate irrigation" is defined as irrigation facilities having canal density of less than 50 m/ha, which is not sufficient to deliver water for effective crop growth. "Adequate irrigation" means canal density of more than 50 m/ha.

kilograms. Modern varieties (MV, high-yielding varieties including similar local varieties) originally developed by the International Rice Research Institute since 1966 had spread throughout Asian countries, by 1972–73, to 15.60 million hectares (about 20 percent of the total paddy harvested area, and two-thirds of the irrigated paddies). If this tendency continues, all the irrigated areas will be planted with the MV in a few years, and thereafter paddy production will not be able to meet the ever-increasing demand due to the population explosion. In other words, further drastic increases in production must depend on effective water management at the farm level.

Another problem is the fluctuation in paddy production over time. Figure 1 shows that the extent of the fluctuation of per-capita paddy production (Asian averages) is about 13 percent, which is considered to be attributable to year-to-year differences in rainfall. A closer study of the statistical data (Figure 2) shows that the ranges of variations were large in countries with less de-

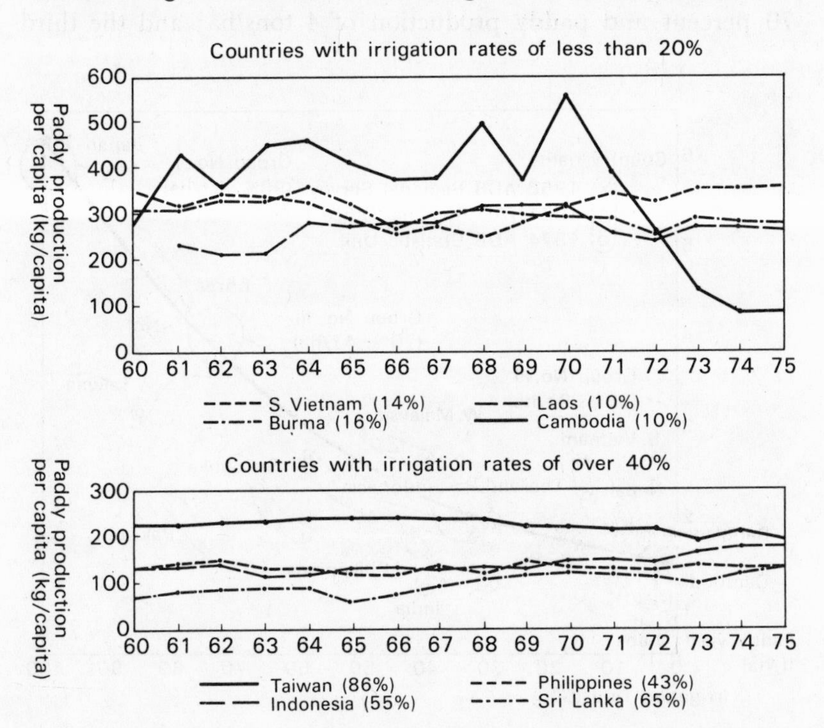

Fig. 2. Relation between paddy production stability and irrigation rate.

veloped irrigation facilities (for example, they were 51 percent in Cambodia where the irrigation rate is 3 percent; 23 percent in Taiwan where the irrigation rate is 86 percent; and 13 percent in Japan where the irrigation rate is 98 percent). This phenomenon often misleads government officials into relaxing their efforts toward increasing rice production when good harvests continue for two years or longer. It is essential to carry out long-term continuous efforts at improvement of irrigation not only in order to increase rice production but also in order to stabilize production irrespective of meteorological or climatological change.

The major factors affecting rice production include the rice variety, fertilizer, agricultural chemicals, and irrigation, but among these the closest correlation is between irrigation rate and rice production. As shown in Figure 3, the countries in Asia can be divided into three groups. The first group contains only Japan, with an irrigation rate of 98 percent and production of 6 tons/ha; the second group, South Korea and Taiwan, with irrigation rates of 70 percent and paddy production of 4 tons/ha; and the third

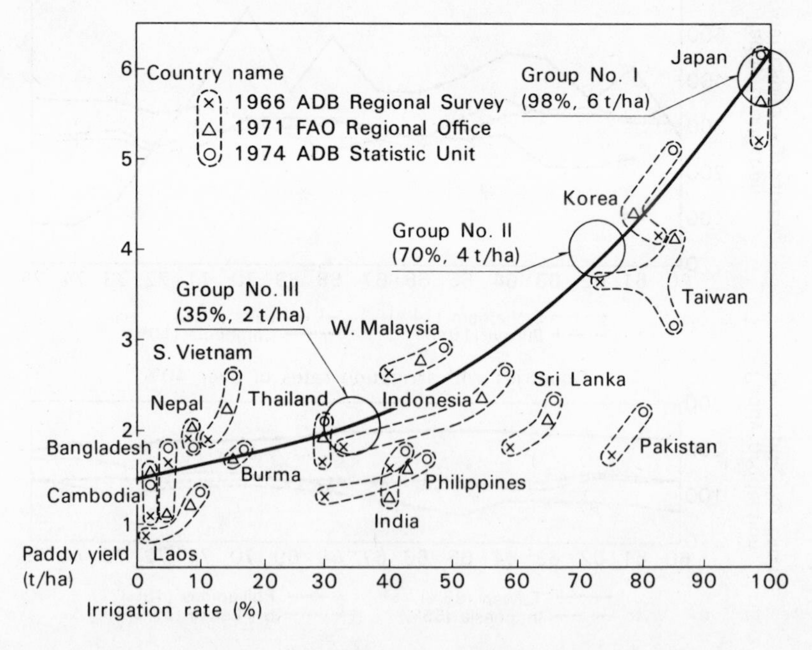

Fig. 3. Relation between irrigation rate and paddy yield.

group, the rest of the countries, with irrigation rates of 35 percent and production of 2 tons/ha in 1974. Figure 3 also shows the combined statistics for 1966, 1971, and 1974. Although there were some countries such as Japan and South Korea where paddy production increased about 1 ton/ha over the eight years, there were decreases in Taiwan and Nepal in 1974. In most other countries, there were slight increases: 0.8 ton/ha in Indonesia, 0.7 ton/ha in South Vietnam and Bangladesh, 0.5 ton/ha in Laos and Sri Lanka, 0.4 ton/ha in Thailand and the Philippines, 0.3 ton/ha in Cambodia and W. Malaysia, 0.2 ton/ha in India, and 0.1 ton/ha in Burma, for an overall average of 0.5 ton/ha. Even if irrigation development is continued at a rate allowing the same dissemination of MV as in the past (1966–74), the average increase over the next 15 years would be only about 1.0 ton/ha, which can hardly meet the rice requirement in 1990.

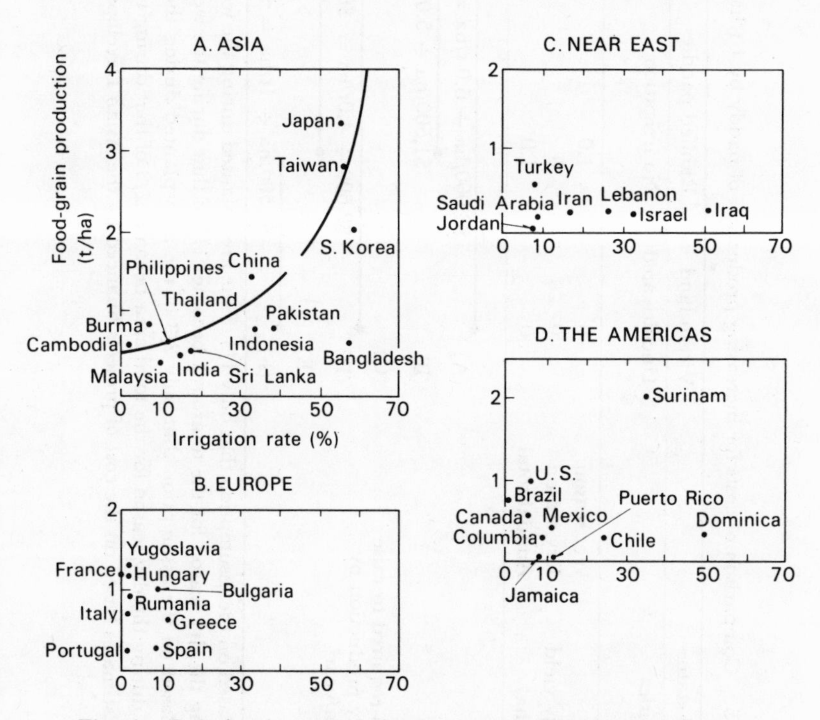

Fig. 4. Relation between irrigation rate and food-grain production.

Fig. 5. Comparison of costs for increasing production of paddy by 1 t/ha/year.

Land status		Virgin land	Rainfed paddies	Inadequate irrigation	Adequate irrigation	
Facilities		Uncultivated	No irrigation	Irrigation canals of less than 50 m/ha	Irrigation canals of more than 50 m/ha	
Paddy yield (t/ha)	Wet season	0	1.0	3.0	3.5	
	Dry season	0	0	1.0[a]	2.5[b]	
	Annual total	0	1.0	4.0	6.0	Investment priority
Costs required to raise paddy production by 1 t/ha/year[c]	(A)	Virgin land → Adequate irrigation: $3,000/ha ÷ 6.0 t/ha = $500/t				(4)
	(B)		Rainfed paddies → Adequate irrigation: $1,500/ha ÷ 5.0 t/ha = $300/t			(2)
	(C)			Inadequate irrigation → Adequate irrigation: $400/ha ÷ 2.0t/ha = $200/t		(1)
	(D)	Virgin land → Inadequate irrigation: $2,600 ÷ 4.0t/ha = $650/t				(5)
	(E)		Rainfed paddies → Inadequate irrigation: $1,100/ha ÷ 3.0t/ha = $367/t			(3)
	(F)	Virgin land → Rainfed paddies: $1,500/ha ÷ 1t/ha = $1,500/t				(6)

[a] Based on the assumption that only 1/3 of the area planted during the wet season can be planted in the dry season, the yield during the dry season for the total area becomes 1/3 of that during the wet season.

[b] Based on the assumption that only 2/3 of the area planted during the wet season can be planted in the dry season, the yield during the dry season for the total area becomes 2/3 of that during the wet season.

[c] Estimates based on the cost of projects financed by the Asian Development Bank from 1968 to 1972 (see Table 6).

Figure 4 shows that this close relation between food grain production and irrigation rate holds true only in Asia. Since wheat and other food grains are the staples in Europe, America, and the Near East, the yield seems to be more strongly influenced by other factors such as soils, varieties, and fertilizers. In the case of paddy, water is an absolute prerequisite: varieties and fertilizer have effects only when there is sufficient water.[5] It should be clearly recognized that water control is the single most important factor in increasing paddy yield in Asia.

Comparative Cost Study of Increasing Rice Production

Broadly, there are two ways to increase rice production. One is to expand the total planted area and the other is to increase yield per unit area. The former method depends mainly on land reclamation (opening new land) and the latter on improvement of existing irrigation facilities.[6] Figure 5 shows a comparison of costs for (A) land reclamation and adequate irrigation, (B) conversion from rainfed to adequate irrigation, (C) conversion from inadequate to adequate irrigation, and (D), (E), and (F) combinations of various cases. According to these data, the cheapest way to increase production by 1 ton/ha/year of paddy is (C), $200/ton, followed by (B), $300/ton, at 1975 constant prices. These cost estimates are based on ten irrigation projects assisted by the Asian Development Bank between 1968 and 1972.

In general, the methods involving new land [(A), (D), and (F)] are not advisable, because they cost more and take longer than others, which further deteriorates their economic returns. For example, (F) costs as much as $1,500/ton, or 7.5 times more than (C). Land suitable for rice production is becoming scarce in Asia due to topographical and soil conditions. Moreover, land reclamation involves resettlement on new land, which raises social

[5] In recent years, the International Rice Research Institute has been studying drought-resistant and flood-resistant varieties which attempt to minimize the adverse effects of inability to control water. This does not mean, however, that there are any varieties which can achieve yields as high as those where water is adequately controlled.

[6] It is also possible to expand planted area by introducing a second crop after improving existing irrigation facilities.

Table 2. Paddy Production Statistics for Various Countries in Asia

	1965						
Country	Paddy production*	Harvested[a] area*	Irrigated area**	Paddy yield*	Irrigation rate**	Paddy production*	Harvested[a] area*
	(1000t)	(1000ha)	(1000ha)	(t/ha)	(%)	(100t)	(1000ha)
1. Afghanistan	380	249	13	1.52	5	480	266
2. Bangladesh	15,751	9,186	460	1.72	5	17,679	9,904
3. Burma	8,055	4,750	710	1.70	15	8,582	4,974
4. Cambodia	2,500	2,290	62	1.09	3	635	555
5. India	45,983	29,300	11,700	1.57	40	60,000	37,500
6. Indonesia	13,660	7,500	2,450	1.82	33	22,732	8,537
7. S. Korea	4,731	1,137	910	4.16	80	6,178	1,205
8. Laos	740	914	22	0.81	2	905	686
9. W. Malaysia	892	339	141	2.63	42	1,813	597
10. Nepal	2,207	1,108	78	1.99	7	2,453	1,239
11. Pakistan	1,975	1,147	860	1.72	75	3,470	1,604
12. Philippines	4,073	3,140	938	1.30	30	5,660	3,539
13. Sri Lanka	756	401	236	1.89	59	1,603	680
14. Taiwan	3,076	824	573	3.73	70	3,250	1,040
15. Thailand	9,199	5,511	1,650	1.67	30	13,175	7,734
16. S. Vietnam	4,822	2,432	262	1.97	11	7,200	2,900
Subtotal	118,800	70,228	21,065	1.69	30	155,815	82,960
17. China (excl. Taiwan)						111,963	34,188
18. Japan						15,618	2,724
Asia total						293,391	123,803
World total						321,818	136,273

Source: * Obtained mainly from the FAO *Monthly Bulletin of Agricultural Economic and Statistics.*

** Obtained mainly from data of the ADB Asian Agricultural Survey and the FAO Bangkok Regional Office, but partly

1974	Estimated food supply and demand in 1974						
Irrigated area**	Paddy yield*	Irrigation rate**	Imported paddy*	Consumption of paddy	Population*	Consumption of paddy per capita	Staple food
(1000ha)	(t/ha)	(%)	(1000t)	(1000t)	(million)	(kg/capita)	
16	1.80	6	+ 4	484	18.80	26	Wheat
495	1.78	5	+ 121	17,800	74.99	238	Rice
797	1.74	16	− 282	8,300	30.27	275	Rice
17	1.14	3	+ 208	843	7.89	107	Rice Maize
16,100	1.60	43	+ 78	60,078	586.06	102	Rice Wheat
4,950	2.66	58	+2,190	24,922	129.12	193	Rice Maize
1,022	5.12	85	+ 547	6,725	33.46	201	Rice Barley
69	1.32	10	+ 105	1,010	3.26	310	Rice
287	3.04	48	+ 294	2,107	11.65	181	Rice
124	1.97	10	− 300	2,153	12.07	178	Rice
1,280	2.16	80	− 822	2,648	68.21	39	Wheat Rice
1,590	1.60	45	+ 444	6,104	41.46	148	Rice Maize
449	2.35	66	+ 392	1,995	13.49	148	Rice
896	3.20	86	—	3,250	15.71	207	Rice
2,860	1.71	37	−1,485	11,690	41,02	285	Rice
435	2.48	15	+ 405	7,605	20.40	373	Rice
31,387	1.86	38	+1,899	157,714	1,107.86	143	
	3.27						
	5.73						
	2.37						
	2.35						

estimated by the writers.

[a] If a paddy field with 100 ha is planted 1.5 times a year, then "harvested area" is shown as 150 ha.

Table 3. Doubling Rice Production Program by Irrigation for Each Country in Asia

Sub-region	No. Country	1974 irrigation rate (%)	Inadequate irrigation to be improved (%)[a]	1974 harvested area	Net irrigated area* to be improved [a] (1,000 ha)	Cost (million dollars)	Rainfed rate (%)[a]
				Conversion from inadequate to adequate irrigation			
		(1)	(2)	(3)	(4)=(2)×(3)×3/4	(5)=(4) x$400	
	1 Afghanistan	6	4	266	8	3	60
	2 Bangladesh	5	3	9,904	223	89	61
South	3 India	43	41	37,500	11,510	4,602	23
Asia	4 Nepal	10	8	1,239	74	29	56
	5 Pakistan	80	64	1,604	771	308	—
	6 Sri Lanka	66	64	680	327	131	—
	(subtotal)			51,193	12,913	5,162	
	7 Indonesia	58	56	8,537	3,580	1,431	8
	8 Malaysia	48	46	597	206	82	16
ASEAN	9 Philippines	45	43	3,539	1,140	456	21
	10 Thailand	37	35	7,734	2,023	810	29
	(subtotal)			20,407	6,949	2,779	
	11 Burma	16	14	4,974	523	210	50
Other	12 Cambodia	3	1	2,290[c]	17	7	63
Parts	13 S. Korea	85	64	1,137	545	218	—
of Asia	14 Laos	10	8	914[c]	54	22	56
	15 Vietnam	15	13	5,100[d]	497	199	51
	(Subtotal)			14,415	1,636	656	
	TOTAL	38%	33%	86,015	21,498	8,597	31%

[a] Taken from Table 2.

[b] Including area under rice cultivation in East Malaysia (103,000 ha × 66% = 68,000 ha).

[c] 1965 figures used to avoid effects of the war.

[d] Including estimated harvested area in the Democratic Republic of Vietnam in 1972, 2,200,000 ha (4,100,000 tons – 2,200,000 ha = 1.86 t/ha).

[e] From this area, 6 t/ha/year are produced.

[f] From this area, 1 t/ha/year is produced.

[g] A total of 328 million tons per year is produced which exceeds the 316 million tons of the target shown in paragraph 16. At this time, the paddy yield is 2.93 t/ha for the harvested area (111,968,000 ha) and 4.19 t/ha for the net

Conversion from rainfed to adequate irrigation		Required cost (million dollars)		Target for 1990				
Net rain-fed area* to be improved (1,000ha)[a]	Cost (million dollars)	Total a mount (15 years)	Annual amount (per year)	Net adequate irrigation area*	Harvested adequate irrigation area (1,000 ha)	Net rainfed area* (1,000 ha)	Irrigation rate (%) (1,000 ha)	Paddy production (1,000 tons)
(7)=(3)× (6)	(8)=(7)× \$1,500	(9)=(5) +(8)	(10)=9 ÷15	(11)=(4)+ (7)+(3)×2%	(12)=(11) × 5/3	(13)=(3)× 34%	(14)=(12) (12)+(13)	(15)=(11)×6 (13)×1
160	240	243	16	173	289	91	76	1,128
6,040	9,060	9,135	610	6,461	10,800	3,370	76	42,190
8,630	12,950	17,552	1,170	20,890	34,820	12,720	73	138,020
694	1,040	1,069	71	793	1,321	421	-6	5,181
—	—	308	21	803	1,338 +225	321	83	5,816
—	—	131	9	341	569	231	71	2,274
15,524	23,290	28,452	1,897	29,471	49,362	17,154	74	194,609
683	1,024	2,455	164	4,433	7,400	2,900	72	29,500
164[b]	246	328	22	382	637	203	76	2,493
742	1,112	1,568	104	1,953	3,260	1,200	73	13,090
2,240	3,360	4,170	278	4,418	7,370	2,625	74	29,185
3,829	5,742	8,521	568	11,186	18,667	6,928	73	74,198
2,487	3,735	3,945	263	3,109	5,190	1,690	75	20,360
1,441	2,162	2,169	145	1,504	2,510	780	76	9,860
—	—	218	15	568	946 +216	171	87	4,229
511	768	790	53	583	973	310	76	3,810
2,600	3,900	4,099	273	3,199	5,340	1,731	76	20,931
7,039	10,565	11,221	751	8,963	15,233	4,682	76	59,190
26,392	39,597	48,194	3,126	49,610[e]	83,204	28,764[f]	74	327,997[g] 2.93 (4.19)

area (78,374,000 ha).

In column (1), 2% is considered adequately irrigated. Therefore (2) = (1) − 2% is the rate of inadequate irrigation which needs improvement.

Since the target in each country for 1990 is to be 66% of all paddies adequately irrigated, figure (6) is 66% − (1). Since the inadequately irrigated area of (2) − (3) includes net area in wet season and 1/3 thereof in dry season, multiply by 3/4 to obtain net area (4).

The harvested adequately irrigated area (13) is obtained by multiplying the net area × 5/3 because the net area in wet season is 2/3 thereof in dry season.

* A 100ha "net area" can be used as 150 ha harvested area, if paddy is planted 1.5 times a year.

problems. It is a mistake to regard the increasing of rice production as a mere economic or physical problem. People have an instinctive desire for a better life, and this is reflected in the conspicuous migration of the population from rural areas to urban areas, a phenomenon common to many Asian countries.

A Master Plan for Irrigation Improvement

We have delineated a master plan for irrigation improvement which forms the core of the Doubling Rice Production Program in Asia with 1990 as the target year on the basis of the various points mentioned above. The year 1970, which saw the best harvest in history (on a per-capita basis) will be taken as the reference year of approximate self-sufficiency. As can be seen in Figure 1, the population of Asia (excluding China and Japan) was 1 billion and annual paddy production was 150 million tons in 1970. On the assumption that the demand for rice will increase by 3.8 percent annually[7] (2.5 percent for population increase plus 1.3 percent for per-capita consumption increase), it will be necessary to produce 316 million tons of paddy by 1990 for a population of 1.64 billion.

In order to meet this demand in 1990, the irrigation rate in the Group III countries should be raised from the 30 percent of 1970 (1.8 tons/ha) to 66 percent (3.8 tons/ha), by the cheapest method, which is basically farm ditch construction. As is shown in Tables 2 and 3, 26.39 million hectares of rainfed area and 21. 50 million hectares of inadequately irrigated area are to be converted to adequately irrigated areas in the fifteen years between 1976 and 1990 throughout Asia. The total cost is estimated at $4.82 billion at 1975 constant prices.

Based on our experiences in executing irrigation projects, the following three elements are essential for successful adaption of agricultural technology in each project, as shown in Figure 6:

(1) Experimental farms, for conducting experiments with modern agricultural techniques and scientific studies of physical and biological relations among varieties of crops, soils, fertilizers,

[7] If the rate of population growth could be lowered appreciably before 1990, the increasing demand for rice would be smaller accordingly.

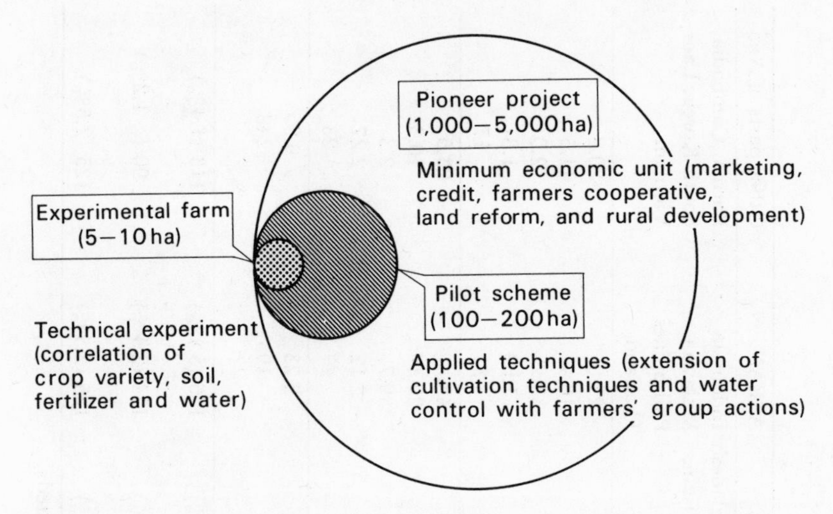

Fig. 6. Three elements essential for irrigation development.

and water. Experimental farms usually have an area of 5–10 hectares.

(2) Pilot schemes to demonstrate applied techniques obtained from the experimental farms and to train formers in irrigation water management. A pilot scheme usually requires 100 to 200 hectares of land. The irrigation network of this pilot scheme should be constructed according to the same designs as other parts of the project.

(3) Pioneer projects. Various activities such as those of marketing, credit, and farmers' cooperatives should be established in a minimum economic and social unit (1,000 to 5,000 hectares) of a full-fledged irrigation project.

Table 4 compares paddy production records in 1965 and 1974 for three sub-regions: South Asia, ASEAN, and other parts of Asia. Although these nine years are considered the height of the Green Revolution, the irrigation rate increase only from 30 percent in 1965 to 37 percent in 1974, and will be 48 percent in 1990 if this trend continues, which is much below the target of 66 percent. In South Asia, the increases in the irrigation rate were particularly slow (32 to 36 percent), while the ASEAN sub-region had the highest increases (31 to 47 percent). In the other parts of Asia, the irrigation rate increases were very low (17 to 23 percent),

Table 4. Paddy Production Statistics for Sub-regions in Asia

	Sub-region	Asian total	South Asia	ASEAN	Other parts of Asia
	Country	15 countries	Afghanistan, Bangladesh India, Nepal, Pakistan, Sri Lanka	Indonesia Malaysia Philippines Thailand	Burma, Cambodia, South Korea, Laos Vietnam
1965	Paddy production (million tons)	115.7	67.0	27.8	20.8
	Harvested area (million ha)	69.4	41.4	16.4	11.5
	Irrigated area (million ha)	20.5	13.3	5.2	2.0
	Paddy yield (t/ha)	1.67	1.62	1.69	1.81
	Irrigation rate (%)	30	32	31	17
1974	Paddy production (million tons)	152.6	85.7	43.4	23.5
	Harvested area (million ha)	81.9	51.2	20.4	10.3
	Irrigated area (million ha)	30.5	18.5	9.7	2.3
	Paddy yield (t/ha)	1.86	1.67	2.12	2.27
	Irrigation rate (%)	37	36	47	23
	Population (100 million persons)	10.92	7.74	2.23	0.95
	Paddy consumption per capita (kg/capita)	139	110	195	248
1974/1965 (Annual increase)	Paddy production increment	131 (3.1%)	128 (2.8%)	156 (5.1%)	113 (1.4%)
	area increment	118 (1.9%)	124 (2.4%)	124 (2.4%)	90 (1.2%)
	Yield increment	110 (1.1%)	103 (0.3%)	125 (2.5%)	125 (2.5%)

Source: Data are mainly from FAO, ADB, but some figures have been estimated.

mainly because of the war. Annual increase rates of paddy production in the three sub-regions were 2.8 percent for South Asia, 5.1 percent for ASEAN, and 1.4 percent for other parts of Asia, averaging 3.1 percent for all Asia.

General criteria for selecting priority irrigation projects are as follows:

(1) Top priority should be given to projects for which effects can be achieved quickly and cheaply, including improvement of existing irrigation projects and pump irrigation, on a small or medium scale. Full participation of local farmers is considered a great advantage in view of employment effects and involvement in the projects.

(2) Medium scale multi-purpose dams with provision for irrigation, hydropower, and flood control may require a considerable amount of construction machinery, cement, iron and steel, contractors' work, and consultants' services, which in turn would stimulate the economies of developed countries which export these goods and services.

(3) Large-scale projects under consideration would be difficult to complete by 1990 as they require at least five years for surveying and designing plus another ten to twenty years for construction. These include the Mekong River basin (requiring a total investment of $20 billion up to the year 2000, according to the Indicative Basin Plan compiled by the Mekong Committee of ECAFE in 1970), the Indus (Pakistan), the Ganges (Bangladesh and India), and the Kalimantan (Indonesia) projects.

As to the economic viability of these irrigation projects, there would be no problem with a high to moderate internal rate of return. For example, the Angat-Magat Project in the Philippines financed by the Asian Development Bank in 1973 (total cost, $17.7 million ÷ 70,000 hectares = $250/ha; farmgate price of milled rice: $88.5/ton; paddy production expected to increase from 2.0 to 4.0 tons/ha) had an internal rate of return of 24.2 percent. As of 1975, with the costs inflated 1.5 times ($400/ha) and the rice price three times ($265/ton), the internal rate of return is considered to be higher than that initially expected, and the project thus has become more feasible.

Fertilizer, Chemicals, and Farm Machinery

Fertilizer requirements will increase rapidly once irrigation facilities are completed. Based on the assumption that 60 kg/ha of N, 75 kg/ha of P_2O_5, and 30 kg/ha of K_2O are required for the production of 4 tons/ha/crop of paddy, the current amount of fertilizer used in Asia (17 kg/ha of N, 7 kg/ha of P_2O_5, and 3 kg/ha of K_2O) will have to be increased by 11.5 million tons[8] by 1990 for an estimated paddy area of 83.20 million hectares. Considering that the cost of a fertilizer plant with a capacity of 260,000 tons/year is $200 million,[9] $8.8 billion will be required for fertilizer plants producing 11.5 million tons/year. As a short-term stimulation measure, current excess stocks of fertilizer resulting from the high prices might be released at lower prices.

When irrigation facilities are complete and the area of double-cropping with heavy application of fertilizers is increased, agricultural chemicals will be required to cope with insects, pests, and weeds ($800 million). Since seasonal cultivation must be completed in a short time, agricultural machinery modified for Asian agriculture (such as tractors, power tillers, sprayers, rice planters, and harvesters) are also necessary ($5 billion). The increased demands for rice mills and storage facilities would require an additional $4.1 billion, and the total of the above investment will come to $9.9 billion.

International Service Center

Two other reasons for the difficulty in modernizing Asian agriculture are that the farms are small in size (average of one hectare per household) and the production system is very closely connected with institutional problems and human relationships in the village society. For example, a tenant who cultivates a small land area has little incentive to invest in the expensive fertilizer required for

[8] N: 60 kg − 17 kg = 43 kg
P_2O_5: 75 kg − 7 kg = 68 kg
K_2O: 30 kg − 3 kg = 27 kg
} 138 kg × 83.2 million ha = 11.5 million tons.

[9] International Bank for Research and Development: "Fertilizer Requirements of Developing Countries—Revised Outlook in 1975" (August 12, 1975).

increased yields, because the majority of the profit resulting from increased production would go to the landowner. This is a well-known fact, but at the same time it is extremely difficult to achieve land reform, which involves major political issues. Government policies also play a major role in the formation of credit institutions, farmers' cooperatives, and extension and training services, all of which provide essential support to paddy production.

Since these technical, institutional, economic, and social problems are location-specific, the solutions could be different project by project. Solutions also require policy decisions by the government at the national level. Finally, there must be a link with an International Service Center which can generalize and standardize matters for Asia as a whole. Because of the complexity of these problems, a three-tiered mechanism seems to be far more effective than the single-tier structure of most regional institutes and centers. An International Service Center, working in cooperation with and in support of national research and training centers, could in turn conduct location-specific pilot projects at the field level, in a schema like that shown in Figure 7.

This Center would stress both research and training.[10] The location and the organization of the International Service Center is properly subject to open discussions by all concerned. However, ther permanent staff of the Center should be kept small. Staff members will be experienced in Asian agriculture; the greatest possible use of expertise available within the Asian region is recommended. The budget for fifteen years is tentatively estimated at $100 million.

Problem Areas

Table 5 shows the total financial requirements for this Program. At 1975 constant prices, the amount will be $67 billion for fifteen years or an average of $4.5 billion per year. Net disbursement of

[10] In Japan, there are currently about 15,000 extension officers for rice cultivation on 2.67 million hectares. Supposing that the density of extension officers in Asia should be at least half of that in Japan, the number of extension officers in Asia should be increased from the current 40,000 persons to 140,000 for 49.94 million hectares of irrigated paddy by 1990.

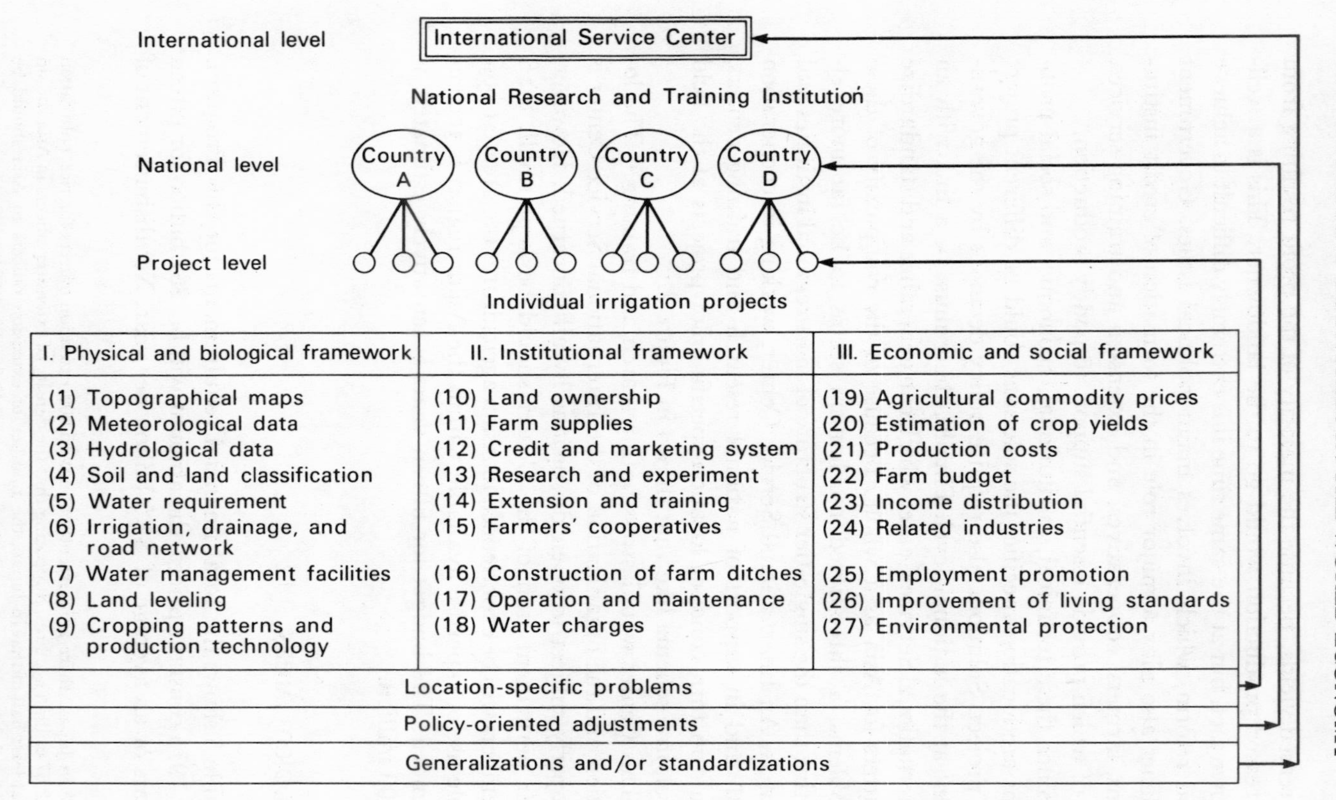

Fig. 7. Three-tiered mechanism for promoting irrigated agriculture in Asia.

Official Development Assistance (ODA) from seventeen DAC countries in 1974 amounted to $11.3 billion, or 0.33% of GNP. Assuming that Asia shares 40 percent of the world total ($4.5 billion), of which 13 percent would be invested for the agricultural sector ($0.6 billion), and that an equal amount is borne by developing countries, the total investment to Asian agriculture is estimated at $1.2 billion in 1974. Supposing that (1) the economic growth of the developed countries would continue at a certain annual rate, (2) the rate of ODA against GNP would be improved, and (3) the share of the agricultural sector in ODA would also be increased, it may not be totally unrealistic to achieve the target

Table 5. Financial Requirement for the Program

(Unit: $100 million)

	Total amount (1976–90)				Annual amounts			
	Asian total	South Asia	ASEAN	Other parts of Asia	Asian total	South Asia	ASEAN	Other parts of Asia
Irrigation	482	285	85	112	32	19	6	7
Fertilizer plants	88	52	20	16	6	4	1	1
Farm machinery etc.	99	59	18	22	7	4	1	2
International Service Center	1	1	0	0	—	—	—	—
Total	670	397	123	150	45	27	8	10
Percentage	100%	59%	19%	22%				

of $4.5 billion in an average of fifteen years (for example, starting from $3.0 billion for the first year of the Program and reaching $6.0 billion for the last year). We consider it to be not impossible but within a reasonable range of possibility, although great efforts would be required.

We admit that the Program has several limitations. First, it has been prepared on a macro-physical basis, considering Asia as one area. Second, no consideration was given to possible changes in the present geographic distribution of paddy fields. Certainly, each developing country must have its own policy for food production and strategy for agricultural development. In order to optimize the Program, further studies may be necessary both on an individual country basis and on a regional basis.

Table 6. Irrigation Projects Financed by the Asian Development Bank 1968–1972, before the Oil Shock

Type	Project	Country	Total cost ($1,000)	Irrigable area (ha)	Unit cost ($/ha)	Conversion to 1975 prices ($/ha)	Foreign component (%)	Paddy yield with project (t/ha) Wet season	Paddy yield with project (t/ha) Dry season
A. Land reclamation and adequate irrigation	Walawe	Sri Lanka	26,455	13,220	2,000	Average 2,165 × 1.5	32	4.2	4.2
	Tha Ngon	Laos	1,957	840	2,330	≑ 3,000	50	5.0	5.0
B. Conversion from rainfed to adequate irrigation	Tajum	Indonesia	3,503	3,600	974		28	4.0	4.0
	Cotabato	Philippines	4,577	7,430	616	Average 1,030 × 1.5	55	3.5	4.0
	Besut	W. Malaysia	7,105	5,100	1,393	≑ 1,500	59	5.0	5.0
	Sempor	Indonesia	16,400	16,240	1,110		56	4.0	3.2
	Kankai	Nepal	6,900	5,000	1,380		65	4.0	4.0
	Binh Dinh	S. Vietnam	6,000	8,500	706		42	5.0	5.0
C. Conversion from inadequate irrigation to adequate irrigation	Gawargan	Afghanistan	8,510	25,300	336	Average 258 × 1.5	61	(wheat) 3.0	—
	Gambarsari	Indonesia	4,869	20,300	179	≑ 400	75	4.0	4.0

Knowing the several problem areas still to be studied, we consider the Program workable. If Asian countries can jointly or individually formulate a "specific program" for increasing rice production in their own countries, it will certainly attract the interest of developed countries all over the world, and they may be induced to participate positively in the implementation of this Program. We hope that active discussion and thorough study may take place in international forums, so as to lead to a concrete action program in this very important area.

Dynamic Division of Labor and the International Order

When thought is given to the future international order, the relationships between rich and poor countries, the North and the South, are of obvious importance; hardly less important, however, is the order among the rich and among the poor countries. In particular, the principle of free trade, which has been a regulating force in the market economy countries, has felt the brunt of both prolonged stagnation of the world economy and high unemployment rates in the industrialized countries—pressure which seeks to modify the working of the principle of free trade. Moreover, when consideration is given to the diversity which is becoming common among the developing countries, it becomes evident that there should be different policies for different economic groups of countries. Even though it is possible to think of the South as a political monolith when discussing North-South issues, it would be quite difficult to entertain similar thoughts in an economic context.

The developing countries may be divided into four categories: (i) the oil-exporting countries, (ii) the rapidly industrializing developing countries, (iii) the intermediate developing countries which account for the largest part of the Third World and which heavily rely on exports of primary commodities, and (iv) the low-income developing countries.

The members of the oil exporters' category do not necessarily have similar economic conditions. Indonesia and Nigeria, for example, belong to OPEC but also have features of the fourth category. Circumstances thus defy neat division into four categories. Many of the oil exporters are now important capital exporters. Nevertheless, with regard to their domestic economic development, they must, because they still display aspects of underdevelopment, receive technology, know-how, and other inputs from the advanced industrial nations.

Typical examples of rapidly industrializing developing countries exist in Asia and include South Korea, Hong Kong, Taiwan, and Singapore, as well as in Latin America: Mexico and Brazil, to cite just two. These countries have succeeded in rapidly expanding industrial output and in attaining rapid growth of their GNP and export trade. What is necessary for these countries is that the industrially advanced nations open their domestic markets to goods exported from this category of countries while also providing capital which they require for development. This supply of capital need not necessarily be on soft aid terms but may be at commercial or near-commercial terms, the important point being the access to supplies of capital rather than the cost of that capital. In the case of low-income countries, what is necessary is a transfer of resources from developed countries at very soft terms or in the the form of grants.

The basic approach to the provision of development aid should be, according to the Pearson Report, to provide assistance to those developing countries which can effectively use it: "Increases in foreign aid should be clearly aimed at helping the developing countries to reach a path of self-sustained growth at reasonable levels. . . . Countries growing at a rate of 6 per cent per year will be able gradually to raise their rate of capital formation. If they give adequate attention to the fostering and promotion of exports, they should, before the end of this century, be able to participate in the international economy as self-reliant parners, and to finance the investments and imports they need for continued rapid growth without foreign capital on concessional terms. . . . This is why increases in development aid should in the future be closely linked to the economic objectives and the development performance of the aid-receivers."[1] The approach suggested by the

[1] Lester B. Pearson: *Partners in Development:* Report of the Commission on International Development, 1969.

Pearson Report may thus be called the provision of aid according to the "efficiency principle."

However, later criticism held that this efficiency principle was of little use in dealing with the poorest countries. If performance in these countries is poor and they are assigned low priority as aid recipients, then the gap separating those poor countries from the others would be made wider.

Consequently, in the past few years, the argument that international aid should preferably contribute to the direct improvement of the living standards of the impoverished masses in the poor countries has become stronger. The emphasis on the fulfillment of "basic human needs" is typical of this new argument. It can be viewed as being based on the pursuit of income redistribution on a global scale, as a "welfare principle" by which aid is to be provided.

The Rapidly Industrializing Countries

Some of the developing countries, when domestic and external conditions are favorably combined, experience explosive economic growth, as is shown in the case of the Japanese economy in recent years as well as the experience of several other countries.

Development has been particularly remarkable in East and Southeast Asia. Recapitulating the process whereby Japan caught up with the Western nations by dint of her economic growth and development, in recent years some of the East and Southeast Asian countries have been rapidly catching up on Japan. In 1976, the total exports of South Korea, Taiwan, Hong Kong, and Singapore amounted to 43 percent of Japan's total export trade. Traditional markets for Japan's textiles and other light industrial products, such as the United States, are rapidly being captured by these newly industrializing countries. Moreover, their exports to the Japanese market have increased sharply, necessitating structural adjustments in Japanese industry.

In the case of the countries of North America and Western Europe, conditions requiring adjustments are present, due both to an increase in the import of labor-intensive products from the rapidly industrializing countries and to an increase in the import of more advanced industrial goods from Japan. These conditions are exerting forces which are shaking the very principle of free trade, which the developed countries have been strong to advocate.

Further, an international order desirable for those developing countries possessing the ability to produce high-quality products for export at low costs necessitates that the importing countries impose as few constraints as possible, in accordance with the principle of free trade. Regarding this, the RIO (Reshaping the International Order) Report observes: "The industrialized countries, on their part, will have to introduce *policies of adjustment*, develop specialization in knowledge-intensive products and gradually introduce and enforce environmental protection standards. This implies a further reduction or even abolition of the tariffs imposed by the industrialized countries on the semi-manufactured and manufactured products of the Third World, a trend that would contribute towards combating inflation in the industrialized countries. Likely to be of even greater importance is a *reduction of non-tariff barriers* since these form a major hindrance to intra-industry trade. If this is not possible without the inclusion of some escape clauses, it should be ensured that temporary protection mechanisms are *degressive*, i.e. are in accordance with a specific time-table and strictly connected with adjustment measures" (original italics).[2] In this sense, these developing countries may consider that the old economic order offers advantageous conditions for future development.

The Lima Declaration of 1975 contains the objective of increasing the Third World's share of world industrial output from the existing level of 7 percent to 25 percent by the year 2000. Generally speaking, it may be possible that this objective be attained by those developing countries which are attaining dynamic growth through the international division of labor—countries which will further expand their exports to the advanced nations and, moreover, be joined by more countries which enter their group.

In the advanced industrial countries there is at present a gradual transition from demand for goods to demand for services. At the same time, as incomes are rising, society's industrial discipline is tending to become weaker. As an overall trend, while interest in the production of more goods is waning in the rich countries, in

[2] Jan Tinbergen: *Reshaping the International Order*, Report to the Club of Rome (New York: E.P. Dutton, 1976).

the developing countries increasingly wide segments of the population are receiving better education and acquiring new technical skills, and production efficiency is improving. At the same time in these countries, the demand for the fulfillment of material needs and desires, such as for food, textiles, and fertilizer, is at a very high level. Moreover, in many of the developing countries there is a relative abundance of labor; in particular, as a recent result of demographic trends, the forthcoming increase in the youthful section of the work force will constitute a favorable condition in regard to production.

However, if the Lima Declaration objective is to be attained, it is vital for the developing countries that the developed countries adhere to the principle of free trade. There is a strong tendency for old industrial countries to be reluctant to adapt to rapid change. In these countries, social structure is becoming rigid and political and social resistance to rapid change in the industrial structure is present: even though it may be objectively seen as desirable economically to move toward utilizing comparative advantages, political and social factors may prevent it. But if the advanced industrial countries move toward a hardened stand on protectionism, the result for world economic development and for the economic welfare of individual nations will be stagnation. As was experienced during the interwar period, the erection of trade barriers leads to a decline in world trade, stagnation in economic growth, an increase in unemployment, and, in total, a brake on the economic activity of the entire world.

Therefore, it becomes necessary, when giving thought to a future international order, that we adopt the standpoint of seeking to facilitate the responses of the world's countries to a dynamic international division of labor. For the rapidly industrializing countries, while adherence to the principle of free trade is desirable in principle, as a matter of practical concern exporting countries may at times be obliged to accept voluntary export restraints and orderly marketing arrangements in order to make adjustment policies feasible for the advanced industrial countries. The importing countries on their part may resort to safeguard measures.

Moreover, the emergence of rapidly developing LDCs will also present a problem in terms of splitting the existing groups of countries—notably the Group of 77. Although this group shares a common historical background, some of its members have attained very high rates of economic growth. From the viewpoint of attaining a rational, new economic order, reclassification of developed and developing countries will be required from time to time.

One way of approaching this would be to classify those developing countries which have surpassed a certain level of per-capita GNP, say $1,000, as belonging to the "intermediate stage" of development and those countries which have passed, say, $2,000 as "developed." The intermediate countries would be exempt from both the obligations imposed on developed countries and the privileges given to the developing countries under UNCTAD resolutions.

From the viewpoint of the developed industrial countries, a boomerang effect may be anticipated for the rapidly industrializing countries. When these countries rapidly acquire technical and managerial skills from the advanced industrial countries, because they are well endowed with abundant and low-cost labor, it becomes possible for them to rapidly improve the export competitiveness of their industrial products. As these countries are using capital and technology imported from developed industrial countries and are becoming their competitors, at least in the short run they may constitute a potential threat to the industries and employment in the advanced countries. That is, the boomerang thrown by the developed industrial countries may well return to strike them. Of course, from the viewpoint of the world economy, this effect is not undesirable: poor countries acquire capital and technology from the richer countries, gradually develop and increase incomes and then increase their imports of more sophisticated products from the industrialized countries. For countries faced with this problem, the conditions exist which could lead to the adoption of protectionist practices; on the basis of the dynamic international division of labor, however, the developed industrial nations have, in the long run, no choice but to strive to open up new frontiers.

Intermediate Developing Countries

The intermediate developing countries are, essentially, countries with a high dependence on the export of primary commodities. Among them, countries which are exporting primary commodities under internationally advantageous conditions are attaining relatively high economic growth rates, and some of them have gradually moved into the stage of industrial development. Examples include Malaysia, the Philippines, Thailand, and some countries in Latin America. For these countries the area receiving most attention is the stabilization of revenues from the export of primary commodities, especially through the vehicle of commodity agreements. These agreements are beneficial to importer country and exporter country alike since they smooth out market price fluctuations, which otherwise could be volatile, and a number of these agreements have already been signed. If the terms are improved in favor of the exporting developing countries, then trade in primary commodities will have the function of redistributing income, by transferring it from relatively wealthy countries to relatively poor countries. If this element is overemphasized, however, it will make it difficult for exporting and importing countries to reach necessary agreement.

Regarding issues related to trade in raw materials, there are resource-rich rich countries, resource-poor rich countries, resource-rich poor countries, and resource-poor poor countries. Given this, increases in the relative prices of primary commodities will not by themselves automatically resolve the North-South problem. Since such agreements could be beneficial to resource-rich rich countries but not to resource-poor poor countries, caution is required regarding the selection of the commodities to be the subject of agreements, and to the implementation of the agreements.

The promotion of efficient and equitable resource development would be beneficial to the entire world. It opens the way for international institutions, international taxation, and the development of resources without excessive dependence on transnational corporations which have hitherto dominated many development efforts. When there is a transfer of resources through the vehicle of a commodity agreement, the incidence of such a transfer is sometimes arbitrary; it may favor a country possessing resources and not a country lacking resources. In other words, it need not necessarily be in the interest of all the poor developing countries. This makes it advisable to study the possibilities of a transfer mechanism which functions more equitably among countries. One such mechanism is compensatory finance for export earnings. A suitable step in this direction would be expansion to a global scale of STABEX (Stabilization of Export Earnings), created under the Lomé Convention.

Also important to the countries within this group is the promotion of the processing of primary commodities with a view to obtaining a larger share of the total value-added. On the part of importer countries, it is necessary to modify the existing tariff escalation structures by which taxes are levied on products in direct relationship to the extent of processing prior to importation. For the countries of this group, then, increased processing of export products must be promoted. Hereafter, we may expect that a number of the countries within this group will join the group of rapidly industrializing countries. Further, it is also necessary to give thought to the expansion of markets through regional cooperation, and by promotion of trade among developing countries to eliminate the problem of small domestic markets which is an impediment to effective import substitution policies.

Low-Income Countries

The problems of low-income countries are central to the entire North-South problematique, and the eradication of absolute poverty is a joint responsibility of all nations, rich and poor alike. It is generally accepted that a nation should seek to eliminate poverty from within its own borders; the extension of this welfare stage concept to the global level can also be considered perfectly logical as an objective of human society. Such a viewpoint is contained in the growing recognition of the necessity, as expressed in discussions on "Basic Human Needs," to aid the poor people of the poor countries so as to help them attain at least the minimum standard of living which each deserves as a fellow human. Included in basic human needs are adequate nutrition, medical care, and basic education. Although it is difficult to adequately describe all basic human needs in specific, quantitative terms, I believe that the world has been entrusted with the task of fulfilling them on a global scale.

Aid for the fulfillment of basic human needs has sometimes been criticized as being cast into a bottomless hole. Certainly, if poor countries were to rely for a prolonged period of time on aid in order to maintain certain standards of living and to meet the basic human needs of their people, there would be a danger of becoming firmly locked into positions of dependency. Nevertheless, poverty and malnutrition, because they threaten human existence, are adverse elements of the highest order, and it will not do for us to ignore the vicious circle of poverty, malnutrition, and low productivity. It must be recognized that satisfaction of basic human needs, such as the improvement of nutrition, also has productive effects through an improvement in the quality of labor.

A more fundamental policy would be to provide aid for assisting local food production. From the viewpoint of relative production costs, it can be argued that production of rice in Australia or the United States under conditions of mechanized agriculture would be cheaper than production of rice in small-scale units in South and Southeast Asia. But the production of rice in Asia also means the creation of more employment opportunities and more income. Given the rapid rate of increase of the labor force in the Asian region, it becomes evident that there must be more absorption of employment in the agricultural sector.

A survey by the World Food Council indicates that the shortfall in the food supplies of all developing countries will increase from 16 million tons in 1969–71 to 85 million tons in 1985. Of this, the shortage of rice will increase from 3 million tons to 39 million tons. This shortage will be concentrated in the Asian region. In this respect it should be noted that the per-hectare yield in South and Southeast Asia is one-third that of Japan and half that of Korea and Taiwan. It would thus appear that there is ample possibility of increasing food production through the improvement of per-unit area yields.

The Task Force Report, *Expanding Food Production in Developnig Countries: Rice Production in South and Southeast Asia,* submitted at the Bonn session of the Trilateral Commission, recommends that a program be established for doubling rice production in South and Southeast Asia over a 15-year period by investing in water control—especially in irrigation—which would increase the effects of cultivation of high-yielding varieties and in the use of fertilizers. The cost of this 15-year program would be $54,000 million. The annual cost— $3,600 million based on simple arithmetic—would be about double the current annual investment in irrigation in the region by national and international bodies. Of course, the supply of all the requisite inputs must be integrated, and, in particular, the production of high-yielding varieties of rice would require a high level of technology. A considerable expansion of agricultural research and extension activities would thus also be required.

This investment in Asia would contribute substantially to increasing both employment and incomes; it should also be evaluated for the effects it could have in fulfilling basic human needs through local increases in production.

The fulfillment of basic human needs is an important element in the North-South issue. It should not, however, be presented as a substitute concept for the efficiency principle described in the Pearson Report: both are vital in the total development aid effort.

Conclusion

In today's world we have economic stagnation, idle production facilities, and unemployed manpower in the developed industrial countries. At the same time we witness a great demand for investment—in food production, industrialization, infrastructure—in the poor countries. The developed industrial countries are increasing their investment in domestic construction and seeking to stimulate personal consumption, but if a part of that were directed, for example, to construction of irrigation projects or buildings for the fertilizer industry in developing countries, the purchasing power of those countries would be augmented, the exports of developed countries would be increased, and imports by developed countries of primary products from developing countries would also be expanded, thereby contributing to improvement of world economic conditions.

In the global investment policy which would be needed for this task, the constraints imposed by available resources would need to be fully considered. For example, as part of the Global New Deal, investment policies should be directed at raising production ceilings for renewable resources such as foodstuffs, at the development of the related infrastructure, and at the development of non-exhaustible sources of energy. At the same time, at least in the medium term, we should shift our emphasis away from the use of petroleum for fuel to other sources of energy, such as natural gas, coal, and nuclear power.

Today we must deal with the problem of linking the surpluses in savings accumulated in the industrialized countries and OPEC members to the investment needs of the developing countries. Consequently, we must think in institutional terms of combining measures to combat the recession in the advanced countries, to utilize the capital accumulated in oil-producing countries, and to meet the investment needs of the developing countries. While it is desirable that the growing surpluses in the oil-producing nations are effectively mobilized for productive uses on behalf of the development of the world economy, since those surpluses only represent a conversion of the non-renewable resources possessed by those countries into currency, it is understandable that those countries would want to have hedges against the depreciation of currency value and would want to use the currency as profitably as possible. As one possible solution, oil capital might be loaned to a greater extent than at present to the rapidly industrializing developing countries as development funds, at commercial or near-commercial rates.

With regard to the intermediate-income countries, the capital surpluses of the oil-producing countries should be used together with the private capital of the advanced industrial countries and their concessional government-based aid. In addition to this, a semi-soft capital supply, such as through the Third Window of the World Bank, might be encouraged.

Regarding the low-income countries, it is necessary to work toward the satisfaction of basic human needs through the provision of aid funds on very soft terms or as grants. Perhaps the creation of a World Welfare Fund, which would pool the resources and distribute them according to need, would eventually become necessary in order to avoid direct bilateral dependency in the supply of basic requirements.

A slowdown in the economic growth of the developed countries is projected for the future of the world economy. According to conventional thinking, economic recession in the advanced industrial countries causes stagnation in world trade and a slowing down of both the exports from and the economic growth of the developing countries. If the gap between the advanced countries and developing countries is to be narrowed, or if international targets, such as that adopted by the UN Industrial Development Organization (UNIDO), are to be achieved, the means must be found for enabling the economies of the developing countries to grow quickly, even if economic growth in the developed countries slows. That is, the economic growth of the developing countries should not be directly governed by economic growth in the developed countries. Ways to achieve this include the expansion of production and consumption in domestic markets and the promotion of regional cooperation among developing countries. On the part of the developed industrial countries, it is necessary to embark on institutional reforms in order that acceptable employment conditions may be attained in a low-growth environment. These are the basic long-range policy issues which both the developing and the developed countries will have to face in the course of coming decades.

Transfer of Resources to Developing Countries

The world economy has been in a state of disequilibrium since the advent of the oil crisis in late 1973. The quadrupling of oil prices aggravated the inflationary situation which already existed at that time in the developed countries and at the same time created massive deficits in international balances of payments. For that reason the over-all restrictive demand policy adopted in many countries led to worldwide recession and increases in unemployment.

The non-oil-producing developing countries, particularly those identified as "most seriously affected," suffered a drastic deterioration in their balance-of-payments positions due to large increases in the prices of both oil and industrial goods. Since, at the same time, shortfalls in the supply of foodstuffs occurred in those countries, they face a serious problem of domestic adjustment.

Plagued by the problems of recession, inflation, and disequilibria in balances of payments, the world economy is confronted with a crisis of grave dimensions, and changes are required in the international currency and trade systems which have supported postwar economic development. All of these problems are related by means of the transfer of capital, goods, services, and the like, and efforts to resolve them must take into account these interrelationships. It is particularly vital to remember that efforts to solve the problems afflicting developing countries are important not only to overcome the present crisis but also because they may have long-term effects on the future economy of the developing countries.

This chapter is reprinted, with permission, from the United Nations *Journal of Development Planning,* No. 10, 1976.

Developed countries are trying to create purchasing power through domestic-oriented measures such as tax reductions and expansion of civil works programs in order to overcome the current recession. It is necessary, however, to regard these policies from an international viewpoint. That is, the developed industrial countries are increasing their investment in domestic road and housing construction and seeking to stimulate personal consumption, but if a part of that investment were directed, for example, to constructing irrigation projects or fertilizer industries in developing countries, the purchasing power of those countries would be augmented, the exports of developed countries would be increased and their imports of primary products from developing countries would be augmented, the exports of developed countries would be increased and their imports of primary products from developing countries would also be expanded; thus, a contribution towards the improvement of world economic conditions would be made.

Recently, some developed countries have increased their reliance on exports and, hence, they need to find ways to stimulate not only their domestic economies but their export industries as well. Because there is a lack of purchasing power in the developing countries, the transfer of resources would help to create additional import capability. Moreover, if such a transfer of resources is directed towards the increase of food production, it will contribute in the long run to overcoming food shortages in the developing countries.[1]

Farmers in some poor countries do not earn enough to purchase fertilizer, which has risen in price; this has an adverse influence on production of foodstuffs. If financing could be made available on soft terms to developing countries to enable them to purchase necessary commodities, including fertilizer, this would help to in-increase food production.

Just as the New Deal adopted by the United States of America during the 1930s increased public investment and contributed to the recovery of the economy, what is needed at the present time is a global New Deal to increase investment in production—es-

[1] See Saburo Okita and Kunio Takase: *Doubling Rice Production Program in Asia* (Tokyo: The Overseas Economic Cooperation Fund, 1976), reprinted as the third chapter in this volume.

pecially of foodstuffs—in developing countries and also to ensure that facilities and labor in developed countries do not become idle.

Against the background of high labor costs in developed countries, the developing countries are gaining comparative advantage in labor-intensive sectors such as the textile industry. This will enable those industries to grow in labor-surplus developing countries and to export their products to developed countries. In order to facilitate such a process it is necessary for the developing countries to improve management efficiency, give greater attention to productive activities, and be cost-conscious.

Government policies today still place national interests foremost, but policymakers are coming to realize that increasing relationships of interdependence and a gradual structural change of the world economy are inevitable. These changes will require each country to formulate its national policy within a framework of international cooperation rather than of international confrontation. The decisions made by the United Nations General Assembly at its seventh special session in 1975 constitute a welcome step in this direction.

Investment of Oil Funds

Many institutions have published statistics and projections with regard to the influence of increases in oil prices on the world economy and the future outlook. Those statistics and projections which concern the middle-term outlook vary according to the assumptions of the institutions and, especially, according to their view of future trends in the price of oil and the growth of imports of members of the Organization of Petroleum Exporting Countries (OPEC). In general, although in early 1974 it was expected that the surpluses accumulated by OPEC members would be enormous, when information for 1974 became available early projections were adjusted downwards.

Therefore although the projections vary in scale, an accumulation of a high current surplus by OPEC as a whole is anticipated, and it is expected that this will greatly influence the world economy. Further, to the extent that there is agreement among OPEC members, it is likely that they will continue to increase their oil revenues.

The recycling of oil money to finance the deficits in the balances of payments of oil-importing countries has been crucial in maintaining the stability of the international financial system. According to International Monetary Fund (IMF) information for 1974, oil money was recycled to oil-consuming countries primarily by means of international short-term money markets, and this has played an important role in offsetting oil deficits. Nevertheless, the pattern of circulation of oil money shows a bias in favor of developed countries; while providing a measure of ease in those countries, oil money did not circulate in sufficient quantities in the countries where it was most needed, thus giving rise to a North-South problem in financial circulation. That is, the non-oil-producing developing countries, in addition to having to bear the increased burden of paying higher prices for oil, largely because of the decrease in demand for and decline in prices of primary products, suffered from deficits in their current accounts which exceeded those of the previous year by $21 billion and approached $30 billion for the year 1974. Moreover, in 1975 there was little prospect for improvement and it is likely that the deficits will further increase to about $4.5 billion, making it a matter of the greatest urgency that more funds be recycled to the non-oil-producing developing countries.

According to estimates of the Development Assistance Committee (DAC) of the Organisation for Economic Co-operation and Development (OECD),[2] the total volume of aid provided by OPEC members and disbursed in 1974 was $2.2 billion, an almost five-fold increase over the previous year. This increase was much greater than that of DAC members' aid (7.8 percent). Also, OPEC members' commitments in 1974 amounted to $5.3 billion ($3.8 billion as bilateral aid and $1.5 billion as multilateral aid), but these figures exclude contributions to IMF, the World Bank, and other international organizations. Iran, Kuwait, and Saudi Arabia accounted for a majority share of these commitments (see Table 1).

[2] Organisation for Economic Co-operation and Development, Development Assistance Committee: "Flow of Resources from OPEC Members to Developing Countries" (Paris, 1975).

Table 1. Volume of Concessional Aid Provided by OPEC Members, 1974 (millions of dollars, except as otherwise indicated)

Country	Commitments			Estimated disbursements				
	Bilateral	Multilateral	Total	Bilateral	Multilateral	Total	Ratio to oil reveuue (percentage)	Ratio to gross national product (percentage)
Algeria	3	114	117	3	32	35	0.9	0.3
Algeria	1,247	23	1,270	378	23	401	2.0	0.9
Iraq	347	68	415	210	27	237	3.3	1.8
Kuwait	575	221	796	328	56	384	4.6	3.1
Libyan Arab Republic	182	195	377	73	24	97	1.4	0.8
Nigeria	2	10	12	2	9	11	0.1	0.1
Qatar	83	65	148	42	9	51	2.8	2.6
Saudi Arabia	995	461	1,456	710	100	810	2.7	2.3
United Arab Emirates	376	197	573	107	30	137	2.6	1.8
Venezuela	20	91	111	20	41	61	0.6	0.2
TOTAL	3,830	1,445	5,275	1,873	351	2,224	2.4	1.4

Source: Organisation for Economic Co-operation and Development: *Development Co-operation: 1975 Review* (Paris, 1975), p. 182.

However, many problems are anticipated in connection with this rapid increase in bilateral and multilateral aid provided by the oil-producing countries. First, the stagnation of the world economy, coupled with the growth of imports by oil-producing countries, is serving to greatly curtail the current surpluses of these countries. The recovery of the world economy would have some influence, but if oil revenues continue to decline, it is likely that the provision of aid by the oil-producing countries will also decline.

Secondly, the oil-producing countries control the distribution of investment of oil income, including its use for development. Development of their own countries of course takes precedence among the governments of oil-producing nations, and, in accordance with the expanded economic development plans of the oil producers, the current surpluses are therefore likely to be reduced. Inevitably, the pipeline for circulating oil surpluses to the economies of non-oil producers would become narrower.

Thirdly, the oil producers' development aid is concentrated among (*a*) Arab countries and (*b*) countries of West Asia. The same can be said of the circulation of oil dollars by means of trade. In comparison to the rapid growth in OPEC members' imports from the Middle East and African countries during 1974, their imports from South and Southeast Asia and Latin America increased very little. Thus the recycling of oil money to non-oil-producing developing countries shows a clear regional pattern.

Consumer countries have attempted to offset oil deficits by reducing oil consumption and increasing exports to oil-producing countries, but, during the same time, under the pressure of "stagflation," every consuming country has experienced a slow-down of its economic growth rate. Because it is feared that rapid advances in offsetting the deficits could further aggravate both the recession and unemployment and tend to concentrate balance-of-payments deficits in certain countries with weaker economies, adjustment of the world economy by means of close cooperation among countries is needed.

A particular disadvantage to countries which export primary products is that their exports to the oil-producing countries are at low levels, even though the latter countries are rapidly increasing their imports. This is because the greater share of imports of oil-producing countries are capital goods such as steel and machinery or durable consumer goods, and the majority of non-oil-producing developing countries either cannot supply these or have only weak supply capability. Therefore, while industrial countries are expanding their exports to the oil producers, very little expansion of the exports of the developing countries is evident. Further, for the non-oil-producing developing countries, the influence of oil price increases has not been limited to the general area of imports but also, by the medium of the recession in developed countries, has caused a softening of demand by the latter for primary products, factors which in combination have brought about a critical situation regarding their foreign reserve holdings. This situation will continue for as long as the economies of the developed countries fail to recover, so that for the time being there is little prospect that exports of primary products will improve rapidly.

A number of international conferences have already been held in order to establish channels whereby finance may be provided to ease the burden of oil deficits, and as a result of those meetings a Financial Support Fund (FSF) has been established with 20 billion special drawing rights (SDRs) on the International Monetary Fund (IMF) in order to provide financing to member countries of OECD over a two-year period; it has also been agreed that, for non-oil-producing countries, IMF's Oil Facility created by contributions from oil-producing countries will be increased in scale from 3.05 billion SDRs (87 percent from oil producers) to 5 billion SDRs. In particular, for the most seriously affected countries, even a relatively small amount of funds circulated to them by means of the Oil Facility will be of great value in offsetting deficits. For the non-oil-producing developing countries, for which the channel of funds from the oil producers by means of aid and private money markets (such as the Euro-dollar market) is very narrow, the Oil Facility is the last resort for obtaining foreign exchange.

However, in most instances, these systems and countermeasures, as emergency steps taken to combat crises in balance of payments, are weak and do not attempt to deal directly with the adjustment of the deficits. From the long-term viewpoint of balanced world economic development there is a clear need to consider a combination of (*a*) the capital and markets of the oil-producing and the developed countries, (*b*) the technology of the developed countries, and (*c*) the needs of the developing countries. Also needed is a new international recycling system centered on long-term investment in production—in short, the establishment of a new concept of development cooperation.

According to a report of the Trilateral Commission,[3] in order to attain an average annual growth of 2.1 percent in per-capita gross national product for the one billion persons in countries where income is less than $200 per capita, and in view of the expected futher lowering of incomes in these countries due to worsening of the inflation-plagued world economy, an increase in development finance of at least $6 billion per year during 1976–80 is necessary. It is estimated that disbursements of government-based aid from OPEC members as a whole during 1976–80 will be on the order of $3 billion annually.

It was proposed by the Trilateral Commission that, of the remaining $3 billion, funds would be acquired at the interest rate of 8 percent from the oil money of OPEC members and loaned to non-oil-producing developing countries at 3 percent, and that the difference between interest rates would be borne equally by the developed countries and OPEC members. This proposal is now partially being carried out by the creation of the World Bank's "Third Window."

The increases in oil prices compelled oil-importing developed countries to practice a form of forced savings, but this form of savings, if used effectively on behalf of the world economy and particularly on behalf of the development of the economies of the poor countries, will not necessarily be a detrimental phenomenon. The deceleration of the growth of the economies of developed countries has a favorable aspect in that it may promote conservation of natural resources and protection of the environment. If, in this case, the economic growth of developing countries can be accelerated, this will contribute to reduction of the North-South differential. The dilemma is that, if the economic growth of developed countries slows down, world trade expansion will also

[3] See Richard N. Gardner, Saburo Okita and B. J. Udink, rapporteurs: *OPEC, the Trilateral World, and the Developing Countries: New Arrangements for Cooperation, 1976–1980* (New York: the Trilateral Commission, 1975). The Trilateral Commission is a private North American–European–Japanese initiative on matters of common concern.

slow down and this will, in turn, have adverse influences on the economies of the developing countries which depend heavily on trade. In the long run, it is probably essential to create a world economic system in which the growth of developed countries is slowed down and at the same time the growth of the developing countries is speeded up.

Pricing of Exports to Effect a Shift in the Terms of Trade toward Developing Countries

Primary commodities in developing countries accounted for about 80 percent of their total exports in 1970–72 and thus are very important means of obtaining foreign currency. According to a report of the International Bank for Reconstruction and Development (IBRD), the commodity price index for the 34 main primary commodities (excluding oil) of developing countries has continued to decline since 1950–51, the time of the Korean conflict (see Table 2). In 1972–74 it went up rapidly. Major reasons for this rise were: simultaneous upswing of business conditions in the major industrial countries, speculation stimulated by the increase in money supply, collapse of the postwar international monetary system based on the gold-dollar standard, contraction of the supply of agricultural commodities due to bad weather, and the repercussion of high oil prices. The commodity price index rose by 119 percent from mid-1972 to mid-1974, and by 39 percent,

Table 2. Commodity Price Index for 34 Commodities (Excluding Petroleum) (1967–1969 = 100)

	1950–52	1955–57	1960–62	1964–66	1967–69
Current dollars	111	109	91	103	100
Constant dollars	133	123	99	106	100

	1970	1971	1972	1973	1974	June-July 1975
Current dollars	109	103	112	168	234	204
Constant dollars	100	88	88	112	128	101

Source: International Bank for Reconstruction and Development: *Price Forecasts for Major Primary Commodities*, Report No. 814.

on the average, from 1973 to 1974. But the subsequent recession in the developed countries, easing of the oil supply situation, and stagnation of speculation owing to the spread of the tight money situation in the developed countries are pushing the price of primary commodities down sharply. Though the price of industrial products did not go up as rapidly as that of primary commodities in 1973 and 1974, it remained at high levels because of the continuation of inflation in the developed countries. On the other hand, the price of primary commodities declined sharply and the purchasing power of the exporting countries fell. The 1975 *Annual Report* issued by IBRD estimated that the purchasing power for industrial and other products, obtained by exporting primary products, would go down by about 13 percent in 1975 relative to the preceding year. Seventy-five percent of total exports in developing countries are directed to the OECD markets, and the prices of the primary commodities are thus greatly influenced by business trends in the developed countries.

The developing countries, depending heavily on production and export of primary commodities, have taken every opportunity to press for price stabilization of primary commodities and improvement of terms of trade, particularly since the oil crisis. The Declaration and the Programme of Action on the Establishment of a New International Economic Order were adopted by the United Nations General Assembly at its sixth special session in May 1974 (resolutions 3201 (S-VI) and 3202 (S-VI)), and the Charter of Economic Rights and Duties of States was adopted by the General Assembly at its twenty-ninth session in December 1974 (resolution 3281 (XXXIX)). Both the Programme of Action and the Charter for the most part represented the demands of the developing countries, but the developed countries did not respond favorably. More recently, however, the developed countries have tended to be more cooperative, as evidenced by the Lomé Convention signed by the European Community and African, Carribbean, and Pacific countries in February 1975, and by the developed countries' proposals at the IMF and IBRD joint annual meeting and at the seventh special session of the General Assembly. Moreover, at the fourth session of the United Nations Conference on Trade and Development (UNCTAD), held in May 1976, commodities were the most important topic on the agenda, and discussions were focused on the "integrated commodities program" and the "common fund" advocated by the developing countries.

So far, various schemes for primary commodities have been proposed; some of them have actually been implemented. It is necessary to examine these schemes, several of which are outlined below, from two viewpoints: first, the degree to which they will prevent violent fluctuations in prices of primary commodities or cushion the impact of such fluctuations; and, secondly, the degree to which they will promote a transfer of resources from wealthy nations to poor nations by improving the terms of trade in primary commodities for developing countries.

Commodity agreements

(a) *Export quotas*. Under this scheme supplier countries regulate the quantities placed on the market by allocation of production and exports. This scheme tends to protect inefficient producers and to discourage improvement of products. It is effective, however, in improving the terms of trade of the exporting countries and is often used as a supplementary measure to the buffer stock scheme.

(b) *Internationally controlled buffer stocks*. Under this scheme, there is selling on the international market when the price rises above the fixed level and buying when the price goes down below the fixed level in order to stabilize the international market price in a predetermined range. So far, agreements have been made for tin and cocoa.

For the buffer stock scheme there are many problems to be solved: (*a*) selecting suitable commodities for this scheme; (*b*) determining the appropriate stock scale; (*c*) sharing the initial cost for establishment of the stock; and (*d*) sharing the cost of maintaining this scheme. Among these, the first two may be resolved by means of technical studies, but the real problem lies in the latter two. Expansion of the stock and function of the IMF Buffer Stock Financing Facility (established in 1969) may be desirable.

(c) *Integrated commodities program*. This scheme, proposed by the Secretary-General of UNCTAD, combines plans for: (*a*) establishing an international buffer stock of major primary commodities and adjusting supply and demand; (*b*) establishing a common fund to finance international commodity buffer stocks; and (*c*) a diversified trade arrangement intended to provide the necessary guarantees related to both supplies and sales prices of particularly important commodities or products.

Compensatory financing facilities

In case prices of primary commodities or earnings from exports of primary commodities fall below the negotiated level, compensatory financing is automatically made to the developing countries which export the specified commodities. This measure does not intervene in the market system and is not accompanied by as many problems as in the case of buffer stocks.

This facility, for specified commodities, was set up by IMF in 1963, and, for export earnings, it is provided for in the Lomé Convention. In this connection, a proposal of the United States of America at the seventh special session of the General Assembly recommending guaranteed financing for total export income deserves attention.

The Lomé Convention points towards a new style of aid relations between developed and developing countries. It includes the following items: (*a*) a primary commodities export revenue stabilization plan; (*b*) free entry into the Common Market of all industrial goods and agricultural prodocts from associated states in Africa, the Caribbean, and the Pacific (ACP) except certain products covered directly or indirectly by the common agricultural policy of the European Economic Community (EEC); (*c*) abolition of reverse preference to EEC members; (*d*) abolition of import tariffs; (*e*) industrial cooperation; (*f*) cooperation in the supply of funds and technological know-how; and (*g*) export income guarantees.

The approach evidenced in the Lomé Convention, which is regional in scope, should be expanded to be global.

Indexation

This measure involves a sliding scale of prices of primary commodities matched against price increases of industrial products. Since higher oil prices have been depreciated in real terms owing to the inflation in the developed countries, some of the oil-producing countries have insisted on the necessity of an indexation that links the prices of products imported from developed countries to the export price of oil.

For indexation, the following methods are among those which may be considered: (*a*) linking the indexation of export prices of primary commodities to import prices of manufactured foods from developed countries; (*b*) linking the prices of primary commodities to the prices of manufactured goods using these commodities as materials; (*c*) linking the prices of primary commodities to the product cost; (*d*) linking those prices to the currency value fluctuation.

If the prices of all commodities are raised mechanically without giving due consideration to the balance of supply and demand and relative price changes among commodities, excessive rigidity may be introduced in the commodity price structure. There is also a danger of price spiraling.

Unions of primary commodities producers

The purpose of these unions is to fix the prices of primary commodities at high levels by limiting the supply. This method is very effective for such commodities as petroleum, because demand is inelastic and the supply may be easily controlled by producer countries and, further, the supply of substitutes is limited and the commodity is absolutely necessary for industrial activity and the functioning of modern societies. There are relatively few primary commodities other than petroleum which have the above-mentioned properties. Moreover, for some commodities, rich countries are major suppliers and the producers' union is not always suitable for developing countries from the point of view of income transfer.

There are other measures such as development of resources, improvement of the quality of primary commodities, and increase of value added by the promotion of processing resources. The developed countries and international organizations should furnish funds, technology, and knowledge to the developing countries for these purposes.

In considering these various measures, it is useful to think of the countries of the world as belonging in four different categories: (*a*) those rich in resources and economically rich; (*b*) those rich in resources but economically poor; (*c*) those poor in resources but economically rich; and (*d*) those poor in resources and economically poor. Issues related to primary commodities can be viewed as relationships among these groups. Therefore, the transfer of resources from rich to poor by means of higher commodity prices is not simple. It may be necessary to combine commodity agreements with export compensation schemes.

Developed countries should also be encouraged to modify their tariff structures, which sometimes put higher tariffs on processed goods as compared to raw materials, and to increase imports of processed goods from developing countries.

New Sources of Finance

At present, the idea of what in Japan is called a "civil minimum"—that is, the guaranteeing of a minimum level of well-being for the daily life of individuals and a minimum level of social infrastructure—is popular in developed countries. In the future this idea could be expanded worldwide, particularly, at the outset, to those countries whose per-capita income is very low. As economic conditions and the social climate vary from country to country, each country should plan individual national civil minimums. This would comprise one criterion for the allocation of aid by national governments and international organizations. Moreover, as a long-term strategic goal, a world tax would be created and, in accordance with the world civil minimum, financing would be provided to low-income countries. A prerequisite for this provision of funds would be that the recipient countries exert maximum efforts to increase domestic production and attain a more equitable distribution of income domestically.

In its proposals for the Second United Nations Development Decade, the Committee for Development Planning suggested the establishment of a world solidarity contribution in order to create new development fund sources.[4] According to that proposal, a special consumption tax would be imposed on specific goods in all countries (e.g. automobiles, television sets, refrigerators, etc.) the

[4] *Towards Accelerated Development* (United Nations publication, Sales No. E. 70. II. A.2), page 28.

possession of which indicates a relatively high living standard. The tax revenue thereby gained would be used for international development finance as a contribution to world solidarity. The tax rate should be uniform—for example, 0.5 percent of the purchase price. Every country would collect the tax as its own responsibility.

One expert has proposed the creation of a world grain bank to stabilize agricultural prices and to assist food-importing countries to increase their agricultural output.[5] The bank would purchase grain at fair prices and developed countries could purchase grain from the bank according to their solvency, while developing countries could purchase grain at reduced prices. This differentiation in purchase price would be better than the provision of subsidies to poor countries. The revenue from the price arrangement mentioned above would then be used for the purpose of promoting food production in food-deficit countries.

Japan has the experience of using production-sharing systems for development of forest resources and oil in developing countries. This system is worthy of adoption for developing countries which have abundant resources but lack development funds and technology. The contents of this system are as follows:

(a) The enterprise which is to develop the natural resource is established in the developing country concerned. The control of management of this enterprise will be held by government officials or persons from the private sector of the host country.

(b) The partner from the developed country may supply the enterprise with a capital loan or supplier's credit and technical assistance. The enterprise pays debts and fees with its products.

The managers of multinational corporations, in order to maximize the profits of the corporation (or group of corporations) and to minimize tax payments, may utilize differences between the taxation systems of different countries. In such a case, it is conceivable that the multinational corporations active in developing countries could be obliged to make contributions to international organizations, or that a tax be applied to their profits to obtain development funds.

[5] Harrison S. Brown, in a discussion with the author concerning the Club of Rome's study, *The Limits to Growth* (New York, Universe Books, 1972); the discussion was published in Japanese in *The Chūō Kōron* (August 1975).

In another section of the present report reference is made to the fact that, in the event that development of deep-sea and continental shelf resources is jointly and internationally controlled, a portion of the profits thereby obtained might be diverted to use for the economic development of developing countries.

Improved Access to Private Capital Markets

First, the existing international capital markets must be utilized more positively. We can enumerate the existing international capital markets, such as the Euro-dollar market, New York market, or Asian-dollar market. In connection with these existing markets we must devise ways whereby developing countries will be enabled to absorb funds easily through measures including the issue of bonds. According to an IMF survey of the borrowers of Euro-dollars during 1974, developed industrial countries borrowed $16.6 billion and developing countries borrowed $9.1 billion. This accounts for 61 percent and 33.5 percent, respectively, of the total. Among developing countries, high-income countries borrowed $6.6 billion, accounting for 71.8 percent of the total amount borrowed by developing countries.[6] In contrast, medium-income countries and low-income countries borrowed $1.8 billion (28.2 percent). (The rest of the borrowers among developing countries were oil-producing countries.)

The following measures could be considered as ways of deriving development funds from the existing international capital markets: (*a*) both governmental and non-governmental entities could obtain funds from capital markets through the issue of bonds; (*b*) international financial organizations, such as the World Bank and the Asian Development Bank, could issue bonds in markets; and (*c*) enterprises of developed countries could obtain funds from markets in order to invest in developing countries.

Secondly, there is the matter of securing funds from the oil-producing countries. In addition to intergovernmental arrangements, it is conceivable that oil funds could be utilized by joint arrangements between companies, including companies in developed countries.

[6] *IMF Survey,* 17 February 1975.

Thirdly, the circumstances of the recipient countries in receiving foreign capital must be consolidated. For example, if a stock market exists where there is free trading of stocks, it could introduce portfolio investment from foreign countries without management participation.

The creation of local capital markets is important in order to facilitate economic development. The enterprises in developed countries could introduce funds freely from private capital markets, acting on their own initiative. But in the case of developing countries, there is almost no basis for receiving such funds. Developed countries, which supply developing countries with capital and technology, could think about ways to enhance the local capital availability. Following are some of the possibilities:

(a) *Separate transfer of capital and technology*. Governments of developed countries could dispatch managers and technicians to developing countries using their technical cooperation budgets. In addition, governments of developed countries could make loans to development banks of the host countries on concessional terms out of financial cooperation budgets. The banks could then make subloans to the local enterprise concerned. Thus, the enterprise could utilize capital and technology while retaining control of management. Technology and funds from a developed country would thus be linked inside a developing country.

(b) *Gradual tranfer of management*. It is difficult for private investors in developing countries, who have extremely limited capital and technological resources, to hold a large share at the outset of a joint venture with a foreign investor. But the foreign share should be reduced gradually, preferably by providing the shares to local partners. If both partners conclude a long-term agreement on technical cooperation apart from the ownership of capital, the enterprise could obtain technical aid even after the transfer of the foreign partner's share.

The Relationship between Terms of Aid and the Level of Development

Since 1973, the sharp increase in world inflation and oil prices and the recession in developed countries throughout the world have had a great influence on the developing countries and have promoted the differentiation of several groups among the developing countries.

The oil producers and some other countries succeeded in accelerating their growth because of the higher oil prices and the economic boom in those countries, but, on the other hand, the poorest countries were barely able to maintain even low economic growth during the first half of the 1970s and fell into such a critical situation that there is no hope of their achieving significant growth by 1980.

The implications of these new conditions must be considered in connection with economic cooperation and the need at all levels for the development of the developing countries.

The problem is, basically, how to fit the quality and quantity of aid to the needs of developing countries.

The developing countries may be divided into the following four groups: (*a*) the most seriously affected and the poorest countries; (*b*) countries producing and exporting primary commodities; (*c*) countries exporting manufactured goods; and (*d*) oil-producing countries that have large financial surpluses.

The first group consists of most seriously affected countries and the countries with low per-capita income, low literacy, and low proportion of employment in secondary and tertiary sectors—the least developed among the developing countries.

The countries belonging to the second group depend on primary commodities for their earnings of foreign currency for economic development, and they are plagued by the fact that they cannot stabilize export income because of the instability of primary commodity prices and terms of trade.

The third group of countries are those promoting export-oriented industrialization and in need of expanding foreign markets. So far, they have generally been attaining high rates of economic growth in recent years.

The fourth group consists of the oil-rich countries which are accumulating large capital assets by exporting oil.

The task before the first group is to establish a basis for the stabilization of their people's livelihood and economic development by eliminating starvation, rolling back inflation, improving the balance of payments, and rebuilding the budget.

Emergency aid like food or commodity aid should be provided to these countries. But at the same time, because of the need to improve the standard of living, to liberate people from the bonds of poverty and improve the physical and human infrastructure which forms the basis of economic and social development, aid which increases social capital (such as better primary education, medical care, and training of skilled manpower) should also be considered. In particular, aid for projects to increase food production should be emphasized so that starvation may be eliminated and food imports, which adversely affect the balance of payments, can be reduced.

Emergency aid, aid for the preparation of infrastructure, and aid for projects to increase food production should be provided as grants or soft loans. Measures such as rescheduling or refinancing should be considered so that the amount of aid provided may not be in effect decreased substantially by debt payments.

The amount of funds available for transfer from developed countries under soft terms is limited. Thus, when soft terms are offered to countries outside the first group, the differential between those terms and commercial or near-commercial terms should be transferred to the most seriously affected countries or to low-income countries that export primary commodities.

Some countries belonging to the second group have expanded export earnings and have made progress in industrialization as a result of the boom in primary commodities since 1973. But as the economies of these countries depend on the international price of specific goods, they are very unstable. To achieve economic growth, these countries must promote the stabilization of the prices of primary commodities, increase the level of processing, and diversify their primary commodities. Therefore economic cooperation provided to these countries must take the form of commodity agreements including use of the export revenue compensation and international buffer stock schemes mentioned elsewhere in the present paper and also such cooperation through trade as reduction of tariffs and abolition of nontariff barriers. Moreover, support should be provided for increased processing of goods prior to export and the preparation of related infrastructure. Developed countries need to cooperate positively by paying in the funds for buffer stocks or export revenue compensation through international organizations. As the development stages of the countries belonging to this group vary greatly, aid terms must be determined separately for each country, according to its development stage and level of per-capita gross national product.

Securing markets for their manufactured goods is the most important matter for those countries promoting export-oriented industrialization—that is, the third group. Developed countries need to open their markets to these developing countries gradually by reducing and eliminating tariff and nontariff barriers while adjusting their own industrial structures. On the other hand, it is necessary that developing countries depend on domestic savings as well as on the transfer of capital and technology from developed countries to cover the increase in the demand for capital and technology which accompanies the progress of industrialization, and they should create an environment favorable for this. Developed countries may also assist the development of industry and financial institutions through bank loans. This could be done on a commercial or near-commercial basis. Although these countries' debt service ratios are usually high because of the introduction of large amounts of foreign capital in the process of industrialization, they can bear the burden of external debt by greater promotion of industrialization and expansion of exports. Developed countries, however, must pay continual attention to the developing countries' external debt situation, and when developing countries fall into a critical situation concerning the external debt payments, refinancing and rescheduling may have to be considered at multilateral meetings such as those held by creditor countries or consultation groups.

The oil-rich countries, which form the fourth group, have enough funds to purchase the necessary technology and materials for their social and economic development. Developed countries should cooperate with them, especially in the provision of technology, on either a commercial or technical-aid basis. These countries should be encouraged to transfer their surplus funds to other developing countries, to support the development of the latter.

According to a DAC report,[7] the furnishing of funds transferred from developed countries to developing countries recently tends to

[7] Organisation for Economic Co-operation and Development: *Development Co-operation: 1974 Review* (Paris, 1974).

give the priority to the least developed among the developing countries. Classifying the developing countries into groups by per-capita gross national product and tracing the aid flow to each group, it was found that the group of lower-income countries had been furnished with more funds and on softer terms than the others. This tendency grew more and more marked from 1969 to 1972 and it should be promoted even more. It is also important, however, to provide facilities for financing development of less poor developing countries through commercial or near-commercial channels.

Multinational Corporations as a Channel for Financial Transfers

The role played by multinational corporations in the process of financial transfer from developed countries to developing countries during the past ten years has been enormous. The net direct private investment flow from DAC countries to the developing countries increased from $2.5 billion in 1965 to $6.7 billion in 1974, while the share of those flows in total transfers increased from 22 percent to 27 percent over the same period.

The balance of payments of non-oil-producing developing countries has steadily deteriorated, as a consequence of the increase in import prices of oil, the combined influence of higher import prices for industrial products, lower import levels in the developed countries resulting from the economic downturn, and the softening of the market for primary products. To cope with this situation, the non-oil-producing less developed countries, by acquiring Euro-funds, by borrowing from IMF and other international organizations, and through bilateral transactions with OPEC members, have in the short term staved off the effects on their international balance of payments which were brought about by increases in the price of crude oil and other commodities, and have been able to hold their position by adopting restrictions on imports. However, having recourse to borrowing will not necessarily solve the basic problem which persists in the form of obligations to repay the principal and interest on loans. If such conditions continue for a few more years, the debt burden of the non-oil-producing developing countries will become exceedingly grave. While it is thought that the effects will be most serious in those countries which were forced to acquire funds in the Euro-market and other money markets at a commercial and hence high rate of interest, nevertheless many developing countries with medium and high income levels were able to borrow in the Euro-market to offset deficits in their current accounts caused by the higher oil prices. For some of those countries the debt service ratio has crossed the danger line (23.5 percent in Mexico; 22.2 percent in Argentina), while it has risen above 10 percent in others (in the Republic of Korea, 14.2 percent; in Brazil, 13.6 percent), and the increase in borrowing during 1974 is considered to have caused widespread deterioration of debt positions. Further, with regard to the most severely affected countries, the Ministry of International Trade and Industry of Japan estimated the amount to be repaid in 1975 at $800 million, which is equivalent to 45.6 percent of those countries' government-based aid receipts in 1973, providing one measure of the severity of the conditions which must be anticipated.[8]

It is self-evident from the foregoing that, for the non-oil-producing countries that confront this difficult problem, government-based aid from oil-producing countries and developed countries is of paramount importance and, moreover, that this problem enhances the importance of the role played by multinational corporations which have the capability to transfer, in a package, capital, technology, management abilities, and other inputs and to contribute to the economies of recipient countries.

There is, however, the very real possibility that the multinational corporations, by dint of their enormous scale and near-monopolistic control of their areas of business, will exert political influence and acquire control of crucial sectors of the economy in the host countries. A condition desirable to these corporations from the viewpoint of effectiveness in their own operations will not necessarily be similarly seen as desirable by the host governments. Further, it is possible that these corporations will act in a manner not in accord with the policies of the host governments. A situation which Raymond Vernon expressed with the

[8] Ministry of International Trade and Industry: *White Paper on International Trade* (1975).

title of his book, *Sovereignty at Bay*,[9] has developed. Research and study on the multinational corporations has increased, and several international bodies are now investigating the possibilities of regulating the activities of the multinationals, reflecting concern with these conditions. Drafting of a code of conduct for the multinational corporations is now being done within OECD and the United Nations. Because, as mentioned above, improvement of the difficult situation which the developing countries confront depends greatly on the actions of the multinational corporations, it is necessary in any code of conduct to augment the merits of the multinationals and reduce their demerits.

Fund procurement by subsidiaries of the multinationals has in the past primarily made use of internal resources such as internal reserves and amortization and depreciation, but recently they are combining loans from financial institutions in the host countries and income from bond issues in the Euro-market with the use of internal resources. Considering that, at the present time, a worsening of the international balance of payments may be seen not only in the developing countries but also in the developed countries, increased use of these new methods of fund procurement is to be expected. Although there is a disadvantage which has recently attracted attention in that the augmented relations between the multinationals and the Euro-market can lead to a transfer of the "hot money," there is the even greater advantage that it becomes possible to absorb Euro-bonds which no single developing country could absorb on its own. Considering further that large quantities of oil dollars have been flowing into the Euro-bond market, the role of the multinationals in bringing oil dollars into the developing countries is very important.

The issue at hand is not merely to acquire capital in the amounts required but rather how to use that capital so that it effectively contributes to the development process. This makes it incumbent on the investment-receiving country to plan its own economic and social development and determine development priorities.

Further, with regard to general conditions applicable to incoming foreign investment, or to actual administrative schemes, it is desirable to have the relationship between an investment and

[9] Raymond Vernon: *Sovereignty at Bay: The Multinational Spread of U.S. Enterprises* (New York: Basic Books, 1971).

the program for economic and social development lucid at all times and to make necessary corrections speedily. At the same time, the multinationals should exercise care so that their investment plans are in accord with priorities set in the economic and social development programs of the host countries and should prepare a realistic program for implementing the investment.

One effective means of attracting direct investment is the adoption of an import-substitution policy, strengthening trade barriers by such means as raising tariffs and imposing quantitative restrictions on imports, but the developing countries whose development is greatly constrained by their balance-of-payments positions should give precedence to export-oriented foreign investment. Because of the general decline in competitiveness of the labor-intensive industrial products of developed countries, it is necessary for developing countries to aggressively attract investors possessing pertinent technology, and for this purpose it may sometimes be useful to improve and expand free trade zones. On the part of developed countries, it is necessary to open their doors further to industrial products exported by developing countries which have international comparative advantages.

In addition to being one form of capital transfer, direct investment, at the time the investment is made, is a positive factor in the international balance of payments of the host country. Conversely, however, when profits are earned and then repatriated, they are a negative factor. During the early stage of investment, the former exceed the latter, but if the amount of the outstanding investment is high and the growth rate of new investment is low, the latter will exceed the former and in net terms the investment will have an adverse effect on the balance of payments of the host country. Owing to considerations related to the balance of payments, developing countries at times impose restrictions on the overseas remission of dividends and royalties, but it is an issue of basic importance in attracting foreign investment that assurance be provided regarding repatriation of profits. For the developing countries suffering from chronic shortages of foreign exchange and sources of revenue, however, the reinvestment of profits in effect is an attractive source of revenue, so that reinvestment of a portion of the profits may be encouraged.

The role which the multinationals can play in the expansion of their host countries' exports is immense. It is often their marketing and production know-how which makes it possible to produce goods that can be sold abroad. Japanese trading companies, for example, have global networks and have done much to expand the exports of developing countries. Owing to increases in production costs and growth of demand in Japan in recent years, Japan now imports large quantities of goods which were formerly available from domestic sources. Most of these imports are brought into the country by the trading companies. In 1965, Japan imported textile products worth $55 million; by 1974 the value of such imports had risen to $1,829 million and Japan had become the world's largest importer of textiles, behind the United States of America. Thus, many of these trading companies can be utilized not only to sell goods to Japan but also for export to third countries.

Governments of developing countries often make a sharp distinction between manufacturing and commerce, but they are then obliged to take realistic steps to increase earnings of foreign currency. Marketing in order to attain that goal often requires technical know-how as complex as that needed for constructing production facilities. The opinion is often advanced in developing countries that foreign capital is only seeking to exploit the cheap labor of the developing countries. International trade, however, is based on differences among the production factors of capital, labor, and raw materials. It is natural that the cost of labor will be low in countries where the per-capita national income is low, and that is one essential condition which enables those countries to attain larger exports. In principle, larger exports, by relieving a shortage of foreign exchange, are conducive to larger imports and, subsequently, a higher level of domestic economic activity. From this viewpoint, the developing countries may make good use of the multinationals for their own benefit.

Rising economic nationalism in the developing countries is seen to be resulting in increased use of "fade-out formulae," and this will probably also influence the pattern of capital supply by the multinationals. Because the capital markets in developing countries are undeveloped and the capacity of local investment partners to supply capital is limited, the local equity share (particularly in the case of big projects) is necessarily low, and at the same time there is increased need to rely on borrowing or on deferred payments for imports as a means of obtaining capital. To the developing countries, this amounts to a shift away from direct investing and towards greater borrowing and use of credits. It is desirable for international organizations or investment institutions in developed countries to participate in joint ventures and to provide soft loans when possible to the local partners either directly or indirectly through the intermediary of a local investment bank. It will probably be worthwhile to take note of the proposal announced at the seventh special session of the General Assembly by the United States of America recommending a fourfold increase in the capital resources of the International Finance Corporation.

Under the present circumstances there seems to be a possibility of triangular agreements for the development of the developing countries, whereby funds from OPEC, technology from developed countries, and land and labor from the developing countries would be combined. Importation of technology was more important than the importation of capital in the process of Japan's economic development, but in the non-oil-producing developing countries domestic savings are still insufficient to meet the demand for investment capital, which means that both capital and technology must be imported by one means or another. The general practice up to the present has been for the multinationals to provide capital, management, and technology as one package, but if it it should prove to be possible to separate the importation of capital from technology by such means as triangular agreements, multinationals would probably increasingly enter the developing countries under other arrangements.

Sea-bed Resources

Ocean beds, which cover about 70 percent of the earth, hold abundant mineral resources. Exploitation of these resources, however, has hardly begun. Three-fourths of the sea-bed area is deep sea, with depths of 3,500 to 11,000 meters, and the rest is the continental margin (continental shelves, slopes, and rises).

The mineral resources deposited on the deep sea beds which are the subjects of greatest interest are the nodules which contain copper, nickel, cobalt, and manganese as main components. As huge amounts of nodule deposits are believed to exist, as many as 30 companies and several governments of the advanced countries are showing much interest in the exploratory study and technical development of the nodule mining industry. They have so far invested several hundred million dollars in this field. A United Nations report, based on an analysis of the announced programs and estimated data for the leading entrepreneurs developing international systems in this field, projects that commercial exploitation of the nodules might be begun in the near future (some time before 1985) and that total production would amount to the order of 15 million tons in 1985.[10]

To facilitate the development of the nodule industry, consideration should be given to (*a*) profitability of recovery and processing of minerals, (*b*) guarantee of the safety of investment made for work in specified regions, and (*c*) the means of financing.

Regarding the first two of these points, it is necessary to set up at an early date an international scheme to rationally regulate and facilitate orderly development of the nodule recovery. With regard to financing, because the required investment is estimated to be $120–$180 million for the economical production scale of 1 million tons per year and $150–$240 million for 3 million tons, the nodule mining industry must be attractive enough in its profitability to allow the entrepreneurs to secure capital from financial sources.

Several estimates suggest that the profitability would be such that it could be commercially viable, although many uncertain factors are involved. In the above-mentioned report, the United Nations roughly estimated the profitability on the basis of information made known by leading firms of the United States of America. According to the estimate, the annual rate of return would be, at the lowest, 43 percent of investment cost for an annual capacity of 1 million tons and 54 percent for 3 million tons. The nodule industry thus seems attractive.

The most attractive resources in the continental margins, which in some cases extend 800 miles offshore, are oil and natural gas. Exploitation has become much more attractive because of the depletion of economically recoverable land deposits, considerable

[10] *Economic Implications of Sea-bed Mineral Development in the International Area* (United Nations publication, Sales No. E. 75. V. 5).

technical development for offshore exploitation and, especially, current energy problems. In the early 1970s, offshore oil was already accounting for 18 percent of total world oil production. As many as 130 oil companies are now engaged in oil exploration and development in the offshore area of about 80 coastal countries. Sea beds can now be economically exploited for oil to a maximum depth of about 200 meters but this depth is expected to be increased to more than 1,800 meters by around 1980, in line with the progress of technical development. As a result it is projected that the share of offshore oil will go up to about 35 percent of the total world oil production in 1980.

The deep sea bed thus has great potential for development. According to the present continental shelf treaty, however, each country may extend its ocean territory for development to such an extent as the exploitation technique of the country can reach. This possibility could result in a stage of sea-bed exploitation wherein most of the ocean area would be divided by a limited number of advanced countries as their territories for resource development.

With a view to avoiding such a situation, the General Assembly, at its twenty-fifth session, adopted the Declaration of Principles Governing the Sea-Bed and the Ocean Floor, and the Subsoil Thereof, beyond the Limits of National Jurisdiction (resolution 2749 (XXV) of 17 December 1970). The Declaration has made it clear that the sea-bed area beyond the limits of national jurisdiction and resources shall be the common heritage of mankind and no country shall have sovereignty over the area. The Declaration has programmed the set-up of an international regime to regulate the development of the area. The subject, as a part of the comprehensive ocean problem, has been discussed by the United Nations Conference on the Law of the Sea. At a recent session of the Conference in New York, a "profit-sharing scheme" was adopted regarding the exploitation of mineral resources at distances beyond 200 nautical miles, by which means, after a five-year period of grace, a set proportion of profits would be paid to an international organization.

If a part of the profits from developing sea-bed resources becomes available to the United Nations system, the income will be an important autonomous source of funds to be used for development activities.

Conclusion

Various changes have taken place during the past 30 years with regard to the relationships among developed countries, among developing countries, and between developed and developing countries, and currently a new international economic order is being sought. At present, each nation continues to assign greatest importance, in formulating policies, to national interests, but it is necessary to realize that mutual interdependence exists among the developed and developing countries and that it is necessary to plan a gradual change in the structure of the world economy. Each country must adjust its formulation of national policy to operate within a global framework of cooperation, not confrontation.

Because of the increase in oil prices, oil-consuming developed nations have been obliged to transfer many more resources to oil-producing countries, but if such transfers can be effectively utilized for the world economy—in particular, if they can be used for the development of the economies of the poor countries—the increase in oil prices will by no means have only negative effects. If developing countries could speed up their economic growth, it would narrow the gap between the North and the South. There is a dilemma, however, in that if the growth of developed countries' economies slows down, growth of world trade too will slow down, and undesirable effects will be felt by the economies of developing countries dependent on trade. In the long-term perspective, it is necessary to attain a speed-up in the economic growth of developing countries, while a slow-down is likely to appear in the economic growth of developed countries.

Commodity agreements have been recommended as one important means of transferring resources and were vigorously discussed by UNCTAD at its recent fourth session. Nevertheless, many issues remain unsettled with regard to the question of whether commodity agreements would be effective in the transfer of resources from rich to poor nations. As mentioned in the section on pricing of exports, with regard to resources, nations may be divided into four groups, that is, rich countries rich in resources, rich countries poor in resources, poor countries rich in resources and poor countries poor in resources; issues related to primary commodities should be taken up not merely as a matter between the North and the South but as one concerning all four groups. Therefore, in addition to commodity agreements, other measures must be taken, such as compensatory finance for shortfalls in export earnings or, in the long run, the establishment of a world development budget and taxation system.

At present, the transfer of financial resources which are essential for the development of developing countries depends to a great extent on the domestic policies of the donor countries involved, and there is great uncertainty as to the amount of capital flows. Various global measures discussed in the sections on new sources of finance and sea-bed resources would, if implemented, guarantee a long-term, autonomous development fund, and would be effective in creating additions to existing channels of resources flow.

Worldwide inflation and recession have had a strong and varied impact on the developing countries. This structural change in the Third World must be reflected in the provision of economic aid and cooperation to help supply the varying needs of the different groups of developing countries.

Through their transfers, in one package, of capital, technology, and managerial know-how; their promotion of exports; or their contribution to the economic growth of host countries, multinational corporations are steadily increasing their role in development. However, because of their enormous size and, in some instances, their monopolistic position, these multinationals may exert influence on politics in their host countries or become dominant in certain sectors of the economy. To offset these demerits, it seems necessary to regulate them by means of an international code of conduct to which they would be bound to subscribe. It is also essential that the developing countries utilize with greater objectivity the merits which the multinationals can offer most effectively.

Most of the developed countries make extensive use, in their domestic policies, of price supports for farm products and redistribution of income through taxation and other measures which do not necessarily operate through market mechanisms. But in the international arena these same countries often oppose price supports for primary commodities and redistribution of income; thus, the same logic does not apply to international policies as to domestic policies. Simply to defer and deny as inappropriate the nationalism in relation to resources seen in developing countries, as well as those countries' demands for price supports and transfer of resources, may invite political opposition. It would be advisable in any case to listen to any rational request or proposal.

It is necessary at the same time for developing nations that have often ignored price mechanisms and assigned too much power to planning to reconsider their actions. For example, it would be desirable for them to give more thought to comparative cost advantages and price competitiveness in their industrialization programs and work out an effective relation between the market mechanism and planning.

It is thus essential for the developing countries to adopt measures to utilize both domestic and foreign resources more effectively by means of better planning and implementation. Of course, the selection of measures and instruments must be left to the developing countries themselves. Cooperation and transfer of capital will be made more effective if external transfer commitments are linked to the effort to mobilize domestic resources to meet the basic needs of the people of the developing countries. By means of such cooperation among countries, it should become possible eventually to introduce policy strategies into global planning.

PART II

The Japanese Example

Developing Economies and the Japanese Experience

It is my great honor to deliver the Azad Memorial Lecture today, not only because my predecessors have been such prominent persons as Jawaharlal Nehru, Arnold Toynbee, Lord Atlee, among others, but also because this lecture was instituted to commemorate a distinguished person who devoted himself to one of the most important subjects of the human being, education. This is really very significant and what I am going to talk about now partly concerns the importance of education in the economic development.

As for myself, I was involved in the process of postwar economic reconstruction as a planner and as an economist. My first visit to India dates back to 1950 when the Indian Planning Commission had just been created. Since then I have made about a dozen visits to India and have continued interest in the development of the Indian economy.

My assignment today is to express my view on the implications of Japan's economic growth for the developing countries. In order to achieve the task, I should like to draw your attention first to a simple but important fact: economic growth of a country is essentially a result of economic efforts made by the people who live there, and nothing else. To put it like this, however, is not to mean that those who are living in the underdeveloped economies—evidently a big majority of mankind—have not paid enough attention to developing themselves. Rather, what I would like to

This chapter is the text of the XV Azad Memorial Lecture, which the author delivered on December 13, 1977, under the aegis of the Indian Council for Cultural Relations. The text of this lecture is printed separately in book form by the ICCR and the copyright vests with the Indian Council for Cultural Relations, Azad Bhavan, Indraprastha Estate, New Delhi 110002, India.

emphasize here is that there is no cure-all medicine for economic development; each country has its own background, history, religion, and traditions. No economic development scheme can be planned without paying due attention to these factors.

It is often asked whether the modernization of Japan was possible owing to exceptionally favorable circumstances or whether it was carried out by some sort of necessity and design. Those who ask this question are evidently interested in the latter alternative and try to draw some "lessons" from the Japanese experience. To be sure, learning from old "wisdom" may be useful unless the old wisdom is in fact merely conventional wisdom. One should notice, however, that the old wisdom may be only stupidity under different circumstances.

The fact is that Japan is neither an ideal model case nor an utterly useless case for developing countries today; the truth is perhaps somewhere in between. Incidentally, a study is now being undertaken by Professor Kazushi Ohkawa, a well-known economic historian of the International Development Center of Japan, with the collaboration of several foreign scholars on the relevance and irrelevance of Japanese experience to other countries.

Talking about Japan's experience of economic growth, I would therefore like to emphasize that modernization is not a synonym for Westernization. Japanese society today maintains many elements that are far from being Western, and still Japan is the only non-Western country that has, more or less, succeeded in modernizing its economy. Many traditional elements played a vital role in the success of this process.

As all of you know, it is said that the modernization of Japan started in 1868 when the feudal system was replaced by a more outward-looking and modernization-oriented government. Although this is broadly correct, we must not forget that the new authorities inherited from the past a lot of factors favorable for economic growth. One such example is education, especially at the elementary level. During the feudal age, there had already developed many private educational institutions where elementary reading, writing, and arithmetic were taught rather systematically. Although such education had never been obligatory, it was considered that these "three R's" were basic necessities of human life. Even in rural areas, the educational standard was reasonably high as shown by the fact that the literacy rate at the time of the initiation of the new educational system in 1872 was already about 30 percent.

The education policy followed by the new Meiji authorities strengthened and complemented this traditional tendency. While high-level education—at the university level—was given comparatively less emphasis, a lot of resources were allocated to improve primary and vocational education.

The relative neglect of higher education and the emphasis on elementary education characterized the Japanese education system for a long time. On the negative side, we were noted as lacking in creativity, intellectuality, and so forth. On the positive side, we became rather pragmatic, being able to catch up with and improve advanced technology in order to develop the economy. In short, Japan developed, during the early stage of modernization, a pyramid-shaped education structure, with a broad base of primary and vocational education, rather than a pillar-shaped one.

I am sure there are pros and cons to such a policy orientation. One might argue the importance of higher education for one reason or another. To be sure, we should not neglect the negative aspect of such educational policy. With these reservations, however, I dare say that such an orientation of education policy basically reflected the pragmatic choice of the policy makers at that time. Incidentally, I was invited in 1966 by the Indian Education Commission, chaired by Dr. D.S. Kothari, to prepare a report on Japan's experience in education and economic development. I made a few comparisons in that report between India and Japan. One of the findings I remember was that the number of students at the higher education level in India accounted for 3.9 percent of their age group in 1965 while in Japan in 1920—the year corresponding to India's 1965 in terms of per-capita steel production and electricity generation—the ratio was 1.6 percent of the age group.

Let me now turn to industrial policy. Industrial policy by itself is a very big topic. We have actually had two types of policy since the early period of modernization. One policy was to establish industries to serve defense needs, examples being the development of the steel and ship-building industries and some machine-making industries. They were geared specifically towards the needs of the military. In the 1930s the automobile industry was established to produce the trucks and vehicles required for military mobility. Many of the present-day heavy industries originated this way. Thus one source of industrial development in Japan was the overriding need of the government, and these industries were established even if from other points of view they were uneconomic. The government guaranteed their survival, gave them tax concessions, and sometimes even underwrote their dividend obligations. These were the industries which the government considered necessary for the defense of the nation. Secondly, there were industries that developed spontaneously through the mechanism of market forces. The cotton textile industry was a case in point. The cotton industry was imported from England at the beginning of the period of modernization. The cotton textile enterprises, located mostly in the western part of Japan, were proud of their achievements in not depending upon government subsidies or support but rather relying on their own resources.

So, in a nutshell, we started with heavy industries artificially induced into existence for defense purposes parallel with the spontaneous growth of light industries in response to market demand. Japan was a late-comer on the industrial scene so we had the advantage of the accumulated experience of the older industrial nations to guide us. When we compare our industrial policy with that of other advanced countries like the European countries and the United States, we see one clear distinction. They did not derive the benefit of precedence in other countries; their industries grew up *pari passu* with the local market under private initiative. The government hardly intervened, much less set target output goals. On the other hand, our government and our business people very carefully studied the industrial field, searching for those industries with future potential, those in which we would have comparative advantage in the world market, and determined the type of support that should be extended to these industries in their formative years. The automobile industry is one such example. The government closed the door to foreign firms who wanted to invest in the industry in Japan. The policy, simply, was that the automobile industry was a promising field and therefore, until our industry became competitive, no foreign investment should be allowed in that sector. If we had allowed foreign investment too early we would not have developed the sound footing we have in the industry today. The policy was: carefully select industries, prevent ruinous competition at the infancy stage, nurse them up to a competitive stature, and then expose them to outside competition. This has more or less been the industrial policy of Japan. Here Western nations frowned upon our methods, but we felt it was the right policy for the late-comer to pursue.

A developing country should of course protect its infant industries, especially those industries that have a chance of success. But there are also dangers in over-protection. Domestic consumers are unnecessarily penalized with inferior products and high prices. Our policy was to give protection for a specified period and thereafter to gradually phase out all protections. I favor such a policy as an aspect of economic planning—stating the target of production to be achieved in a specified number of years and a graduated program of reducing protection until it is completely abolished. This is necessary because if you keep protection indefinitely, even uneconomic industries will survive, consumer welfare will be reduced, and resources will be misallocated. You will have scarce resources "fixed" in uneconomic industries which will require perpetual protection. Protection means a transfer of tax revenue from the public to certain specific industries. In most countries savings are very scarce and therefore must be used most selectively and not wasted on industry, irrespective of whether it is publicly or privately owned. Whether publicly or privately operated, industries must make a profit after a certain period—not profit from protection but profit from competition.

It is not easy to do this because once protection is granted, vested interests become entrenched. My suggestion is that the government, in principle, should not grant protection for too long a period, say not longer than 10 years, and should phase out protection gradually. If industries cannot compete without protection even in their own home markets, how can they compete in foreign markets? The government will have to make its policy clear on the matter. Then people will be more careful about the types of industries they operate and the appropriate technology they employ since they know that eventually protection will be removed.

They will choose techniques of production that minimize costs and use resources—capital, labor, and raw materials—effectively. I think this is one of the most important aspects of industrialization policy that developing countries should study seriously.

I am of the opinion that industrialization is definitely necessary to increase national income and to attain a reasonable rate of economic growth. At the same time I should emphasize the importance of agriculture as the basis of industrialization. Without a sound agriculture you cannot provide a domestic market for industrial productivity and an initial source of savings to finance industrial development. Granted that industrialization must be an important part of development strategy, the question then is, what are your priorities and sequential targets? What is the orientation of government policy? These are the questions I have tried to answer for the Japanese economy.

Another important aspect of industrialization is the development of small industries. This is a crucial link in the industrial chain. But we need to make the distinction between small industry and cottage industry. People often mix the two up. Cottage industry is mostly based on handicrafts. You can produce souvenirs as a cottage industry but you cannot produce competitive modern industrial products by cottage industry. This is a very important distinction. You can apply electricity and other capital appliances in the small industry and you can enforce some minimum product standards on small industries. They can compete with modern products. In the Japanese case, small industries grew up side by side with the development of large-scale capital-intensive enterprises in terms of both number and range of products. Total industrial output has increased but the small industry has survived. In earlier times hand work was the main source of industrial production. Gradually we introduced machinery, especially small motors. One example is the sewing machine industry. The parts of the sewing machine were produced in the small enterprise, sometimes a family-size enterprise. But the machines were assembled by a big firm. Similarly, in the bicycle industry the parts are manufactured by small unit enterprises. But those small unit enterprises have a system of subcontracting, and the small unit or family enterprise receives technical assistance from the parent company. Thus the small-scale is integrated with the large-scale industry.

The organization of small industries is a very important matter in Japan. In this connection I would just like to mention the role of local governments. The central government often is too remote from the small enterprises, so the local government assumes the responsibility of assisting them. Several years ago the late Professor Gadgil, a well-known Indian economist and one time Deputy Chairman of the Planning Commission of India, visited Japan. He was very impressed with the functioning of our prefectural (local) government. We have some 46 prefectures in Japan. Professor Gadgil was amazed at the extent to which the local administration system was committed to the solution of the problems of small industries in each locality. They local government knew the facts and details of these industries and where they were located. They had departments which offered technical assistance to small enterpreneurs as well as extension services to farmers. This was the aspect of the government machine which impressed him most, and he told me that personally. He remarked that, in contrast, local governments in India were sometimes nicknamed "collectorate" —i. e., the office to collect taxes and nothing else. It was not considered an important part of the functions of local government administration to encourage local industries or assist the agricultural sector. He left Japan convinced that India needed reforms in local government administration to orient it directly towards economic progress and, especially, the development of small-scale economic activity.

Now a few words about technology. One of the favorite topics in development economics today is the transferance of technology. What are the mechanisms? How do you transfer technology from one source to another? How do you adapt imported technology to local needs and conditions? Those are important topics. Sometimes governments in developing countries feel that they must import the most modern technology and all its capital structure without regard to its suitability within the context of the resources in their own countries. So you end up with labor-saving factories in labor-surplus economies. Such a factory does not create much employment but it eats up a very large part of the available scarce capital. A major problem of developing countries today is that in their bid for industrialization they have imported technologies which were developed in the advanced countries where labor is scarce and wages high and capital is relatively cheap. Technology must be adapted to the relative scarcities of resources or else such resources are wasted.

There is also the problem of maintaining the up-to-dateness of the technology. The most modern factory today will be obsolete in five years. This requires that you must yourself build up a technological capability to enable you to modify your technologies and introduce improved innovations. That is what we did, and Japan is sometimes referred to as the "improver" of technology. The basic idea may be imported but we adapt it, toy with it, and eventually improve on it. The most outstanding example is electronics. The transistor was invented in the United States. It was imported into Japan; we tinkered with it, and through continuous improvement our achievements have been outstanding. We are now very competitive in electronics using transistors throughout the world. The story is true of even our iron and steel industry. In the beginning the mills were imported, but after making improvements we obtained higher output than was expected from the designed capacity. I remember the case of one synthetic rubber factory. Their motors were overloaded and they had to replace them with larger capacity motors. The blueprint was originally designed by a foreign engineering firm for an output level of 50,000 tons a year but with modification the factory was producing 70,000 tons. This caused the overloading, but in replacing the motors with larger ones, the factory management succeeded in modifying the original design for more efficient production.

Some industries started in Japan as repair companies. For example, one of the largest companies in the machine industry started as the small repair shop of a copper mine. Repair factories are economically very important. They raise the utilization rate of existing capital equipment considerably.

In short, the basic characteristics of Japanese industrial progress are pragmatism, cost-consciousness, and improvement of technology.

Let me now turn to agriculture. Japanese agriculture is based on small farmer cultivation in small holdings. The average cultivated area per farmer is about 0.8 hectare. Before the Second World War, nearly two-thirds of the farmers were tenant farmers. After the war, far-reaching reforms in the Japanese social system were introduced. The land reform abolished the old tenure system, and tenant farmers became proprietor farmers in their own right. This resulted in intensive farming but did not change the average size of holdings. Foreign observers contend that Japanese agriculture is not agriculture but horticulture. You will find that there are very elaborate ways of doing things on the farm. Until recently, we had a population surplus, especially in the rural areas—a situation which persisted for many decades. It is only recently that, with rapid expansion, the economy has been able to absorb the surplus labor.

As long as land was the scarce factor relative to labor, the main issue was how to raise the productivity of land—in other words, how to obtain the maximum output per hectare of land. That was the essential objective of agricultural policy. We were not, before the Second World War, bothered by concepts of full employment. We concentrated on total employment, not full employment or unemployment. Thus government policy was geared mainly towards realizing higher yields from any given land. Recently it has become necessary to introduce labor-saving technology in agriculture. The agricultural labor force dropped from 38 percent of the total labor force in 1955 to 12 percent in 1975. This sharp decline in the share of agriculture in the total work force has necessitated the substitution of mechanized technology for labor in agriculture. Until then, agriculture was a very labor-intensive activity, and per-hectare productivity was high. For example, a hectare planted to rice in Japan yielded six tons, three times as much as a hectare planted to rice in South and Southeast Asia. The high yields were in part due to the adoption of high-yield varieties. (The high-yield varieties developed in Japan, however, suited conditions in temperate zones. Then several years ago the International Rice Research Institute in the Philippines developed a high-yielding rice variety suited for tropical conditions which was originally developed in Taiwan during the Japanese period before the Second World War.) Thus labor intensity and high productivity from the use of high-yield varieties were the characteristics of Japanese agriculture for many years.

The next important aspect of Japanese agriculture is the role of agriculture cooperatives (*nōkyō*) in the promotion of agriculture. These cooperatives are widespread, and they engage in a number of agriculture-related activities. They organize credit financing, the purchase of such inputs as fertilizers, insecticides, and farm machinery, and the sale of agricultural products. These cooperatives even organize sight-seeing trips to neighboring Asian countries. They promote productivity by linking agriculture to the mainstream of the industrial economy. The government's contribution is its research and extension services. Subsidy payments are also made when the government considers it in the national interest that new technologies should be adopted by the farming sector. For instance, farmers were encouraged through subsidies to adopt better silkworm techniques and humidify their orchards. The *nōkyō* are important in the implementation of such policies.

In spite of the improved agricultural production, dependency on food imports has risen in recent years to about 50 percent of the total consumption measured on an original calorie basis; this includes the indirect consumption of cereals as animal feed. There was a sharp increase in the animal protein intake per person per day from 22.6 grams in 1956 to 40 grams in 1975; half of this was from fish. Another 40 grams of protein intake was from vegetable sources. Fat and oil intake was also doubled during the same period with the improved nutritional level, though the average diet is still much lower in animal protein and fat intake than the Western diet. Life expectancy reached 72 years for men and 77 for women in 1976. Infant mortality has also dropped sharply, to 11 per thousand, one of the lowest in the world and about one-tenth of the figure for the 1930s. Dr. Toshio Ohiso, one of the leading nutritionists in Japan, once wrote as follows:

> The Japanese nutritional experience has potential value for other countries. It illustrates a high level of nutritional state and national health attainable with a largely vegetarian diet, high in carbohydrate, low in fat, and using fish and animal as complementary sources of protein. This is significant for developing countries that must select specific goals for adequate national nutrition and for advanced countries that have the freedom to change their diet.

Here I would like to mention briefly the plan for "doubling

rice production in Asia" which was prepared originally by myself and Dr. Kunio Takase in March 1976.* The 1977 Review of the Development Assistance Committee (DAC) of the Organisation for Economic Cooperation and Development (OECD) included the following paragraph:

> There is large scope for increasing yields through more effective use of irrigation systems, especially throughout the rice culture areas of Asia. The experience of Japanese agriculture, which is characterized by small-scale family farming, provides an excellent example of the possibilities and requirements. It is characterized by integrated use of the components for high yields, the initative and training of small farmers, a high level of effective water control, and the supporting policy of the Government. There is wide scope for increasing yields in most developing Asian countries through improved management and upgrading of existing irrigation systems.

A footnote attached to this paragraph introduces the Okita-Takase plan. The basic idea of this plan is as follows: A majority of the poor people in the world live in Asia, and rice is the major staple food for most people living in monsoon areas. The World Food Council projected 40 million tons of rice deficit in Asia in 1985 unless vigorous efforts to raise production are made. The per-hectare yield of rice in South and Southeast Asia is about one-third that of Japan and one-half that of Korea or Taiwan; for rice cultivation, controlled water supply and drainage is essential. Since there is a close relationship between the rate of irrigation and the per-hectare yield of rice, use of fertilizers and high-yielding varieties of seed should be combined with a better irrigation system. Therefore, a substantial amount of investment is needed for irrigation, and both domestic and foreign resources should be made available for this purpose. In order to double the rate of irrigation in South and Southeast Asia, about 54 billion dollars (in 1975 prices) over a 15-year period is estimated as necessary; this is about twice the current investment for irrigation. I consider this

* Reprinted in this volume beginning on p. 23.

plan one of the concrete projects which will be useful if and when the world requires a "Global New Deal" which may become necessary to fight against a prolonged recession of the world economy.

I have dealt with three topics thus far—education, industrialization, and the role of agriculture. In my view, the economic development of a country should be carried out by paying due regard to many traditional factors. It is wrong to regard these factors only as deterrents to economic growth. What is needed in fact is to think of ways in which these factors may be usefully employed for the purposes of economic growth. Here again, I would like to emphasize the importance of education in development and close my lecture by quoting from an ancient Chinese sage who stated impressively the importance of education: "If you give a man a fish, he can cat it once; if you teach him how to fish, he can eat fish for the rest of his life."

Causes and Problems of Rapid Growth in Postwar Japan and Their Implications for Newly Developing Economies

One of the important changes in economic thinking as compared to the prewar period is the growing consciousness of economic growth. Nowadays, almost every politician, both in developed and developing countries, talks about economic growth. In the developed countries, as the cyclical fluctuations and accompanying unemployment which were the major economic issues in prewar years have more or less been overcome in recent years, people are more concerned with long-term aspects of growth. In the developing countries, economic growth is taken as the vital factor for the improvement of the living standard. In Japan, as in other countries, economic growth is a favorite subject of discussion, not only among professional economists but also among politicians and business people. In particular, since the late Prime Minister Hayato Ikeda made economic growth his political slogan by introducing the idea of an income-doubling plan, economic growth and its accompanying impact has been a very controversial issue in both political and economic life in Japan.

Postwar economic growth in Japan, when compared with that of foreign countries or with her own prewar performance, has indeed been remarkable. The average annual rate for the period of 1955–65, measured in terms of gross national product (GNP) in constant prices, was 9.9 percent.[1] As is shown in Table 1, this figure compares very favorably with that of other advanced coun-

This chapter was written as a working paper for the Japan Economic Research Center (JERC) and issued in 1967 as JERC Working Paper No. 6. The major part of the paper was written during the author's summer 1966 stay at the East-West Center, Honolulu.

[1] Based on the revised series (April 1966) of national income statistics.

Table 1. Rates of Economic Growth (GNP in Real Terms) of Selected Developed Countries

	1950–55	1955–60	1960–65
Japan	12.1*	9.7	9.6
West Germany	9.3	6.3	4.8
Italy	6.0	5.5	5.1
France	4.3	4.6	5.1
U.K.	2.7	2.8	3.3
Belgium	3.1	2.5	4.5
Netherlands	5.5	4.2	4.8
Denmark	2.1	4.7	4.9
Norway	3.5	3.2	5.2
Sweden	3.2	3.6	5.1
Austria	6.1	5.2	4.3
Switzerland	4.8	4.0	5.3
U.S.A.	4.3	2.2	4.5
Canada	4.7	3.3	5.5
OECD	5.2	3.5	4.9
OECD (excl. Japan)	4.7	3.2	4.7

Source: OECD. *1952–55

tries. It was more than double the prewar Japanese rate of 4.6 percent annually for the period 1926–39.

Until around 1958 many observers attributed the high rate of growth mainly to the postwar recovery, and a government economic survey of 1958 stated that since the economy had recovered rapidly, the future growth rate would be considerably lower. Ironically, shortly afterward the economy started an extraordinarily rapid expansion with the result of nearly doubling the GNP in real terms in a matter of six years (1959–64).

Among the Western developed countries, with the exception of West Germany and Austria, there has been a general rise in the rate of growth during 1960–65 as compared to the preceding period of 1955–60 (see Table 1). The success of the leading countries in attaining more rapid economic growth may have had favorable repercussions among the advanced economies of the world. Both in West Germany and Austria the growth rate has recently declined as the postwar recovery factor gradually diminished. In the case of Japan, the growth rate during the period of 1960–65 showed no decline from the preceding period, and this proves that her high rate of growth depends not only on postwar recovery factors but also on some other factors peculiar to Japan.

While many of the advanced countries have succeeded in attaining a higher rate of growth, there has not been much improvement in the case of developing countries, except in a few instances. Considering the fact that the absolute levels of income and output are very low and that population is increasing much faster in developing countries, gaps between them and the advanced countries in per-capita income and output are likely to widen still more. However, the fact that at least a few of the developing countries have succeeded in raising their rate of growth considerably in recent years, as shown in Table 2, is a promising sign.

Table 2. Rates of Economic Growth (GNP in Real Terms) of Selected Developing Countries

	1953–58	1953–58	1958–63
India	3.1	3.6	3.3
Pakistan	1.7	5.1	3.4
Burma	3.9	6.2	5.1
Thailand	3.8	8.1	5.9
Malaysia	2.3	6.0	4.1
Philippines	5.4	4.7	5.0
China (Taiwan)	6.7	7.2	7.1
South Korea	5.4	4.3	4.8
Argentina	5.0	0.3	2.6
Chile	2.9	3.3	3.1
Colombia	3.8	5.4	4.5
Venezuela	8.3	4.3	6.3
Equador	4.5	4.3	4.4
Israel	11.7	10.4	11.1

Source: Bank of Japan: *Japan and the World,* March 1966.

Table 3 shows the annual rate of growth of GNP in Japan in terms of current and constant prices. As seen from this table, the rate of growth shows fluctuations from a high rate of about 15 percent to a low rate of about 3 percent. It seems that the changes in the rate of growth correspond with the approximate four-to-five-year business cycle. It is noteworthy that even at the bottom of the cycle, 3 to 4 percent growth rate was maintained.

With the above-mentioned high rate of growth, the level of in-

Table 3. GNP, Per-capita National Income, and Rates of Growth (Japan)

	GNP (in billion US dollars)	Per-capita national income (in US dollars)	Annual rate of growth of GNP	
			current prices (%)	constant prices (%)
1952	16.8	162	—	—
1953	19.4	183	15.1	7.2
1954	21.7	203	11.9	6.5
1955	23.7	217	9.4	9.4
1956	26.4	237	11.5	8.3
1957	30.8	275	16.4	11.5
1958	31.5	283	2.4	3.7
1959	35.6	310	12.8	10.3
1960*	42.6	374	19.6	15.4
1961*	51.7	438	21.5	15.5
1962*	58.0	493	12.2	7.3
1963*	65.7	551	13.3	7.7
1964*	76.8	629	17.0	13.8
1965*	84.6	694	10.1	4.0

Source: Economic Planning Agency: *Annual Report of National Income Statistics,* April 1966.

* Revised Series, December 1966.

come and output has risen rapidly. As Table 3 indicates, the per-capita national income rose from 162 dollars in 1952 to 694 dollars in 1965.[2] Similarly, during the corresponding period, the GNP rose from 17 billion dollars to 84 billion dollars.

In rough measure, Japan's per-capita national income in 1965 was about half that of the U.K., West Germany, and France, and about one-quarter that of the United States. Compared with the developing countries in Asia, however, Japan's per-capita national income is several times higher. As compared to the U.K., Germany, or France, while Japan's per-capita output is about half, its population is about double, so that Japan's total economic output is approaching that of those countries. As is shown in Table 4, as of 1964 Japan ranks, in terms of GNP, number five among noncommunist countries of the world. If the U.S.S.R. were included it would come second to the U.S.A. The economic output

[2] Converted from yen into U.S. dollars on the basis of the official exchange rate, 1 dollar = 360 yen. This rate was unchanged from 1949 to 1971.

Table 4. GNP and National Income of Major Countries (1965)

	GNP (in billion dollars)	National income (in billion dollars)	Population* (million)	Per-capita (dollars) GNP	Per-capita (dollars) national income
U.S.A.	676.3	554.7	194.6	3,475	2,850
West Germany**	112.1	85.4	59.0	1,900	1,447
U.K.	98.6	79.2	54.6	1,806	1,451
France	94.1	70.8	48.9	1,924	1,448
Japan	84.6	68.2	98.3	863	694
Italy	56.8	45.6	51.6	1,101	884
Canada	48.3	36.1	19.6	2,464	1,842

Note: Conversion into dollars based on official exchange rate.
* Population at mid-year, U.N. *Demographic Yearbook, 1965.*
** including West Berlin.

of China is uncertain. If we assume its per-capita national income to be about 100 U.S. dollars and its population to be 750 million, China's national income is around 75 billion dollars, which is about as large as the corresponding figure for Japan in 1965.

The leading factor in Japan's recent economic growth has been the rapid expansion of manufacturing industry. The production index of manufacturing industry (1960 = 100) rose from 46 in 1955 to 171 in 1965. Among various branches of industry the expansion of heavy and chemical industries (machinery, metals, and chemicals) was most conspicuous, as is shown in Table 5. The expansion of the machinery industry was the most remarkable; the textile industry has registered a relatively small expansion.

As a result of the above-mentioned development, the share of the heavy and chemical industries in the total output of the manufacturing industry reached 56% in 1960,[3] which was higher than that of West Germany (53 percent in 1958), the U.K. (54 percent in 1958), and the United States (50 percent in 1958).[4]

As a result of the rapid expansion of industrial production, Japan's share and rank in world production have risen remarkably, as indicated in Table 6.

Compared to manufacturing industry, the growth of primary

[3] Ministry of International Trade and Industry, Japanese Government.
[4] *UN Statistical Yearbook 1962.*

Table 5. Industrial Production Index (1960 = 100)

	1955	1965	1965/1955
Textiles	62.0	147.2	2.4
Paper and pulp	53.4	153.2	2.9
Chemicals	49.5	201.9	4.1
Petroleum & coal products	39.7	209.7	5.3
Ceramics	51.2	159.6	3.1
Iron & steel	43.8	177.7	4.1
Non-ferrous metals	42.2	161.2	3.8
Machinery	28.5	196.4	6.8
Mining	78.3	106.1	1.4
Total (industrial production)	47.0	173.1	3.7

Source: Ministry of International Trade and Industry (MITI), Japanese Government.

Table 6. Share and Rank of Japan's Industrial Production in the World (1963)

Items	Units	Production	Rank 1963	Share in World Production 1963	1953
Crude steel	(million tons)	31.5	4	8.1	(3.3)
Cotton yarn	(thousand tons)	480	3	12.4	(15.2)
Synthetic fiber	(thousand tons)	239	2	17.9	(3.8)
Pulp	(million tons)	4.57	5	6.7	(3.9)
Fertilizers	(million tons N content)	1.28	2	9.1	(10.8)
Cement	(million tons)	29.9	3	8.1	(4.9)
Shipbuilding	(million registered tonnage)	2.37	1	27.7	(10.9)
Passenger cars	(thousand units)	408	7	2.5	(0.1)
Radio	(million units)	18.0	2	25.0	(6.4)
TV	(million units)	4.88	2	22.2	(0.2)
Electric power generation	(billion kwh)	160	4	5.6	(4.4)

Source: *UN Statistical Yearbook.*

industry (agriculture, forestry, and fishing) has been relatively slow, and its relative share of the national income has declined from 22 percent in 1954 to 12 percent in 1964. The labor force in primary industry as a percentage of the total declined from 45 percent in 1953 to 27 percent in 1964. The overall production index of primary industry (1960 = 100) rose from 87.4 in 1956 to 108.5 in 1964, but it has leveled off since 1962. As indicated in Table 7, the production of cereals, including rice, has started to decline, while livestock production is increasing. With rapid growth of the economy accompanied by basic changes in labor conditions and in the demand structure for agricultural products, primary industry in Japan is undergoing fundamental changes.

Table 7. Production Index (1960 = 100) of Primary Industry (Japan)

	1956	1962	1965	1965/1956
Overall index	87.4	107.1	110.1	1.26
Agriculture	85.4	107.4	111.9	1.31
Cultivation	86.6	100.4	99.9	1.14
(Rice)	84.7	101.6	96.8	1.14
Livestock	76.5	148.3	186.7	2.44
Forestry	100.7	97.8	95.4	0.95
Fishery	81.0	116.9	119.2	1.47

Source: Ministry of Agriculture and Forestry.

With a limited supply of agricultural products from domestic sources and a paucity of indigenous resources with which to meet the growing demand for raw materials, Japan's economy depends heavily on foreign imports. Rapid postwar growth of the economy was made possible only by a corresponding expansion of foreign trade. During 1955–65 export trade expanded from 2.01 to 8.45 billion dollars, about a fourfold increase (Table 8), and the average annual increase during this ten-year period was 15 percent, more than twice as high as the rate of expansion of world trade as

Table 8. Export Trade of Major Trading Countries (in billion US dollars)

	1965	1955	1965/1955
U.S.A.	27.00	15.38	1.76
West Germany	17.89	6.14	2.91
U.K.	13.72	8.47	1.62
France	10.06	4.85	2.07
Japan	8.45	2.01	4.20
Canada	8.11	4.42	1.83
Italy	7.19	1.86	3.87
India	1.68	1.28	1.31

Source: OECD: *Main Economic Indicators*. For India, IMF International Financial Statistics.

a whole. Accordingly, the share of Japan's export trade in the world during the same period rose from 2.2 to 4.6 percent. Such a rapid expansion of export trade has enabled Japan to import foodstuffs, petroleum, iron ore, cotton, and other commodities to meet the growing demand caused by a larger industrial output and the higher living standard of the people.

Causes of Rapid Growth

As indicated in the preceding section, postwar economic growth in Japan is outstanding compared both internationally and with her own historical record. The reasons for such rapid growth are a matter of great interest to both Japanese and foreign observers. The author has participated in various discussions on this subject and has contributed a number of articles to Japanese and foreign publications.[5] Here, in this chapter, the author tries to explain the causes for this rapid growth as systematically as possible.

The phrase "vicious circle" has often been used in connection with the obstacles in developing underdeveloped economies. It also been referred to in connection with the balance of payments dilemma and other difficulties of some of the more advanced economies. Contrarily, postwar Japan presents a case where several favorable factors have worked together in accelerating growth, and this process may be called a "virtuous circle."

Broadly speaking, the causes for rapid growth or the factors of a "virtuous circle" may be grouped into four categories: (i) postwar recovery and reforms; (ii) semi-backwardness of economic structure; (iii) policies and attitude; and (iv) international environment.

In the following pages a detailed account of the above factors will be presented.

Postwar recovery and reforms

Under this category there are three major factors: i) recovery from the deep trough of economic activity due to defeat in the

[5] See, e.g., "Japan's Economic Prospect," *Foreign Affairs,* October 1960; "Economic Growth of Postwar Japan," *The Developing Economies,* September – December 1962.

war; ii) postwar reforms which have revitalized the economy; and iii) abandonment of colonies and reduction in military expenditures.

Recovery from the trough. At the end of the Second World War economic activity came to almost a complete standstill, and the level of industrial production was only a fraction of the prewar level. In the course of recovery existing facilities were available, and with a relatively small additional investment production increased substantially.[6] Even agriculture was in serious dislocation during the early postwar years because of a lack of fertilizers and implements, although the rural population bulged considerably due to the disappearance of employment opportunities in urban areas and to several million repatriates from former overseas colonies, including the demobilized servicemen.

By around 1955, ten years after the end of the war, per-capita national income recovered the prewar (1934–36) level. The immediate recovery factor gradually diminished as time went on, and the other factors have become more important at later stages. However, some economists, including the author of this article and Professor Shunichi Ichimura,[7] argue that in measuring the recovery not only the absolute levels of production and income should be taken into consideration but also a comparison with the long-term growth trend.

One of my earlier writings includes the following paragraph:

> Suppose that we did not enter the war and that the average trend of economic growth, 4.6 percent a year during 1926–39, were maintained without being interrupted by the war—the national income of 1959 would have reached a level about 2.5 times that of 1939. This is about 60 per cent higher than the actual level reached in 1959. Therefore, without the War we could have realized a much larger economic output and a much higher living standard for the people by now. In other words, the present level of economic output is still considerably lower than the long-term trend of Japan's economic growth. Of course, theoretically there is no guarantee of

[6] During 1946–51 industrial production rose average 29 percent annually.

[7] *Nihon Keizai Seisaku No Kaimei* (Studies on Japan's Economic Policy), Vol. I (Toyo Keizai, 1962), p. 7.

> returning to the old trend line. However, the process of recovery from a temporary interruption may have some relationship to the trend because the "potential" of economic output is likely to be influenced strongly by such factors as level of education, accumulated "know-how," and ability of business management, which may have grown without much interruption even during the war. Therefore the process of recovery may continue beyond the point where the absolute absolute level of prewar economic output was regained and gradually narrow the gap between the potential and the actual economic levels.[8]

By 1965, however, even with the above consideration, the postwar recovery factor seems to have worked itself out as the output has surpassed even the prewar trend line.

Postwar reforms. Some of the postwar reforms, although they were introduced under the pressure of occupation authority, have had favorable impact on economic growth. Land reform, encouragement of the labor union movement, and the dissolution of *zaibatsu* were the major items. Land reform, for example, stimulated farmers to introduce better methods of production as well as to improve their living standard. The labor union movement, although it brought about some confusion, as a whole was a stimulant through its demand for higher wages, better management, and higher efficiency. The dissolution of the *zaibatsu*, although its implementation was much mitigated at a later stage, had a stimulating impact on industries. Even the purge of business leaders provided chances to introduce new blood into management.

The departure from the past glory of Empire has reduced various internal and international commitments. Abolition of nobles, disbandment of army and navy, de facto cancellation of government internal debts through inflation—these events have also contributed directly or indirectly to more vigorous economic activity. Because of the defeat people were more easily convinced of the necessity of harder work, an austere life, and larger savings. Professor G. C. Allen wrote in one of his books as follows:

[8] *Nihon Keizai No Shorai* (The Future of Japan's Economy), 1960, pp. 112–113.

The disaster that has overtaken her former policy was so complete that she was impelled to set out on a new course undistracted by regrets for past ambitions. She may have been fortunate in being left with only a single rational choice in 1945, the acceptance of temporal political subordination and co-operation with her victors in economic rehabilitation. Once she had crossed that threshold she seems to have allowed no regret for the past to haunt her journey into the new world.[9]

Abandonment of colonies and reduction in military expenditures. As the result of defeat Japan abandoned all her colonies and parts of several older territories. She also lost her "sphere of influence"—Manchuria and North China. It was rather fortunate for Japan to have lost colonies when in many parts of the world colonies were turning from assets to liabilities, economically. Moreover, the rising tide of nationalism would have made it impossible anyway for Japan to maintain colonies, even if she had not entered the war. Around 1935 Japan was investing about 3 percent of her national income in her overseas colonies and sphere of influence. Moreover, maintaining colonies entailed substantial military expenditures. In the prewar years, during the relatively normal and peaceful period of 1934–36, Japan was spending about 7 percent of national income for military purposes. After the war, because of the occupation policy of demilitarizing Japan and the new Constitution which prohibits the use of military forces as a means of solving international disputes, as well as the anti-militaristic feeling of the people prevailing in the country, expenditures for defense have been substantially reduced to the level of around 1.5 percent of the national income. The Security Treaty with the United States is another factor in decreasing defense cost by dispensing with expensive major weapons. If we assume the postwar saving of military expenditure as compared to the prewar years to be about 6 percent of the national income and that this saving is used for constructive investment, then the additional rate of growth will be about 2 percent annually.[10]

[9] G. C. Allen: *Japan's Economic Expansion* (Oxford University Press, 1965), p. 261.
[10] Assuming capital-output ratio as 3.

Semi-backwardness of economic structure

Japan's economy, though highly developed in many ways, still retains various elements of backwardness, and this semi-backward stage of development has occasioned conditions conducive to rapid growth. In view of the recent experience in Japan, some of the newly developing countries may also succeed in the future in creating a favorable combination of factors for economic growth. In the course of transition from an underdeveloped to a more developed stage of the economy, there is a possibility of realizing a process of "virtuous circle" accompanied by explosive economic growth.

A more detailed account with respect to Japan's case is given under the following headings: i) technological catch-up, ii) high productivity and low consumption, iii) abundant supply of labor, iv) dualistic structure of economy, and v) employment and wage practices.

Technological catch-up. Throughout the history of Japan's modernization since the early Meiji period, the importation of foreign technology played a crucial role in promoting economic progress. This happened again in the course of postwar development. During and shortly after the war Japan was separated from the technological progress of the outside world. As contacts with foreign countries were restored the import of "know-how" from highly developed countries increased sharply. The postwar investment boom—in particular, that of 1959–64—was based mainly on the importation of technology and its application in the actual production process. The large gap which existed after the war between foreign and domestic levels of technology and the resulting catching-up process stimulated investment and promoted rapid economic growth.

Such a gap, or even a much larger gap than in Japan's case, exists in many of the newly developing countries, and this forms one of the most promising factors for the future possibility of faster growth in these countries. So far in Japan, the quality of labor, the accumulation of capital, the social atmosphere, and other basic conditions have been favorable to the effective absorption of foreign technology. Also in many instances the process of adaptation of imported technology to local conditions has been conspicuous. In importing "know-how," sometimes selections were made to take best advantage of local conditions, and such selections were often made not by the conscious policy of the government but by the working of market forces. Enterprisers are keenly cost-conscious in introducing new lines of production, and they are led to achieve the most profitable factor combinations. In the earlier history of its modernization Japan was forced, under the pressure of the Western powers, to abandon autonomy in fixing tariff rates on imported commodities. The maximum tariff rate was set at 5 percent *ad valorem*, and it was only in 1899 that Japan regained tariff autonomy.[11] With this lack of tariff autonomy, Japanese industries were compelled to be cost-conscious and aware of international competition right from the beginning. On top of this historical background, some of the basic industries which had been heavily protected by the government because of military considerations were also exposed after the war to outside competition. Under such circumstances, cost factors were taken into serious consideration in importing and applying "foreign know-how."

Another characteristic of Japan's technological imports is the constant improvement of imported technology. On many occasions, because of such improvement, factories built originally with foreign design reach in the course of time a much higher output than the designed capacity set by the foreign supplier of "know-how." Thus, blast furnaces of the iron and steel industry originally designed for a daily output of 1,500 tons actually operate at 2,500-ton capacity. A synthetic rubber factory with a designed capacity of 50,000 tons a year operates at 70,000 tons. With such improvements cost of production, in particular capital cost, was considerably reduced. Sometimes in newly developing countries officials believe simply in buying the most modern equipment existing in the world without giving due attention to cost aspects and to the factor combination of capital and labor. Sometimes

[11] Masao Baba and Masahiro Tatemoto: "Foreign Trade and Economic Growth 1868–1937," working paper for the International Conference on Economic Growth: Case Study of Japan's Experience, Tokyo, September 1966, sponsored by the Japan Economic Research Center.

they also overlook the fact that the most modern equipment can become obsolete in a few years' time if the ability for continuous improvement is not developed in due course.

High productivity and low consumption. Rapidly improving technology brought about both by the aggressive importation of "know-how" from abroad and by the continuous effort of research and development in the country has resulted in a rapid rate of improvement in the overall labor productivity of the nation as a whole. On the other hand, the consumption pattern has remained relatively unchanged until recent years. The combination of modern, efficient production and the traditional pattern of consumption has created a favorable condition for a high rate of saving which, in turn, provides the capital necessary for rapid expansion. In addition, change in the consumption pattern is a relatively gradual process, and when productivity improves rapidly there appears a gap between production and consumption due to the time-lag effect of the latter. Therefore, the rapid economic growth itself has tended to raise the rate of saving and investment.

Concerning the productivity-wage relationship, a similar development is noticeable. In most branches of industry productivity was rising rapidly while wages were rising at a somewhat slower rate. This was more conspicuous during the 1950s and early 1960s though in recent years there have been signs of reversing this trend (Table 9).

The gap between the rise in productivity and the rise in wages in favor of the former created a margin for reducing the cost of production. It enabled enterprises to earn a higher profit margin and to make larger plough-back investments which in turn resulted in a rapid expansion of industrial output. The productivity-wage gap has also strengthened the competitiveness of Japanese products in the world market, as most of the exporters of industrial manufactures have been experiencing a faster rise in wages than in productivity and, consequently, rising labor costs. Moreover, as the result of active investment, most of the equipment and machinery in industries is new and modern and this again has strengthened export trade. Stronger export trade has provided the larger imports necessary for meeting the growing domestic demand without incurring serious balance-of-payments difficulties. The above is a typical case of the "virtuous circle" mentioned earlier.

Table 9. Productivity and Export Trends in Manufacturing Industry: International Comparison

	1958–65 annual average rate of increase (%)				1958 = 100 1965	
	Production	Labor productivity	Wages	Export quantity	Labor cost	Export price
Japan	15.1	9.4	9.3	17.8	103	94
Italy	8.9	7.3	8.6	16.7	107	95
West Germany	7.1	5.8	8.7	9.3	121	104
U.S.A.	7.6	4.0	3.2	6.2	93	106
U.K.	4.3	3.9	5.9	3.8	114	109

Source: Economic Planning Agency: *Economic Survey, July 1966*, p. 107.

Table 9 gives some statistical background on export expansion and the productivity-wage relationship. It indicates that during 1958–65 the productivity-wage relationship was generally favorable for Japan and that exports expanded at the highest rate among industrialized nations. The export price index declined 6 percent during this period, and this also reflects factors other than the wage-productivity relationship, such as improved technology and more efficient equipment.

Abundant supply of labor. One of the reasons for a favorable productivity-wage relationship is the relative abundance of the labor supply as compared to other industrial nations. Although this abundance has been gradually diminishing since around 1960, still unlike other industrialized countries, the labor supply is not a major limiting factor for growth. In the case of West Germany, a full-employment economy was reached in around 1958, and the growth rate has come down from about 8 to 5 percent per annum mainly because of the labor shortage. Japan has not yet reached the 1958 German labor force condition.

Before the war Japan was known for its chronic overpopulation, especially for overcrowded agriculture with an average of only two acres of land per farm household. The agricultural labor force was nearly 80 percent of the total at the beginning of modernization, and it came down to about 40 percent before the Second World War. Throughout these several decades, the labor force in agriculture stayed at about the same level, while the total population was doubled from 34.8 million in 1873 to 71.4 million in 1940. After the war, the population increased sharply due to repatriation from overseas, a temporary postwar baby boom, and a sharp decline in the death rate. The pressure of overpopulation was felt much more seriously than in the prewar days, and at that time many people felt it was almost impossible to support a rapidly increasing population on the four major islands with an area of 370,000 square kilometers (141,000 sq. miles).

Contrary to the above pessimistic outlook, the actual development so far has been a rapidly expanding demand for labor, and, for the first time in Japan's history, signs of labor shortage have appeared since around 1960. However, a large number of people are still working in low-productivity sectors, and there still exists a large reserve of underutilized labor in agriculture, small-scale industries, small retail shops, etc. The shift of a worker from a low-productivity sector to a high-productivity sector will sometimes result in a several-fold increase in his output. Therefore, the expansion of modern industries with high-productivity employment has contributed substantially to the high rate of economic growth. In the highly developed countries, although there are sufficient numbers of high-productivity employment opportunities, the labor supply is the major bottleneck limiting growth. In the underdeveloped countries, although there is surplus labor in most cases, the quality of labor has not been sufficiently developed to equip workers with the necessary educational and training background required by modern employment. Moreover, the total accumulation of capital is not large enough to provide every worker with high-productivity employment opportunity. In the case of postwar Japan, the combination of an abundant supply of labor with an adequate quality of labor and the continuing process of capital accumulation in the form of productive assets has been realized.

Another characteristic of the labor supply condition is its age structure. Because of the relatively recent decline in death rate and the sharp postwar decline in birth rate, the work-age population accounts for a larger portion of the total as compared to other countries. In highly developed countries, because of the longer average life expectancy the proportion of the older age group is generally high. In the underdeveloped countries, because of the shorter life expectancy in the recent past and a sharp rise in live births after the war, the younger age group population expanded much faster than the total. Therefore, compared with both developed and underdeveloped countries, Japan has a relatively high ratio of work-age population and a low ratio of both old-age and childhood population. This means a larger portion of the population is gainfully employed with a smaller number of dependent family members. In this respect, the age composition of the population of present-day Japan is favorable for economic growth. Table 10 indicates the age composition of Japan as compared with several other countries.

Table 10. Age Composition of Population (as percentage of total population)

Age groups	0 – 14	15 – 59	60 and over
Japan (1960)	30	61	9
Japan (1965)	25	65	10
Japan (1995, projected)	18	63	19
U.S.A. (1964)	31	56	13
U.K. (1964)	23	58	19
France (1964)	25	57	18
West Germany (1964)	23	60	17
India (1961)	41	53	6

Note: Figures for Japan (1995) are based on the population projection prepared by the Population Research Institute, Ministry of Welfare; figures for other countries are from United Nations statistics.

Dualistic structure of the economy. The dualistic structure of the economy, often pointed out as one of the peculiar characteristics of the Japanese economy, implies in a broad sense the parallel existence of traditional and modern sectors of the economy. Professors Ohkawa and Rosovsky write as follows: "In the Japanese economy, modern sectors are those which use techniques and forms of organization imported from the West. Traditional sectors employ techniques and organization indigenous to Japan."[12] Incidentally, Japan's case should be differentiated from other forms of dualistic structure such as the "plural society" or "dualis-

[12] Kazushi Ohkawa and Henry Rosovsky: "Postwar Japanese Growth in Historical Perspective: A Second Look." Working paper for the International Conference on Economic Growth, September 1966, sponsored by the Japan Economic Research Center.

tic society" of colonial society as in the case of pre-independence Indonesia or Burma. Unlike colonial territories, although Japan borrowed techniques and organizations from the West, her economy has never been directly controlled by foreigners, and the dualistic structure of the economy has never destroyed national integrity.

One of the most basic factors in the emergence of a dualistic structure was the fact that, with a limited supply of total available capital for modernization and a large number of the working population seeking jobs, only a portion of the labor force could find employment in modern sectors; the rest had to be left in the traditional sectors. Although the traditional sectors were also making progress, their speed was relatively slow compared to the growth in the modern sectors, and the gap between the two has been apparent since around the time of World War I. The so-called differential wage structure—that is, a discrepancy in average wage levels by size of enterprise—developed around that time, and it continued into the postwar (World War II) period. As shown in Table 11, the average wage of workers (manufacturing industry, 1959) in large enterprises with 500 and more employees was more than twice as high as that in small enterprises with 5 to 29

Table 11. Average Cash Earnings by Size of Enterprise (enterprise in manutacturing industry with 500 and more employees = 100)

	Number of employees		
	100–499	30–99	5–29
1955	74	59	—
1956	72	56	—
1957	71	56	—
1958	70	55	44
1959	70	56	44
1960	71	59	46
1961	75	62	49
1962	78	67	57
1963	79	69	58
1964	79	70	60
1965	81	71	63

Source: Ministry of Labor, Government of Japan: *Monthly Labor Statistics.*

employees. This gap has been narrowing since 1959 due to the beginning signs of a labor shortage, but it was stable or even slightly expanding until then.

The existence of the dualistic structure in Japan has contributed to the rapid economic growth in the following ways:

(1) The existence of a large reservoir of underutilized labor, both in small enterprises and agriculture, has tended to depress the labor market and served to create the productivity-wage gap mentioned earlier. (2) About half of the exports are products of small and medium enterprises. They are mostly labor-intensive products and enjoy advantages in the international division of labor. Foreign exchange thus earned is utilized to finance imports, including raw materials and equipment needed by large enterprises. (3) Larger enterprises can utilize smaller ones as subcontractors and this has enabled larger ones to add flexibility in management in adjusting their levels of production as well as to use indirectly (by subcontracting) relatively cheap labor for their products. (4) With a differential wage structure, total employment has been kept higher than with a rigid wage system, as the employment level is a function of wage level. (5) The existence of a large number of entrepreneurs, through their competition and initiative, contributed to the dynamic adjustment in industries to meet changing market and other conditions.

As mentioned above, the dualistic structure has served as one of the basic causes of rapid economic growth. It was accompanied, however, by some undesirable repercussions from a social point of view, such as the following: (1) A sharp contrast between the conditions of employees in large enterprises and those in small ones. Employees of large enterprises enjoyed not only high wages but also better fringe benefits and security. (2) A concentration of economic power in larger enterprises, relative instability in small enterprise management, and a subordinate position of small enterprises to larger ones. (3) In small enterprises not only wages but also productivity and capital intensity are much lower than in larger enterprises (Table 12). In order to reduce the productivity gap, larger investment to raise productivity in small enterprises will become necessary. Otherwise, prices of the products of small enterprise will rise or many small enterprises will go bankrupt when wage levels rise faster than productivity.

Table 12. Capital Intensity and Wage Level in Industry by Size of Enterprise, 1957

Size of enterprise (number of employees)	Ratio of gross output to fixed capital	Fixed capital per worker (capital intensity)	Labor productivity	Ratio of gross profit to fixed capital	Gross profit per worker	Wage per worker
		(thousands of yen)			(thousands of yen)	
			(2) × (3)		(3) × (5)	(4) − (6)
(1)	(2)	(3)	(4)	(5)	(6)	(7)
1–3	0.139	93	13	0.043	4	9
4–9	0.186	97	18	0.082	8	10
10–19	0.256	90	23	0.133	12	11
20–29	0.269	97	26	0.144	14	12
30–49	0.284	102	29	0.167	17	12
50–99	0.258	136	35	0.162	22	13
100–199	0.221	186	41	0.145	27	14
200–299	0.202	233	47	0.133	31	16
300–499	0.168	345	58	0.119	41	17
500–999	0.146	447	65	0.103	46	19
1,000 and over	0.100	769	77	0.068	52	25
Total	0.133	324	43	0.083	27	16

Source: Ministry of International Trade and Industry: *Analysis of Current Japanese Industry, 1959.*

Thus, the dualistic structure of Japan's economy has been, with its merits and demerits, one of the most important factors in interpreting the process of economic growth and modernization. Many of the newly developing countries are likely to face similar problems in the course of industrialization when they reach certain stages of development. Basically, most of the newly developing countries lack capital accumulation to provide high-productivity employment for all workers. As mentioned earlier in Japan's case, only a portion of the labor force can enjoy the opportunity of finding jobs in modern sectors; the rest are left in low-productivity sectors. There is an important choice for newly developing countries to make, whether they should allow a dualistic structure to develop or should follow an egalitarian approach by introducing regulations against discrepancies in wages, for instance, by enforcing strict minimum wage regulations. If they follow the former course there will be larger employment opportunities and export will be promoted due to better productivity-wage relations. The rate of economic growth will also be higher. On the other hand, there will be strong opposition to such a policy on social and political grounds. If those countries follow the latter course, they may be able to bring about socially more desirable conditions but at the same time rigid control over prices and wages will become necessary; export trade, particularly that of manufactured goods, may suffer from high wage costs; employment opportunities will be smaller; and the rate of economic growth will probably be lower than if the former course had been followed. This is one of the serious dilemmas that newly developing countries are likely to face in the course of economic development.

Employment and wage practices. "Employment with lifetime commitment" and "promotion on a seniority basis" are features of employment and wage practice in Japan often pointed out by both domestic and foreign observers. It is a well-known fact that in most of the large enterprises (and government departments) both workers and staff are recruited from among new graduates of various levels of schooling, and they usually stay with the same company (or ministry) until retirement. Even after retirement, companies often look after their former employees by such measures as providing positions in related enterprises or assisting the establishment of new subcontracting firms. This means lifetime security for the employees, and, in return, an employee is expected to devote his whole energy to the prosperity of his company. In many companies (and government departments) promotions are usually based on the length of service with the company, and a majority of the employees are recruited from among fresh graduates, on the year of graduation from final schooling. This system started in Japan more or less simultaneously with the appearance of the differential wage structure early in this century and is one of the causes of the emergence of such a wage structure.

The above practice is also related to the traditional social backgound of paternalism or groupism as contrasted to Western indidividualism, and this is one of the examples of Japanese industries successfully combining traditional elements with foreign elements imported from more advanced countries. On the same ground, labor unions are mostly company unions, and in many cases there exists a sense of partnership between the management and the union.

So far, such employment and wage practices have worked rather favorably for accelerating growth by bringing about enthusiastic competition among enterprises and creating a stimulating atmosphere of hard work and devotion. There are signs, however, that the lack of mobility of employees among enterprises, due mainly to the above practices, may become an adverse element in realizing the more efficient and more specialized organization of the economy which seems to be a necessity if economic and social conditions in Japan are to approach a fully modernized stage of development.

Policies and attitude

In realizing rapid economic growth, the attitude of the people in general—or more specifically, that of enterprisers, workers, farmers, citizens, and others—toward economic problems has much significance. Government policies are also important elements. It is not always easy to draw a clear-cut line between the government policy and the attitude of the people. Some of these issues have already been dealt with in the preceding pages. Here, however, the following items will be discussed in connection with the rapid economic growth: i) the "economy first" principle; ii) production-oriented policies; iii) expansion of heavy industry; iv) export promotion; v) use of the price mechanism and planning; vi) high rate of saving; vii) financial mechanism.

The "economy first" principle. After the serious disillusionment about the policy of militaristic expansion and the misery and devastation people experienced due to the bankruptcy of this policy, the Japanese people in general have tended to assume an "economy first" attitude. The energy of the people, dissipated in military actions in the past, is now concentrated upon economic rehabilitation and development. Business is now attracting the best brains among young people, and the ability and energy of scientists and engineers is now fully applied to the production and improvement of civilian commodities.

In the field of international policy as well, "Japan has been following a policy of 'economic interest first.' On many international issues Japan has been taking a passive attitude, examining their impact on her economy and protecting her immediate national interests. This attitude has been effective in achieving a rapid recovery and an expansion of domestic economy, and while Japan's economy was weak and struggling to recover from the after-effects of the war, such an attitude was more or less accepted by foreign nations. Gradually, as the economic accomplishments of postwar Japan have become widely recognized abroad, more is being expected of Japan in the formulation of international economic policy and in the discharge of her responsibility as one of the world's leading trading nations."[13]

Production-oriented policies. It has been only recently that people have started arguing that the government should pay due attention to consumers' interest in the betterment of housing and environmental facilities. The criticism has been raised that in the past government policies were too heavily oriented toward production and neglected the problems of the people's daily life. It is true that so far, while industries, agriculture, and trade have had strong voices in influencing government politices, consumers as a group have not had such influence.

In the early postwar years rehabilitation of the basic industries such as coal, iron and steel, fertilizers, electricity, and food production was the major concern of the government. Then policies such as the modernization of basic industries, the establishment of new industries including petrochemicals, export promotion, the protection of agricultural production, etc., attracted government attention. Monetary policy and banking practices have also been heavily oriented toward production, as exemplified by the fact that so far Japanese bank loans are extended mostly to manufacturers and traders and not very often to consumers.

This policy, though it has had some undesirable social repercussions, has certainly contributed to the rapid growth of production.

Expansion of heavy industry. During the early period of modernization, the most popular motto frequently used by the leaders was "to build a rich nation and a strong army." The government took strong leadership in promoting industrialization, and one of the

[13] Saburo Okita: "Japan and the Developing Nations," *Contemporary Japan,* Vol. XXVIII, No. 2, 1965.

important features at that stage and later, until the Second World War, was the combined effort of promoting industries in the private sector basically on a commercial basis, such as the silk and cotton textile industries, on the one hand, and the building and expansion of military-related industries, mostly heavy industries, irrespective of cost and profitability, on the other. Since the war, though military considerations have disappeared, the policy of expanding heavy industries has been persistently followed. The reason for this was probably the recognition by the government and industry of the fact that for higher income and greater GNP, the expansion of heavy industries, particularly the machinery industry, was essential. Heavy industries were sharply expanded before and during the war in order to meet military needs, and the struggle of those industries to survive as commercial enterprises in the postwar years may have been another reason for the improvement and expansion of heavy industries. As a result, machinery and equipment necessary for the rapid expansion of industrial production have largely been supplied by domestic industries. This has had a dual effect favorable to growth: first, it saved foreign exchange otherwise necessary for importing capital goods from abroad; and second, it has multiplied the total industrial output by creating demand at various stages of production, from raw materials to finished products. In many of the present newly industrializing countries and also in prewar Japan, a sharp rise in imports of capital goods and a subsequent shortage of foreign exchange has been and is one of the major bottlenecks in attaining rapid industrial expansion. The expansion of heavy industry has had another important advantage; in foreign trade Japan's export expansion was facilitated by the fact that it has been in line with the expansion of world trade as a whole, in which exports and imports of heavy industry products are expanding much faster than the average.

In 1965 products of heavy and chemical industries accounted for 61 percent of the total export trade of Japan, and this compares very favorably with the figure of 41 percent in 1955.

Export promotion. Export trade has been considered for many years a vital necessity for the survival of the Japanese economy. During the early postwar years Japan was cut off from overseas trade. Because of the pessimistic outlook entertained by most people for the expansion of foreign trade, views were expressed that Japan must live mainly on indigenous resources. However, people realized in due course the economic inefficiency and low living standard which will result when a nation cannot enjoy the advantages of the international division of labor.

Looking back on the progress of Japan's export trade, we may classify it into the following stages: (1) export of primary commodities such as copper, silver, tea, silk cocoons, and even rice; (2) export of semi-manufactured items, in particular raw silk; (3) export of light-industry produccts such as cotton textiles, at this stage mostly directed to low-income markets, due to low quality and low price (4) export of light industry products to high-income markets with the improvement in quality; (5) export of high quality consumer goods and the beginning of the export of heavy industry products to both low- and high-income markets; (6) weakening exports of labor-intensive products due to a growing labor shortage, higher wages, and competiton from newly industrializing countries.

The above stages in the development of export trade may provide some useful reference for newly developing countries. In many of those countries foreign trade has been considered something of marginal importance or a necessary evil, due partly to the memory of past exploitation by the colonial powers. In some countries there is also a feeling of defeatism concerning the possibility of export expansion. India has been one of these: in the course of twelve years (1953–65) export trade expanded only from $1.2 to $1.7 billion while Japan's exports increased from $1.2 to $8.5 billion during the same period. Without expanding export trade a country cannot find the foreign exchange necessary to import capital goods for development. The establishment of industries for import substitution often resulted in larger imports of equipment, semi-processed items, food, and other consumer goods, instead of reducing imports. It is true that the developed industrial nations are still putting various obstacles in the way of increased exports by newly developing countries, as pointed out at the first meeting of the United Nations Conference on Trade and Development held in Geneva in 1964. At the same time, developing countries may find some usefulness in learning Japan's process of export expansion, particularly of manufactured and semi-manufactured items.

Use of the price mechanism and planning. During the war, the economy was under strict government control, and most commodities were allocated or rationed. Immediately after the war similar control was enforced because of the scarcity of food and other commodities. In 1949 rampant postwar inflation was put to an end, and a uniform exchange rate for the yen (1 U.S. dollar = 360 yen) was fixed. With this stabilization program, physical controls were removed one after another, and the market mechanism and free enterprise system started functioning. With the outside stimulus created by the Korean War demand and the internal conditions conducive to vigorous competition, economic recovery was much accelerated. Around 1954, when the Yoshida Cabinet was replaced by the Hatoyama Cabinet, the latter criticized the former as excessively laissez-faire, and officially adopted a five-year economic plan for the first time since the war. Nevertheless, the basic tone of economic policy was not much affected by the change of cabinet, and it continued to follow the line of a competitive market economy.

There were two major exceptions, however, one being the protection of domestic industry from foreign competition by imposing strict control over foreign exchange transactions on the grounds of the balance-of-payments consideration, and the other being the protection of agriculture by guaranteeing both purchases and prices of staple products, particularly rice. It was only around 1960 that the government, somewhat reluctantly, decided to liberalize imports and reduce quantitative restrictions on imports. Industries were given the date of the removal of import controls on competing foreign products and were encouraged to rationalize their management so as to be able to compete with the foreign products when they appeared in the domestic market. In spite of the serious apprehension expressed by some of the industrialists and MITI (Ministry of International Trade and Industry) officials that many domestic industries would suffer serious setbacks through foreign competition, actual import figures after liberalization have not shown any abrupt increase, and most of the domestic industries have survived the liberalization. Although import liberalization and the future relaxation of controls on capital transfers have not yet been fully demonstrated, the general development so far indicates that the policy of step-by-step liberalization has succeeded in strengthening domestic industries by giving them a secure market in their infancy, while still encouraging rationalization and reduction of costs by setting targets for eventual import liberalization. Thus the automobile industry, for instance, might not have developed to the present level if foreign competition had been introduced at an earlier stage.

As mentioned in an earlier section, a price mechanism and market forces are the important factors to effectuate appropriate resources allocation. In newly developing countries there is sometimes the necessity of utilizing market forces as a means of attaining effective resources allocation. Without protection from outside competition, new industries might never be established. Overprotection, on the other hand, may perpetuate high costs and lead to inefficient use of resources. In this regard, newly developing countries may introduce in their economic plans targets of cost reduction and schedules for reducing protection from foreign products.

In connection with the use of the market mechanism, the profit-making of enterprises, both private and governmental, may deserve more attention in developing countries. Profits are often associated with the exploitation of local people by foreign capitalists. Profit-making, however, has two more aspects of importance for economic development. One is the plough-back investment from profits. This is the surest way of financing industrial expansion. Second is the use of profit as a yardstick of management efficiency. Without efficient management scarce capital resources would be dissipated and countries might not be able to develop industries competitive in the world market. The problem is not profit as such but its effective use for economic growth.

Concerning economic planning in Japan,[14] since the first post-war plan of 1955 new plans have been adopted by the government every two or three years. Although the government has economic plans, they are indicative in nature. Frequent revisions of the plan are partly due to the realization of rapid growth exceeding the planners' estimates and partly due to the recognition that planning in a market economy should have sufficient flexibility to meet changing conditions. Plans should be utilized as guidelines

[14] A more detailed account is given in Saburo Okita and Isamu Miyazaki: "The Impact of Planning on Economic Growth in Japan," *Development Plans and Programmes,* OECD, 1964.

for current decision-making by providing future perspectives, and for such purposes a rolling or shifting type of plan may have relevance. Economic planning in Japan has also served the purpose of indicating a set of long-range policies in meeting with possible future problems and bottlenecks and of coordinating different objectives pursued by individual government departments in the light of an overall economic framework and future prospect. It has also served educational purposes in orienting people to a forward-looking and rational-thinking attitude on various economic and social issues.

High rate of savings. As is often pointed out, postwar Japan's rate of savings is extremely high compared both to her prewar record and to other countries of the world. Gross savings were nearly 40 percent of the GNP in recent years, while in other developed countries they are around 20 percent. Personal savings as compared to personal disposable income has been nearly 20 percent in Japan, and this figure again compares very favorably with about 10 percent in other developed countries. Moreover, as shown in Table 13, the rate of savings has been increasing in the postwar period, although it seems to have reached a plateau after 1961. For example, gross savings, 23.4 percent of the GNP in 1953, rose to 37.4 percent in 1964. Incidentally, this rising trend in the savings rate was a perplexity for planners, as they repeatedly underestimated the rate of savings in preparing government economic plans and accordingly projected a lower rate of growth than was actually realized.

Of the total gross savings, about 50 percent is from private corporations (including depreciation allowances), 30 percent from personal savings, and the remaining 20 percent from government savings; compared with other developed economies, the share of personal savings is relatively high. The reasons for the high rate of savings are manifold, and some aspects are discussed in other parts of this paper. There are already several studies on this subject, including those by Professor Shinohara and myself.[15] Some of the salient causes are: a) high productivity, low con-

[15] Miyohei Shinohara: "The Role of Savings in the Japanese Economy," unpublished paper, 1965; Saburo Okita: "Savings in Japan," *Economic Development and Cultural Change,* October 1957.

Table 13. Gross Domestic Capital Formation and Savings

	Gross domestic capital formation as % of GNP	Personal savings as % of personal disposable income
Prewar (1934–36 average)	18.9	—
1953	22.4	6.2
1954	21.4	8.0
1955	19.9	11.9
1956	24.0	11.9
1957	27.2	13.8
1958	26.3	13.2
1959	27.1	14.9
1960	31.0	13.4
1961	34.9	19.5
1962	34.4	18.0
1963	32.7	17.9
1964	32.8	18.0
1965	31.3	18.4

Source: Economic Planning Agency: *Annual Report on National Income Statistics, 1966.*

sumption; b) consumption lag in a rapidly growing economy; c) insufficient social security; d) the housing shortage; e) a wage system conducive to saving; f) proprietors' savings; g) the increasing share of income from property. Among these, items (a) and (b) have already been discussed.

(c) Insufficient social security

Loss of personal assets due to war and inflation encourages people to save in order to build assets. Insufficient social security may also cause people to save in preparation for old age and illness. However, the fact that the postwar rate of saving was higher compared to the prewar, when social security measures were much less developed, implies that it is not necessarily the absolute level of social security benefits which influences the rate of saving but rather the extent to which people feel insecure about their future. In the past parents depended primarily on the support of their children after retirement. Now the family system is gradually weakening, and many parents feel that they must support themselves in old age; at the same time they do not feel the social security benefits dependable enough. Such a transitional social change may encourage people, in particular those of middle age, to save more. This latter cause explains the observed fact[16] that, in postwar Japan, the personal savings of middle-aged people are higher than the average.

(d) The housing shortage

The loss of houses due to war damage, the rapid progress of urbanization, and the tendency towards smaller family units create a large demand for houses. As the public housing program to supply low-cost houses to medium- and low-income families has been relatively underdeveloped, individuals are accumulating savings for the future purchase of their own houses.

(e) A wage system conducive to saving

In most enterprises, including government departments, bonuses are paid twice a year, in amounts which total about three months' salary. People adjust their normal expenditure to the regular monthly salary, and this gives a larger margin for saving out of bonuses. The government's Annual Economic Survey of 1966 gives statistical evidence that in 1965, while the savings ratio of normal months was 5.9 percent of the disposable income, that of bonus months (June, July, and December) was 24.6 percent. Other statistical evidence shows that in 1964 60 percent of the total annual savings of urban worker house-hold was from bonuses and that 55 percent of the summer bonus and 48 percent of the year-end bonus was actually saved.

f) Proprietors' savings

In the national income statistics, "personal savings" includes the savings of proprietors (farmers and other self-employed people), and a portion of this latter savings represents that for business purposes and inflates the figures for personal savings appearing in the statistics. However, the fact that in postwar years, while the relative importance of proprietors' income is declining, the rate of savings as a whole is increasing, indicates that this factor has limited verification.[18]

[16] M. Shinohara: "The Role of Savings in the Japanese Economy," p. 21.

[17] Economic Planning Agency: *Nenji Keizai Hokoku, 1965* (Annual Economic Survey), p. 278.

[18] The share of the income from unincorporated enterprises in the national income declined from 37 percent in 1954 to 24 percent in 1964.

g) The increasing share of income from property

The share of personal income from property in the national income has risen in the course of postwar years. It increased from 5.4 percent of the national income in 1954 to 10.6 percent in 1964. As the savings ratio is higher in higher income brackets[19] and the income from property is usually larger in high-income families, the increased share of income from property results in a higher savings ratio.

The financial mechanism. Observing the financial aspect of Japan's rapid postwar economic growth, economists have often pointed out that the financial mechanism in Japan has been in a continued stage of over-loan. It has been a general practice among Japanese enterprises to depend heavily upon commercial banks for the supply of funds required for their business expansion and for commercial banks in turn to borrow heavily from the central bank. As a consequence, the percentage of the companies' own capital in their total operating funds has greatly fallen while that of borrowed funds has risen. This practice has made the financial position of Japanese firms very unstable, and commercial banks have often furnished more credits to enterprises than they could normally afford. For this reason, foreign bankers and entrepreneurs have often criticized the management of Japanese banks and enterprises as unsound and unorthodox. However, it should be noted in this connection that equipment investments have expanded so sharply that the funds needed for such investments could not be supplied from the companies' own capital in an orthodox way. On the other hand, the market for long-term capital has been relatively undeveloped, and a major portion of the bank deposits made by individuals has been channeled to industries through banks. It is also true that Japanese bankers and industrialists usually expect that the government or the central bank will do something to help them if they encounter a serious problem which they think is too difficult to solve for themselves. Such an attitude stems from the historical background—the fact

[19] Saving propensity (savings as a percentage of disposable income) of five income groups in 1965 (*Nenji Keizai Hokoku, 1966*, p. 300):

I	II	III	IV	V
(—)	6.0%	8.6%	13.4%	21.0%

that the Japanese economy emerged from the undeveloped into the modernized stage under the strong leadership of the government.

However, such a financial mechanism and practice has made it possible for the central bank to adjust business fluctuations effectively by raising the official discount rate and also by exercising the so-called "window guidance" which implies a central bank control over commercial banks regarding the volume of credit supplied to industries by the banks. When the domestic economy has sharply expanded and imports have increased, aggravating Japan's balance of payments position, the central bank exercises strong influence on industry by restricting loans to the private banks. Then the nation's balance of payments quickly turns into the black. And if international receipts exceed payments for some time and a recession continues, the central bank relaxes monetary restrictions and usually a business upsurge follows.

In short, the state of over-loan enables the Japanese economy to grow at the maximum rate possible until the balance of payments position deteriorates and is then rectified through tight money measures taken by the central bank. This form of financial operation has been an important factor contributing to the rapid economic growth in Japan. In 1965, however, the monetary relaxation by the central bank failed to cause an economic upswing. So the government resorted to a substantial tax reduction and to the issuance of government bonds for the first time since the end of the war in order to stimulate business recovery. As Table 14 shows, postwar government finance has maintained a more or less neutral position in the relation between savings and investments, and personal savings—the surplus of family income over expenditure—have played a leading role in supplementing the funds needed for equipment investments by private firms.

Since 1965, the relation between savings and equipment investments has altered, and capital accumulation and investment in the private corporate sector has come to be balanced; a deficit in the national government budget has come to absorb the surplus in personal savings. It is now essential to maintain stable economic growth by taking combined fiscal and monetary measures to prevent the business fluctuations which Japan has repeatedly experienced in the past. Through their experiences during the

Table 14. Savings and Investment Balance by Sector as Percentage of Gross Capital Formation

		1957	1961	1965 (Tentative)	1966 (Estimated)
Gross capital formation	% (% of GNP)	100 (32.9)	100 (40.8)	100 (34.0)	100 (33.8)
	Fixed equipment	51.6	53.8	45.4	41.3
	Increase in stocks	16.3	13.9	6.6	7.6
	Total (A)	67.9	67.7	52.0	48.9
Enterprise sector	Provision for consumption of fixed capital	28.3	25.6	35.7	35.7
	Savings of private corporations	16.0	14.4	10.9	12.0
	Total (B)	44.2	40.0	46.6	47.8
	B − A	− 23.5	− 27.7	− 5.5	− 1.1
	Investment (C)	22.0	21.8	31.0	32.6
Government sector	Provision for consumption of fixed capital	2.6	2.2	2.7	2.9
	Government saving	20.3	22.5	19.4	16.7
	Total (D)	23.0	24.6	22.1	19.5
	D − C	0.9	2.8	− 8.9	− 13.1
	Investment (housing) (E)	10.0	10.4	17.0	18.5
Household sector	Saving (F)	30.8	30.6	33.1	35.0
	F − E	20.7	20.1	16.1	16.5
Others	Net lending to the rest of the world	− 2.8	− 4.6	3.8	3.0
	Statistical discrepancy	− 0.8	− 0.1	2.1	0.7

Source: Economic Planning Agency, September 1966.

1965 recession, businessmen learned that high dependency on borrowed capital makes a management shaky and that heavy payments of interest on bank loans result in a higher cost of production. Now enterprises are making greater efforts to accumulate as much capital as possible and to become less dependent upon bank loans. When the government decided to issue sizable government bonds in 1965, it also recognized the necessity of building up a sound capital market to insure a stable supply of long-term funds.

International environment

When World War II came to an end with Japan's defeat in August 1945, the Japanese economy was thrown into dire confusion. Japan lost overseas territories whose area accounted for 44 percent of her total area. In the three years that immediately followed the end of the war, the population increased by ten million, due to the presence of several million repatriates from overseas, including demobilized soldiers, as well as to the "baby boom" which occurred during those years. Japan was placed under the control of victorious nations. She lost her prewar supply sources of raw materials and also her traditional markets on the mainland of Asia. Her merchant marine had been destroyed and her international trade suspended, and she was placed under the most difficult international restraints. Many domestic and foreign observers who were familiar with Japanese affairs were extremely pessimistic about the future economic recovery of Japan. They thought that her economic rehabilitation would take a very long time. However, later developments show that the international environment has been rather favorable to Japan's economic resurgence. Among the various factors which have aided her economic rehabilitation are i) occupation policy; ii) the Korean War; iii) international cooperation in expanding trade; iv) success in major countries in preventing depression and in raising the rate of economic growth; and v) substantial reductions in the import cost of raw materials.

Occupation policy. The occupation policy followed by the Allied Powers immediately after the war's end placed emphasis on measures for preventing Japan from regaining military strength and constituting a menace to world peace—in short, on the demilitarization of Japan. The outcomes of this basic policy were the disbanding of the Imperial Army and Navy and the formulation of reparations programs aimed primarily at the removal of heavy industrial equipment which was thought to be a part of potential military strength (although eventually these programs were not carried out). In the early stages of the Allied occupation, occupation authorities were responsible for the prevention of famine and diseases but not for the economic rehabilitation of Japan. A directive given by the United States Government to General Douglas MacArthur at an early stage of the occupation states:

> You will not assume any responsibility for the economic rehabilitation of Japan or the strengthening of the Japanese economy. You will make it clear to the Japanese people that:
> (A) You will assume no obligations to maintain, or have maintained, any particular standard of living in Japan, and
> (B) That the standard of living will depend upon the thoroughness with which Japan rids itself of all military ambitions, redirects the use of its human and natural resources wholly and solely for purpose of peaceful living, administers adequate economic and financial controls, and cooperates with the occupying forces and the governments they represent.[20]

The economic democratization and demilitarization policy aimed at reforming the social and economic structure of Japan in order to prevent and avert the potential danger which Japan might threaten in the future. Such rigid occupation policies were gradually relaxed, and the Allied occupation began to assist in Japan's economic rehabilitation and to bring Japan back into the community of free nations. The aid furnished by the United States to Japan gradually increased until 1950 when the Korean War broke out and Japan started to obtain special-procurement dollar revenue.

During the occupation, the United States repeatedly sent teams of experts to Japan to offer advice on the modernization of Japanese industries. The recommendations and advice given by the American experts during those years on the reform of various systems were not all fit for the actual situation of Japan, but it should be admitted that the occupation carried out extensive reforms and injected new blood into the Japanese society and economy, and thereby laid the foundation for the subsequent vigorous economic activities. It should also be admitted that during the several years

[20] Basic Initial Post-Surrender Directive to Supreme Commander for Allied Occupation and Control of Japan, U.S. Government, November 1, 1945.

immediately following the war, when the Japanese economy was at its lowest ebb and when Japan had very little to export, the aid furnished by the United States enabled Japan to import the commodities required for her economic rehabilitation.

The Korean War. Acting upon the recommendation of Mr. Joseph Dodge, advisor to the Supreme Commander for the Allied Powers, the Japanese government succeeded in putting an end to the rampant postwar inflation in 1949. In the same year, the exchange rate for the yen was set at ¥360 to one U.S. dollar. The inflation was followed by severe deflation, but the stimulus for expansion came from outside. With the outbreak of the Korean War in June 1950, Japan started to earn foreign exchange through the special procurement of goods and services required by the U.S. armed forces. At the same time, commercial exports substantially expanded. Thus Japan became able to import necessary commodities with her export and special-procurement earnings. In 1952 and 1953, nearly one-half of Japan's imports were paid for with special-procurement receipts.

When the Korean War ended, special-procurement earnings directly connected with the Korean War decreased, but Japan continued to gain procurement earnings in subsequent years from the U.S. armed forces stationed in Japan and her neighboring areas which maintained an annual average of nearly 500 million dollars. It cannot be denied that during those years when Japan's commodity exports were still limited, her foreign-exchange earnings from special procurement substantially facilitated the import of materials vital to her economic rehabilitation.

International cooperation in expanding trade. During the interwar period many countries imposed restrictions on their imports and formed themselves into economic blocs. Consequently, international trade was greatly hampered, and this stage of affairs intensified the political tension among the world powers and finally led to the outbreak of World War II. After this costly experience, the world powers of today have been cooperating in relaxing import restrictions and in expanding international trade. Although this trade policy has not necessarily been extended effectively toward less developed countries, trade among advanced nations has steadily expanded at an increasingly higher rate and has served as a favorable factor in promoting Japan's export trade. Japan's exports are mostly manufactured goods because she produces very small amounts of raw materials for export. Taking advantage of this international trade situation, Japan has been able to develop and expand her overseas markets by offering quality products at low prices. The government decided in 1960 to liberalize commodity imports, because people came to realize that Japan could enjoy more benefits from the international division of labor and could further expand her import and export trade by so doing.

Success in major countries in preventing depression and in raising the rate of economic growth. Since the war, most of the developed countries have succeeded more or less in minimizing cyclical fluctuations, maintaining full employment, and attaining higher rates of economic growth. These factors have greatly contributed to the continued expansion of world trade. At the same time, the full employment attained in major industrial countries has enabled them to relax restrictions imposed on their imports of low-priced Japanese manufactured goods, which might have been tightened if these countries had been suffering from depression or unemployment. Under conditions of full employment, imports of low-cost merchandise from other countries help alleviate inflation and enable the importing country to shift local labor and capital to more productive sectors. In short, such imports favorably affect a country's economic growth. For example, Japan's exports to the United States rose steadily from $180 million in 1950 to $1,100 million in 1960, and further to $2,500 in 1965. It is evident that the U.S. imports of Japanese goods have, in general, had favorable effects not only on the Japanese economy but also on the U.S. economy, even though movements for import restriction have been persistently continuing.

Substantial reductions in the import cost of raw materials. In prewar Japan, the lack of raw material resources in the homeland was regarded as a serious handicap to her economic development, and it was used as a justification for her military expansion. Today the lack of raw material resources is a still more serious problem to the Japanese economy, and Japan must import a large quantity of raw materials from abroad. In fact, she imports 20 percent of the cereals she consumes, almost all of the raw wool and cotton she needs, 99 percent of her petroleum, 85 percent of her iron ore, and many other raw materials. Since the war, (a) raw materials can be imported from abroad much more easily and at a lower cost; (b) the construction of mammoth tankers and ore-carriers now enables Japan to import mineral fuels and ores from remote countries at lower cost; (c) for geographical reasons, Japan's major industrial areas are located by the seacoasts, which fact greatly reduces the unloading cost of raw materials brought from abroad. These factors all work together favorably for Japan's economic development. Japan is now one of those countries which produce iron and steel at the lowest cost in the world. It should be noted that Japan imports iron ore not only from nearby countries such as the Philippines, Malaysia, and India but also from such distant lands as Peru, Chile, and Brazil. She also imports coking coal used in her iron and steel industry from the east coast of the United States. Before the war, she used to import coking coal from the northern part of mainland China.

Petroleum is an important material for generating energies which are indispensable to modern society and to manufacturing industries. The fact that Japan is importing a large amount of petroleum from the Middle East now presents no handicap to other industrial nations. In the past, a lack of raw materials in the homeland was always regarded as a great disadvantage to the economy. But today the lack of raw materials at home and the necessary importation of materials from other countries under the most favorable terms have freed this country from the use of uneconomic raw materials necessitated by the protection of domestic industries producing raw materials. Thus, the lack of indigenous natural resources has turned into one of the favorable factors supporting rapid economic growth.

Future Problems and Prospects

As explained already, there have been many favorable factors working together to form what might be called a "virtuous circle." Therefore, in presenting the future economic prospects for Japan, it is essential for us to see if such factors will continue to work together favorably and if other favorable or unfavorable factors will arise and affect Japan's fast-growing economy. At this juncture, it is thought that various factors are likely to gradually slow down

Japan's future economic growth from the present high rate, for a number of reasons:

The narrowing gap between foreign and domestic technologies

As mentioned in the preceding section, the wide gap between foreign and domestic technologies has been an important factor contributing to the rapid economic growth in this country. However, this gap has been steadily lessened through Japan's active importation of advanced foreign technologies. As a result, Japanese industries are now investing more in scientific and technological research to develop new industrial techniques. On the other hand, it has become more difficult for Japanese industries to promote industrial production by combining advanced foreign technologies with the comparatively cheap and abundant domestic labor.

Changes in the labor situation

An abundant supply of labor with considerably high educational standards has been another important factor enabling Japan to attain rapid economic growth. As the economy expands, however, the labor market situation has gradually become tight. In Japan, young laborers are available at lower cost; consequently Japanese firms strive to employ recent school graduates. On the other hand, the ample supply of laborers—young laborers in particular—which resulted from the age composition of the population will start to decline in or around 1970. In the coming years, the number of junior high school graduates who enter senior high schools and of senior high school graduates who enter universities will rapidly increase (Table 15). As a result, the supply of young laborers will fall further. The declining supply of young laborers will unavoidably change the Japanese wage system based on seniority and will narrow the gap in wages between younger and older workers. Such a trend will eventually encourage Japanese industries to use middle-aged workers more effectively. The declining supply of labor will also affect the lifetime employment system and will strengthen the mobility of Japanese workers. At the same time, the labor shortage will narrow the wage gap between large and small enterprises, and large enterprises will find it more difficult in the future to make use of subcontracting arrangements by which they can utilize relatively low-paid workers.

Such changes in the labor demand and supply situation will accelerate the modernization of the Japanese labor market, but at the same time they may tend to slow down the rate of Japan's economic growth.

Until now, the labor unions in Japan have not strongly demanded the shortening of working hours, presumably because the wages have not been sufficiently high and the laborers have chosen to earn more by working for a longer time rather than to get more leisure by working for a shorter time. But the demand for shorter working hours will become stronger in the years to come. In ten years it will become a common practice among large enterprises to adopt a five-day-week system. At the same time, as mentioned earlier, the ratio of older people to the entire population of Japan will increase. Thus the percentage of the most efficient and productive age group will fall and that of the older people who need social support will rise. This trend will be another factor conducive to a lower rate of economic growth in the long run.

Expanding social security and social overhead investments

It has been possible for the Japanese economy to apply a large part of the available financial resources directly to production, and this has been an important factor enabling it to grow rapidly. However, as the economy expands, the social overhead outlays for housing, transportation, city construction, better social environment, and so forth will increase gradually, and direct investments in industries for increasing production will decline relatively. Such a trend will undoubtedly play an important role in bettering the living of the people who have so far been more or less left behind by the ever-expanding economy. However, it must be admitted also that this trend tends to slow down the economic growth of the nation.

In the field of social security, transfer income constitutes a smaller portion of the national income in Japan than in other advanced countries, and this country, in particular, lags behind other countries in the old age pension and other social-aid systems. Under the prevailing employment system with lifetime commitment, expenses required for social welfare activities have often been paid by private enterprises and their employees. On the other hand there are a great many people, including the employees in smaller enterprises and self-employed workers, who receive far less benefit from various social welfare schemes. In order to promote democratization, the government should do its best to lessen the gap between the employees of large enterprises and those outside them.

Likewise, greater importance is now attached to the betterment of the social environment. For instance, public nuisances such as air and water pollution are now arousing no small concern in the general public. Since a large part of the expenses needed for the prevention of such public nuisances are likely to be borne by the enterprises themselves, such expenses will inevitably add to the cost of production.

The density or intensiveness of Japan's industrial activity is already exceedingly high. In fact, the GNP per acre of land in Japan is nearly twice as high as that in the United States. Twenty years from now, Japan's GNP per unit area is expected to be ten times as high as that of the United States at present. Level land in Japan constitutes less than 20 percent of her total area, and, in the future, production activity in this country per unit area of level land is bound to be even more intensive. This state may work to increase the efficiency of the economy, but at the same time expenses for social welfare and social overhead investments will definitely expand, and this is likely to reduce the rate of Japan's economic growth to some extent.

Rise in prices

In Japan both wholesale and consumer prices were stable until around 1959. Since 1960, however, consumer prices have been rising at an average annual rate of 6 percent, while wholesale prices remained stable. Rising consumer prices have pushed up wages. During the five years 1955–60, wages in the manufacturing industries gained an average of 39 percent, but during 1960–

1965 they went up by 63 percent. During 1955–60 consumer prices advanced by only 9 percent but during 1960–65 they rose by 35 percent. Real wages went up by 31 percent during 1955–60 but by only 21 percent during 1960–65. Although nominal wages increased at a higher rate during 1960–65, the increase rate of real wages went down. Productivity in the manufacturing industries rose by 48 percent during 1960–65, or at a lower rate than nominal wages.

Thus it may follow that if consumer prices continue to rise at an average annual rate of 6 percent for a long period, they may affect wholesale prices and eventually slow down the rate of export expansion. The leading cause of advancing consumer prices is generally believed to be found in the fact that the so-called dualistic structure of the Japanese economy is gradually weakening, particularly in that the wages in consumer-goods manufacturing as well as in service trades, which have greatly depended so far upon low-wage labor, have sharply risen.

Expansion of gross demand is another important factor in the price spiral. During the 1965 recession, the Japanese government decided to issue government bonds for the first time since the war. If the government budget and the new issues of government bonds should continue to expand even after the recovery of private investment, such an expansion may cause an inflationary trend and stimulate a price hike. The introduction of a fiscal policy as a means of adjusting business fluctuation will mean progress in economic operations. But every precaution should be taken in following such a fiscal policy, in order to prevent continued expansion of budget expenditure depending on deficit financing.

Japan's future foreign trade

As mentioned already, in the process of Japan's rapid postwar economic growth, sharply expanding exports have been a great contributing factor in the field of international accounts. In the future, Japan's export trade is expected to encounter the following problems:

i) Exports of Japan's traditional light-industry products, which have depended heavily upon an ample supply of labor, are likely to receive a challenge from newly industrializing nations.

ii) As the gap between foreign and domestic technologies is gradually narrowed, it will become less possible for Japanese industries to easily increase the production of competitive merchandise by importing advanced foreign technologies.

iii) Increasing outlays for social welfare activities and social overhead investments will indirectly affect the cost of production.

iv) The Japanese pattern of business management has so far been raising efficiency within each enterprise, but it also obstructs the coordination or merger of different enterprises and the realization of "economies of scale." This factor may weaken Japan's future competitiveness in international markets.

In spite of these factors, which are expected to have adverse effects on Japan's future economic growth, Japan's GNP is still expected to continue to expand at an annual rate of around 8 percent or more in real terms and her exports by 10 percent at least for several years to come, if not at such high rates as those recorded in the past decade. At a later stage, the economy may grow at a more moderate rate. In the course of such development, however, the income of the Japanese people will rise to the level of that of other advanced nations, and inequalities in the benefits from economic progress are expected to be reduced to a considerable extent. Cyclical fluctuations in business activities will also become more moderate. Japan's GNP in 1966 is estimated at 100 billion dollars and per-capita GNP at about 1,000 dollars. It is not so unrealistic to expect per-capita GNP to rise to 2,000 dollars in 1975 and to 3,500 dollars in 1985. This would mean that the Japanese economy would possibly surpass the present level of West European economies and reach that of the United States in the not-so-distant future. At such a stage, it will neither be possible nor necessary for the Japanese economy to grow at the high rate of today.

The Relationship between Population and Development: The Japanese Experience

The purpose of this study was to try to answer questions whose solutions might help solve the growth and population problems facing today's developing countries. In brief, what process of change in the population and labor force enabled Japan's economic development; and, conversely, how did this economic development affect Japan's population and labor force?

Japan is, certainly, poor in both land area and natural resources and plays host to a large population. It is also true that it has overcome numerous obstacles in its economic development, turning disadvantages into advantages. However, the degree of relevance of the Japanese experience to the growth of developing countries today is uncertain. Some very complex factors are involved. Still, a study of how Japan developed its economy and solved its population problems should prove of some value. The words of Irene B. Tauber are particularly fitting here:

> The demographic transition to low fertility along with low mortality, the economic transition to high and increasing productivity, and the social transition to advanced educational and scientific achievements are not limited by re-

This study was conducted for the United Nations Fund for Population Activities (UNFPA) in 1978 by a research team consisting of the author, Toshio Kuroda (Professor of Demography, College of Economics, Nihon University), Yoichi Okazaki (Chief, Division of Migration Research, Institute of Population Problems, Ministry of Health), Masaaki Yasukawa (Professor of Demography, Faculty of Economics, Keio University), and Koichi Iio (Senior Staff Economist, Japan Economic Research Center). It is reprinted from Philip M. Hauser, ed.: *World Population and Development: Challenges and Prospects* (Syracuse University Press, 1979), with the permission of the publisher.

> gion, race, culture, or relgion. The empirical validation of this point is one of the great contributions of the Japanese experience to comparative and theoretical demography.[1]

The researchers all are of the belief, as is UNFPA, that the Japanese experience can be of great value in planning the growth of developing nations.

Time limitations restricted the scope of this study. A comprehensive treatment of the subject would entail discussion of education, health and nutrition, government population policies, and the status of women. In this sense, the researchers have directed their efforts more at a preliminary report than at an all-embracing one, intending it to serve as an introduction to a wider approach in the future.

The researchers would like to express their thanks to UNFPA Executive Director Rafael M. Salas for proposing and supporting this project and UNFPA Associate Hirofumi Ando for his concrete assistance. It is hoped that further work will be done on this subject in the near future.

The Japanese Experience—An Overview

Food

In the Japanese experience, the process of industrialization and development of agriculture which began in the late 19th century had a significant effect on the increase in the urban population and the industry-wide labor force composition. For example, the number of persons employed in primary industries remained almost constant at 14 million from the late 1860s to the 1930s while during that same period the population doubled. The surplus population, therefore, streamed to the secondary and tertiary industries. During the postwar period, secondary and tertiary industries developed to the point where they began to rapidly absorb labor from the primary industries. The case, however, will probably be quite different in today's developing countries. In the

[1] Irene B. Tauber: "New Dimensions in Pacific Demography," 11th Pacific Science Congress, Tokyo, 1966.

Japanese experience, the rate of population increase remained low in the early period of development. In today's developing countries, not only is the rate of population increase high but it is also not timed with industrialization. Therefore, this population increase must be absorbed by the agricultural sector. Economic development will consequently be more difficult.

The age composition of Japan's population proved to be extremely advantageous during its period of rapid growth. This much may therefore be said from Japan's experience: once another country reaches a certain stage of development, it may create conditions extremely favorable to economic growth by sharply cutting down on the number of children produced after it has achieved a working-age-to-over-65 population rate equal to or greater than Japan's.

Let us examine this from another angle. One of the most striking population movements in Japan up until now was the postwar rise in the average life expectancy. In 1935, it was 46.92 years for males and 49.63 years for females. By 1977, it had risen to 72.69 and 77.95 years, respectively, giving Japan one of the longest life expectancies in the world. At the same time, the infant mortality rate, which stood at a high 138 per thousand in 1926, has recently fallen to 9.3. Advances in medicine and hygiene naturally were the major contributors to this decline, but the general improvement in the Japanese nutritional level cannot be ignored. Before World War II, the average Japanese diet consisted primarily of rice, with protein being obtained from soybeans and fish. Postwar economic development and increased exports of industrial goods, however, created a substantial reserve of foreign currency with which it was possible to import large quantities of animal feed. This then increased the availability of meat and poultry. This point should not be overlooked. Industrial development therefore both encourages the increase of urban population and leads to improved diet through acquisition of foreign currency. The former leads to lower fertility; the latter to lower mortality.

The present-day Japanese ingests an average 80 grams of protein per day. The proportion of animal and vegetable protein is roughly equal. Half of the animal protein is derived from fish and shellfish and the remainder from meat and poultry. The proportion of fish and shellfish is consequently much greater in Japan than in Western Europe or the United States. Dietetically, this considered to be a desirable combination. Developing countries should not necessarily aim at achieving the rich diets prevalent in Western Europe and the United States, but should consider diets appropriate to their respective regions. Japan should be considered a case in point. A trial calculation shows that per-capita caloric intake, including calories in animal feed (original calories), is 10,000 per day for Americans and 4,000 per day for Japanese. Japan can therefore feed a population 2.5 times greater than the United States with the same grain supply.

There is all too often a spiral of malnutrition and poverty in developing countries. Food is to man what fuel is to an engine. Without a sufficient quantity of proper, good-quality fuel, an engine will not perform well. Without sufficient food, people cannot work efficiently. A lack of good-quality food or an insufficient amount of food in the childhood years also has serious repercussions on the health of the adult. Malnutrition, further, increases the susceptibility of the human body to various diseases, thus reducing the work efficiency of the community in general.

A vicious circle also exists with high birth rates and poverty. Infant and childhood mortality rises with the malnutrition of mothers. To insure that some offspring survive into adulthood, large families are favored. Extremely poor communities do not have adequate numbers of hospitals or clinics, or adequate communication and transport facilities. Lack of electrical power halts or seriously inhibits economically productive activities within the community at night and thus indirectly results in an increase in the birth rate. Since it is difficult to obtain funds to operate schools and to prevent malnutrition in children, a high degree of illiteracy prevails. The result is that the majority of people remain in rural areas, where the incentives for small families are not as strong as in the cities.

As several Food and Agriculture Organization studies have shown,[2] if the world population continues increasing at its present rate, most of the developing countries will lose almost all hope of improving the nutritional level or food intake of their people. The time factor is extremely important. Should mankind fail to

[2] For instance, *Agricultural Commodities: Projection for 1975 and 1985* (Rome: FAO, 1967).

take effective measures within the next ten years to restrain the increase in population, it may lose the chance to solve the food and population problem altogether.

Solving these problems on a global scale is no easy matter, of course. Japan, however, succeeded on a national scale. The food situation in the postwar period was extremely serious. The government managed to radically improve the health and nutritional conditions of the people by disseminating information on good nutrition and conducting vigorous local campaigns. It enacted legislation promoting the study of dietetics and encouraging improved nutrition, helped train dietitians, and initiated a program of school lunches. Annual surveys on national nutrition were conducted and recommended nutritional standards established. Local campaigns featuring "kitchen cars" and other measures were also under taken. Incidentally, these campaigns were simultaneously used to spread information on family planning and birth control, effectively reducing the psychological inhibitions of housewives toward participation in the latter promotional activities. Excellent results were also obtained from a project combining information on family planning and parasite control. The freer access to information on contraceptive techniques by mothers proved to be a great plus in population control and was probably of significant value in the spontaneous spread of birth control practices.

Education

A study of the interrelationship of economic development and population must not fail to take into account the role of education. Japan had already achieved widespread grade-school education among its people in the late 1860s, and thus has traditionally had a high literacy rate. Japan's early educational pyramid was extremely broad-based. The government expended considerable time and effort on grade school education and less at the high school level. The general trend in developing countries, especially former colonies, is toward a narrow educational base. The propagation of grade school-level education, however, may be considered one of the keys to successful population control and effective family planning.

Higher education in Japan became even more widespread after

World War II. The percentage of students reaching high school rose from 52 percent in 1955 to today's high figure of 93 percent. This has been one of the factors behind the change in the lifestyle of the average Japanese. For example, the considerable expense involved in putting one's children through high school increased the desirability of small families. Higher education among the female population has also encouraged more women to enter the labor pool, a development which is directly related to low fertility rates.

Higher education has even reached the rural areas in Japan. The effect this has had on closing the various gaps between the cities and rural areas should not be overlooked. Education undeniably plays a significant role in changing lifestyles and encouraging lower fertility and mortality rates.

Urbanization

The increase in the urban population which accompanies industrialization stops after a certain stage is reached, and the nature of the urbanization changes: local urban centers start to expand, and the gap between the standards of living in urban and rural areas narrows. Japan has already entered the stage of transition from concentration in the large cities to local dispersion. Developing countries won't have to face this for some time to come. The Japanese experience, however, demonstrates the potentialities of this process.

Attention should be drawn to the role played by social overhead capital, especially the advancement of communication and transportation, in closing the gap between the large cities and local areas. This has been one of the major factors promoting regional migration. Improved communication and transportation facilities encourage the concentration of population at one stage, but conversely enable dispersion at the next. In the past, life in the big cities held a strong fascination for people in local areas, especially the young. Today, however, pollution, the deterioration of the living environment, the rise in housing costs, the increasing distance from natural surroundings, and other factors have reduced their allure. Japan has reached the stage where people are reevaluating medium-sized and small cities. Therefore, a certain stage in economic development, particularly development of the infrastructure, may be thought of as having a large effect on the regional distribution of population.

Income and population dynamics

Japanese data may be used to clarify the relationship between income and birth and death rates. When the per-capita income in Japan reached the U.S. $200 to $300 level, there was a sudden drop in both rates. Of course conditions differ in other countries, but plotting data from several Asian countries on a graph, as has been done in Figures 1 and 2, shows that this trend is widespread.

There are exceptions. For example, the birth rate has refused to drop in Latin American countries even though the per-capita income has reached a fairly high level. Several complex factors are involved here, primary among which are religious beliefs and income distribution patterns.

It is widely believed in some advanced nations that increases in the income of developing countries will only lead to larger

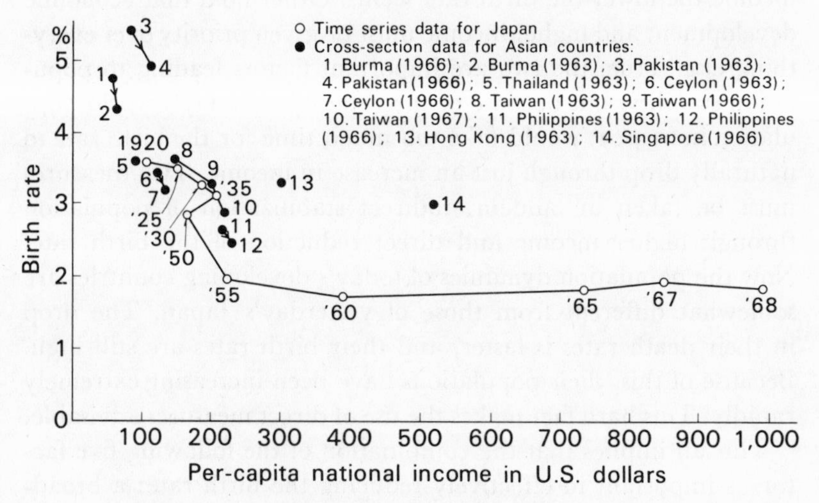

Fig. 1. Birth rate and per-capita national income.

Sources: UN Demographic Yearbook, 1967
UN Statistical Yearbook, 1968
Vital Statistics, Ministry of Health and Welfare, Japan

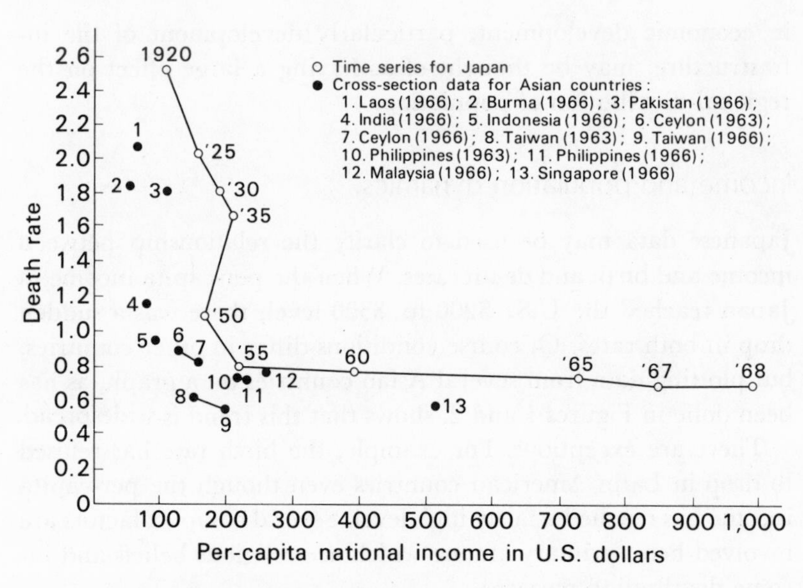

Fig. 2. Death rate and per-capita national income.

populations. This is not necessarily true; indeed, the higher the income the lower the birth rate seems. Other hold that economic development and higher income must be given priority over everything else. True, the two are important factors leading to population stability, but because of the rapidity of today's world population increase it would take too much time for the birth rate to naturally drop through just an increase in income. Two measures must be taken in tandem: indirect stabilization of population through higher income and direct reduction of the birth rate. Now the population dynamics of today's developing countries are somewhat different from those of yesterday's Japan. The drop in their death rates is faster, and their birth rates are still high. Because of this, their populations have been increasing extremely rapidly. This hard fact makes the use of direct measures advisable.

This all implies that the combination of the following five factors is important in effectively reducing the birth rate: a broad-based grade school education, an increase in the income level, improved nutrition, a rise in the social position of women, and decisive governmental action in population policies.

The demographic process which led to Japan's modernization was condensed into a relatively short period. It is possible to trace the roles of employment, education, nutrition, and other factors in the process of Japan's transition from an undeveloped to developed society. And since Japan began collecting statistical data at a relatively early date, it is also possible to obtain relatively long-term time series deta. The fact that Japan has historically not experienced major changes in its national boundaries nor massive external migrations means that its economic development was achieved in a kind of pure culture medium. Japan's experience in economic development and population movement should, therefore, provide many useful hints on the best future path for modern developing countries.

Demographic Transition and Economic Development

Modernization and population in Japan

Both economic development and the population trends acting upon it are topics of great significance in the 100-year history of Japan's modernization. Japan's modernization began with the first attempts at copying and imitating Western European civilization. Although the process of development was not always straight, it was for the most part steady. At the time, Japan was blessed with both a large population and a plentiful labor force. The size of the labor force meant workers could be hired for low wages; it was cheaper to employ manual labor than to purchase machinery. Economic development after the late 1860s was assisted by both the cheap and ample labor supply and, on the reverse side, the greater amount of work the people had to perform because of their low wages and renumeration. Japan's characteristic thirst for knowledge and other factors also contributed significantly to rapid development.

The hard life of the people created a "poverty mentality" which has lasted even till today and has had the effect of suppressing over-population. In other words, it was commonly believed that the smaller the population, the better life would be. In 1868, Japan had a population of 35 million. Today, it has more than three times as many people, 110 million, and its economy has developed to the point where its GNP ranks third in the world.

A threefold rise in population over 100 years might seem rapid at first glance, but it actually amounts to only a one percent increase annually. Looking back, Japan's population increase has been fairly low since the start of its modernization. The economic growth rate from 1868 to 1912 is estimated to have been approximately 4 percent per year; consequently an average 3 percent improvement per year can be inferred for the standard of living during that same period.

Postwar population trends

Japan's population passed 100 million in 1967 and reached 114.15 million in 1977. This means that there was an increase of 38 million, from the 72 million in 1945, in only a 30-year period. From a contemporary viewpoint, the population at the end of the war might seem to have been small; however, these 72 million were living in a war-devastated, defeated country and were hovering around the starvation line. The people became conscious of the dangers of overpopulation because of food shortages.

At the same time there was a vast influx of soldiers and civilians returning to the islands. Even with the large-scale repatriations of Koreans, Taiwanese, and other nationals from Japan, these soldiers and civilians swelled the population by another 5 million. Peace also brought with it a temporary explosion in the birth rate, resulting in 8 million more children in the three years from 1947 to 1949. By 1950, the population had thus risen to 83 million.

The effect of newly introduced medicines and hygienic practices on the death rate soon became felt. The death rate dropped from the postwar 16 to 17 per thousand, finally settling at the slightly over 6 per thousand of today.

Though the birth rate had shot up to 34 per 1000 from 1947 to 1949, it was subsequently brought under control. People were too busy providing for their existing families to want to produce more dependents, and the rate of births began to follow the downward path taken by the death rate. In less than ten years, it had already halved, and by 1957 it had dropped to slightly over 17 per 1000. Bottoming out at 17.0 in 1961, it hovered for a while and then showed a slight upturn as the young people born during the 1947 to 1949 baby boom reached the marrying age. (The 13.8 recorded in 1966 was a special case due to the traditional folk belief that girls born in this year would make poor wives.) The birth rate rose slightly from 19.2 in 1971 to 19.4 in 1973, but dropped again to 18.6 in 1974 and continued falling, reaching 17.1 in 1975, 16.3 in 1976, and 15.5 in 1977. This signified the end of the second postwar baby boom.

The economy of Japan during the postwar period was fraught with confusion and inflation, but the outbreak of the Korean War in 1950 set Japan on the path toward steady economic reconstruction. As for population, the number of births declined, the burden of child raising lightened, and a potential for high purchasing power built up, a factor of value in economic development. The government formulated a program to double income by 1960 and was subsequently able to achieve rapid growth.

The government had a difficult time providing people with food and employment in the first ten years after the war. The economic programs of the late 1950s, however, eliminated the danger that the pressure of the increasing labor force would make modernization of the low-productivity sectors difficult.

After 1960, technical revolutions stimulated the growth of the heavy and chemical industries. The changes in the industrial structure caused by Japan's rapid growth resulted in different conditions in the labor market and brought about a need for a larger labor force. Up until then, migration in Japan had been due to pressures from overpopulated rural areas. This changed with Japan's increasing industrialization and urbanization: the attraction of urban areas became the impetus for migration, and it is the cause of today's crowded cities and underpopulated rural areas. What needs to be discussed is, rather than the migration itself, the effects of the migration on the community.

The period up until the late 1960s or early 1970s is known as Japan's high-growth era, or "golden age." All effort was directed to achieving the economic goal of boosting the GNP. Japan managed to develop its economy to a level comparable with that of the advanced nations and emplanted the concept among the people that Japan was an economic giant. It was here that Japan's population problem became detached from the food problem. The traditional population problem disappeared.

Demographically, Japan changed quickly to a nation characterized by low fertility and low mortality, as exemplified by the change in the average life expectancy. In 1971, it finally broke through the Western European level of 70 years for males and 75 years for females and by 1977 had reached a record 72.69 years and 77.95 years respectively. It might appear from this that Japan had solved its population problem, but in reality this was not the case.

Although Japan managed to join the ranks of economically advanced nations, it simultaneously became burdened with new population problems. A high level of industrial productivity serves to increase the consumption of its beneficiaries. Consequently, consumption of natural resources rises, and the problems of ecological damage and pollution as well as of energy shortages then become added to the list of national considerations. As noted above, even the slow population increases in advanced nations have now become problematical. Considering this along with the population explosion now occurring in the developing nations, it becomes clear that the world will soon be pressured by population on one side and limited resources on the other. The only path remaining for the survival of the human race is controlling births to match the declining death rate. Of course, conditions differ in each country, and in applying this principle a more sophisticated approach must be used, taking into consideration various internal factors.

Japan has recently entered a stage of low economic growth, and labor surpluses are troubling the industrial world. Surveys show that during the high-growth era of the 1960s, city residents, who formed the majority of the total population, felt that living conditions were too crowded, and there was a shortage of people in productive sectors. Today, Japanese society has become more diversified; there are more regional variations in population and a distorted age distribution.

The regional variations in population were caused by population concentration in the cities. The problem is excessive concentration and over-dispersion. The distortion in age distribution manifests itself as an extreme bulge in the age composition caused by the postwar baby boom. The large numbers of children born during that period have now reached 29 to 31 years of age. The bulge was followed by a decline in births, and there is consequently a deep depression in the youthful population after that.

The increase in the average life expectancy of the Japanese has also produced larger numbers of senior citizens. Social security and medical insurance for the elderly have now become important issues. Vigorous efforts to adjust the population imbalances and the distorted age distribution for the future welfare of society have become essential.

Demographic transition

Studies of recent structural changes in Japan's population reveal the great significance of postwar population movements. Especially important were the drop in the death rate and the subsequent fall in the birth rate. Figure 3 shows the trends in Japan's population movement since 1900. The postwar period is particularly noticeable. But first, let us examine the population movement caused by changes in the economy and society.

There is a basic relationship between population and the economy. Countries with high birth and death rates rank low in economic development. Countries with highly developed economies conversely have low rates. Every highly developed nation had high birth and death rates in the past when it was still economically immature but achieved low rates upon reaching its present position.

The demographic transition in postwar Japan is of particular interest. Western Europe took more than half a century to com-

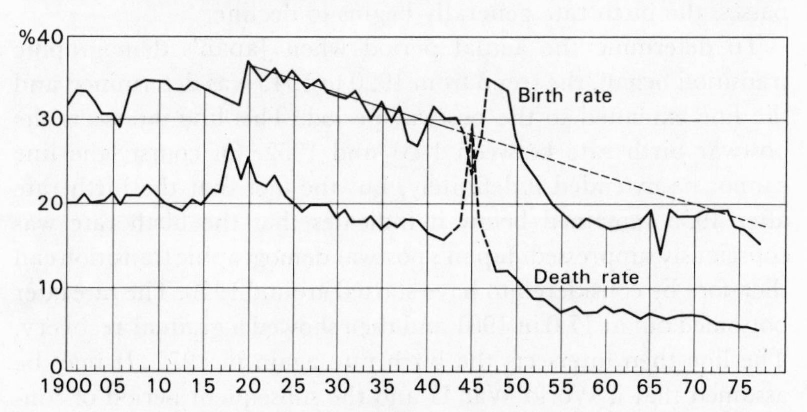

Fig. 3. Birth and death rates.

plete the transition to low fertility and mortality. This same transition was accomplished in Japan in just ten years. The Western European experience, however, is understood as a manifestation of the rapid economic growth of the late 19th century. In Japan's case, the demographic transition was a separate phenomenon, caused by factors unrelated to economic growth, yet proceeding in parallel with it.

Bearing this in mind, take another look at Figure 3. The period directly after cessation of hostilities in World War II is especially noteworthy. The Japanese economy and society were in a state of confusion, and no development was apparent. The death rate, however, began to fall, and a rapid decline was also registered by the birth rate after the 1947 to 1949 baby boom. Both rates declined by more than half in the ten years after the war, an unprecedented world record.

The drop in the death rate resulted from the introduction of new medicines and the dissemination of new hygienic practices; it proves once more that economic development is not necessary for such a drop, as developing countries today are also experiencing.

The drop in the postwar birth rate, similarly, was not caused by economic development but was a product of the confusion which followed the war and the hard life during that period. There was a temporary spurt in the birth rate, causing a "baby boom," but this occurs in all countries after a war with the repatriation of overseas personnel and their return to married life as well as the flurry of marriages. After this temporary period passes, the birth rate generally begins to decline.

To determine the actual period when Japan's demographic transition began, the trend from 1920 to 1945 was determined and the line extended to the postwar period. This line intersects the postwar birth rate between 1951 and 1952. Of course, the line cannot be extended indefinitely, but the fact that the birth rate after 1955 remained below it indicates that the birth rate was consciously suppressed. Japan's postwar demographic transition can therefore be considered to have started around 1950. The rate later bottomed out at 17.0 in 1961 and then showed a gradual recovery. The line then intersects the birth rate again in 1972. It may be assumed that if World War II and the subsequent period of confusion had not occurred, the slow decline of the birth rate which began in 1920 would have continued. Thus, the rapid postwar demographic transition began in 1950 and ended roughly 20 years later in 1972. Japan has now returned to the slow prewar demographic transition which began in 1920. Since, however, the children produced in the postwar baby boom have now come of marrying age and a second baby boom has been experienced, a new situation must be projected for the future. That is to say, the rapid postwar demographic transition ended in 1972. The prewar demographic transition also saw its completion here. This is of particular interest in studying future birth trends.

Let us compare the Japanese experience in its demographic transition with that of Western Europe. In Western Europe, the transition accompanied a continuous process of economic development. Postwar Japan's experience was different in that it resulted from conscious efforts on the part of the people, who at that time faced serious hardships in their daily lives. Thus such a demographic transition need not be coupled with economic growth. This is one of the lessons to be gained from Japan's experience by nations on the road to development.

In brief, Western Europe's demographic transition from the 19th to the 20th century resulted from a prior process of continuous economic development. Japan's demographic transition in the 20 years after World War II, however, was a conscious one proceeding in parallel with the full-scale economic reconstruction starting in 1950. The case of developing countries today is the opposite of that of the Western European nations. If demographic transition in these countries does not precede development, it will be impossible to improve the standard of living of the people.

Migration

Migration is one of the strongest of the structural changes in population that influence population movement. Migration in a stable economy and society is of the outflow type and is caused by population pressure; people are pushed out from rural areas and stream to the cities. Migration is, therefore, only the search for employment opportunites. Even when these people reach the cities, they are forced to work for low wages.

In the context of a technical revolution, however, like that in

Japan in the 1960s with its heavy and chemical industries, labor productivity rises and there is a simultaneous stimulation of related industries. The opening up of new employment opportunities resulted in the start of intake migration. Society itself is modernized through this industrialization, and rapid urbanization is encouraged. The concentration of people from rural areas in the cities intensifies the migration. At the same time, people's lifestyles change and the old ways of life are destroyed. Education becomes more widespread, the average marrying age rises, and even reproductivity is influenced.

The economic expansion of industrialization also leads to the development of new medicines and public hygiene, which brings down the death rate. With migration, however, the decline is generally due to the move from poor, high-mortality areas favoring early marriages and large families to low-mortality areas with greater economic opportunity and higher standards of living which favor late marriages and small families. It must be remembered that this promotes the drop in the death and birth rates. Now, the city not only stirs up the dreams of young people living in backward areas; it also attracts a young labor force because of its industrialization. Therefore, migration affects age distribution and plays a large role in changing the nature of a population.

Population Increase and Economic Development

Japan's population increase

Japan's modern growth period began in 1868, the year of the Meiji Restoration. The approximately 260-year period before that, starting from the establishment of the Tokugawa shogunate government and commonly known as the Edo Period, was also an important phase for Japan. During the Edo Period, Japanese society was basically agricultural in nature and was structured along feudalistic lines. Society was controlled by a strong centralized government. Yet even in those years, conditions were changing.

Two contrasting trends in population in the Edo Period are apparent: strong growth in the first half and weak growth in the second half. Studies by contemporary historical demographers indicate that the population at the beginning of the 17th century was 10 to 12 million people.[3] By the middle of the 18th century, this had risen to about 30 million. This means there was an increase of from 18 to 20 million in about 120 years, or an annual rise of 0.8 to 0.9 percent. This was almost the same as that experienced in the late 19th century, but the reason for this comparatively high rate must be examined.

The population increase in the 17th and early 18th centuries was caused by a rapid rise in both the marriage and birth rates. More than 200 castle towns, including the giant cities of Edo (modern Tokyo) and Osaka, were built throughout the nation. In the rural areas, the small family unit, based around the husband and wife and including the lineal relatives, made its appearance. At the same time, the improved standard of living brought the death rate down sharply, especially for infants and children, and this proved to be another major factor behind the increase.

In contrast to this, the population only increased slightly from the mid-18th to the mid-19th century. The population in 1868 has been estimated at approximately 35 million people; consequently there was an increase of only 5 million in slightly under 150 years, or an annual rate of only 0.1%. In the prewar period, it was theorized that this was due to the loss of vigor of the feudalistic society.[4] Recently, however, historical demography has provided information suggesting that the demographic characteristics of the cities of the premodern society, the high death rate, and the low birth rate were the main causes.[5] This new theory will have to be checked as further studies on the historical demography of Edo Period cities are made. However, it provides a new explanation for the premodern population–economy relationship.[6]

Now, what about the population increase from 1868 to today? Much more reliable statistical materials on population are available for this period. Modern population surveys—that is, censuses—however, were begun only in 1920. The estimates of demographers have to be used for the years before 1920. Table 1 gives

[3] Hiroshi Shinbo, Akira Hayami, and Shunsaku Nishikawa: *Introduction to Quantitative Economic History* (Tokyo: Nihon Hyoronsha, 1975), pp. 42–48.

[4] Ryozaburo Minami *et al.*, eds.: *Encyclopedia of Population* (Tokyo: Heibonsha, 1967), p. 329.

[5] Hiroshi Shinbo *et al.*: *Introduction to Quantitative Economic History*, p. 58.

[6] A representative work on this subject is Society of Socioeconomic History, ed.: *In Search of New Concepts of Edo Period History* (Tokyo: Toyo Keizai Shimposha, 1977).

figures for Japan's population from 1865 to the present. Figures from 1865 to 1920 are based on the estimates of Professor Masaaki Yasukawa of Keio University,[7] while those from 1920 on are from government population censuses and population estimates.

Table 1 reveals the following:

First, the slow population increase which had lasted from the

Table 1(a). Population Increase in Japan

Year	Total population (thousands)	Increase (%)
1865	34505	0.51
1868	35033	0.50
1870	35384	0.64
1875	36528	0.88
1880	38174	0.75
1885	39634	0.69
1890	41020	0.70
1895	42472	0.88
1900	44393	1.07
1905	46825	1.17
1910	49637	1.29
1915	52949	1.11
1920	55963	1.31
1925	59737	1.52
1930	64450	1.44
1935	69254	1.08
1940	73114	−0.25
1945	72200	2.84
1950	83200	1.41
1955	89276	0.91
1960	93419	1.01
1965	98275	1.08
1970	103720	—

Source: 1865 to 1920: Estimates of Masaaki Yasukawa; 1920 to 1970: Population Census.

Note: Rate of increase is the average annual rate compared with the next year.

[7] Masaaki Yasukawa: *Economics of Population*, 3rd rev. ed. (Tokyo: Shunjusha, 1977), pp. 182–83.

Table 1(b). Recent Population Increase in Japan

Year	Total population (thousands)	Increase (%)
1970	104665	1.37
1971	106100	1.41
1972	107595	1.40
1973	109104	1.35
1974	110573	1.24
1975	111940	1.03
1976	113089	0.94
1977	114154	—

Source: Bureau of Statistics, Prime Minister's Office.
Note: Figures after 1970 include Okinawa, though actual reversion was in 1972.

mid-18th to the mid-19th century accelerated once again with Japan's modernization drive. Second, the population increase rate was comparatively low during the period when the government was devising measures to modernize the country and striving for economic and social development. The rate was strikingly different from those of countries now in their early stages of development. Third, the rate of population increase began to rise as the industrial and social base for modernization grew stronger and the economy was set on the road to steady development. It reached its highest levels from 1925 to 1935. Fourth, the rate of population increase gradually declined after 1935. Severe fluctuations in the increase rate were seen during the Sino-Japanese War, World War II, and the postwar period due to disturbing factors such as the dispatch overseas and subsequent return of military personnel and civilian employees and the postwar baby boom. The leap in the increase rate shown after 1970 reflects the attainment of marriage and childbearing age by the group born in the postwar baby boom and the subsequent second baby boom.

Economic development and population increase

The relation between economic development and population

increase from 1968 to the present has changed with each development stage. This suggests that, although it is possible to discuss the relationship between population and development abstractly with a general theory, such a discussion would yield few results of any practical value.

The prewar period. The population increase in the late 19th century was rather slow and consequently, as already pointed out, did not obstruct economic or social development. In fact, the population increase during this period was induced and caused by the development of the economy. In other words, population growth kept pace with the expanding population-supporting capacity on the economic side. Now, while the population was increasing passively in this way, it also served as the source of supply of the labor force required by the growing industries. In this sense, it contributed positively to Japan's early economic growth.

Of note here is the dual structure of the economy which prevailed at that time. Two sectors existed side by side: a growth sector based on the modern industrial plants originally managed by the government and later transferred to private ownership; and a traditional sector consisting primarily of small farms established before 1868. The former demanded more people for its labor force and the latter supplied them. Fertility was high in the traditional farm sector. After the labor force needed for its own reproduction was secured, the excess was sent to the growth sector. Because of this, for example in the roughly 30-year period from 1878 to 1911, although the population had increased by 12.79 million and the number of employed by 7.42 million, there was an increase of only 610,000 persons employed in the primary industries. During this same period, the number of persons employed in secondary industries rose by 3.06 million and in tertiary industries by 3.75 million.[8] As the economy developed in this way, Japan's population increased at an ever faster rate. The economic structure shifted from light industries to heavy and chemical industries and was transformed from a labor-intensive model to a capital- and technology-intensive model. Japan, however, became more and more overpopulated from the turn of the century on.

When the post-World War I economic boom ended, the world

[8] Kazushi Ohkawa (ed.): *The Growth Rate of the Japanese Economy Since 1878* (Tokyo: Kinokuniya, 1956), pp. 130–131.

was thrown into an economic recession. Japan, of course, did not escape its effects. It was then that the seriousness of Japan's overpopulation was realized—directly and indirectly. Scholars began to discuss the problem and the government deliberated on measures to cope with it, establishing in 1927 a special committee to study population and food problems. Two years later the American demographer Warren S. Thompson pointed out the potential threat to world peace of Japan's overpopulation.[9]

Japan's population increase thus gradually began to obstruct rather than aid its economic and social development. A rational solution to the population problem was not found, and Thompson's prophecy finally came true when Japan resorted to war.

The postwar period. In the end, Japan was not able to solve its population problems through force. In fact, the war struck a stinging blow to its economy and swelled the population on the islands by another 5 million people. The military personnel and civilians returning from overseas areas more than offset the Koreans, Taiwanese, and other foreign nationals repatriated from Japan. Added to this was the natural increase of 5 million caused by the postwar baby boom. Thus, from 1945 to 1950, Japan's population grew at the abnormally high rate of 2.84 percent per year, for a total increase of 11 million, and Japan was confronted with a population problem even more serious than in the prewar years.

The only method of birth control open to the people at this time was illegal abortion. Information on contraception and contraceptive implements were still not sufficiently available. The situation changed in 1948 when the Eugenic Protection Law was enacted, legalizing abortions only in certain cases. This law was amended several times, and the conditions under which abortions were permitted gradually relaxed. In 1952, the family planning program and related activities of the Ministry of Health and Welfare began on a full-scale basis.

Because there was a strong conscious desire among the people to keep the number of births down and because of the measures taken, Japan managed to realize a sharp drop in its birth rate. For example, there were 2.68 million births in 1947 for a crude birth rate of 34.3 percent. Ten years later, in 1957, this had fallen to 1.57 million (17.2 percent). Since there was a sharp parallel

[9] Warren S. Thompson: *Danger Spots in World Population* (New York: Alfred A. Knopf, 1929).

decline in the death rate, however, no pronounced decline in the actual rate of population increase was shown. The settling of Japan's population in the postwar period into a low-fertility and low-mortality model was extremely significant from the point of view of economic development.

Postwar Japan was blessed with unexpectedly favorable economic conditions which encouraged its rapid growth. This growth both created the conditions under which low fertility and mortality became possible and set off a massive, rarely seen migration altering the distribution of the population and labor force. While demographic factors had little directly to do with this rapid growth

Table 2. Postwar Economic Growth and Population Increase

Year	Economic growth (%)	Population increase (%)	Difference (%)
1955	6.1	1.0	5.1
1956	7.8	0.8	7.0
1957	6.0	0.9	5.1
1958	11.2	1.0	10.2
1959	12.5	0.8	11.7
1960	13.5	0.9	12.6
1961	6.4	0.9	5.5
1962	12.5	1.0	11.5
1963	10.6	1.1	9.5
1964	5.7	1.1	4.6
1965	11.1	0.8	10.3
1966	13.1	1.2	11.9
1967	12.7	1.1	11.6
1968	11.0	1.2	9.8
1969	10.4	1.2	9.2
1970	7.3	1.4	5.9
1971	9.8	1.4	8.4
1972	6.4	1.4	5.0
1973	−0.3	1.4	−1.7
1974	3.4	1.2	2.2
1975	5.7	1.0	4.7

Source: Economic growth percentages are based on *Annual Report on National Income Statistics* published by the Economic Planning Agency, Government of Japan, annually for the period 1955–75; population increase percentages are based on *Estimated Population in Japan* published annually by the Bureau of Statistics, Prime Minister's Office.

itself, they played an important role in determining its effects.

At the end of its economic reconstruction period, Japan entered a new growth phase. Table 2 shows the economic growth rate after 1955 (real gross national expenditure) and the rate of population increase. The table makes it immediately apparent that the economic growth rate was generally extremely high. While the prewar economic growth rate was an average 4 percent per year, considered high compared with other nations,[10] it more than doubled after the war.

This high economic growth was supported by an uncommonly fast rise in productivity. Despite this, the demand for labor became stronger. The traditional agricultural sector was not able to fill this demand with its excess labor force alone, unlike in prewar days, and was consequently seriously drained of its own manpower. This drain is visible in the absolute and comparative decline in both the number of persons employed in the primary industries and the rural population. In 1955 there were 16 million persons employed in the primary industries, 41 percent of the total number of employed. By 1970, this had fallen to 10 million, or 19 percent. The rural population dropped in the same period from 40 million people, or 44 percent, to 29 million, or 28 percent. In addition, during the high-growth period, approximately 8 million production units, composed of the group born during the postwar baby boom, reached productive age. All this meant that the growth industries were favored with a plentiful new labor force. The rapid economic growth of the postwar period brought a temporary solution to the overpopulation problem—one which the government had previously attempted to solve by force of arms. In addition, it dissolved the old dual structure of the economy which had characterized prewar Japan and spread the practice of birth control from the prewar urban white collar class to the blue collar and farmer classes. An epochal change was realized in population reproduction, with low fertility becoming the pattern nationwide. Together with the simultaneous drop in mortality, this set the population trends of the future and is of great significance for economic development in the years to come.

[10] Kazushi Ohkawa, Nobukiyo Takamatsu, and Yuzo Yamamoto: *National Income* (Tokyo: Toyo Keizai Shimposha, 1974).

Aging of population and economic development

Assuming that the birth and death rates remain stable at their current low levels,[11] it is possible to project fairly accurately the future trends of Japan's population. Table 3 shows the estimated

Table 3. Future Population Projections

Year	Total population (thousands)	Increase (%)	Over-65 group	Proportion of over-65 group (%)
1975	111940	1.0	8865	7.9
1980	117563	0.8	10436	8.9
1985	122333	0.6	11909	9.7
1990	126280	0.6	13909	11.0
1995	130065	0.6	16503	12.7
2000	133676	—	19061	14.3

Source: Institute of Population Problems, Ministry of Health and Welfare: *Estimated Future Population of Japan,* 1976.

size of the population in the future as well as the proportion of the over-65 group. The following trends may be pointed out in relation to the table:

1. The population increase will continue for the time being. By the end of the century, there will be more than 130 million people on the islands. The increase will continue further until a stable population is achieved in the middle of the 21st century.

2. The rate of population increase, however, will gradually decline, falling below one percent a year. At the beginning of the 21st century, the rate of increase will be even more sharply curbed, finally dropping to zero.

3. Both the size of the over-65 group and its proportion in the total population will rapidly rise.

4. The proportion of children (14 years and under) will gradually decline.

5. The proportion of dependents (children and the over-65 group) to the productive age group (15 to 64), or what is known as the dependency ratio, will rise.

Sixth, although there will be almost no increase in the young strata (15 to 39) of the productive age group, the middle-aged stra-

[11] Although the birth rate dropped after 1974, breaking the previous stability, this point is not considered here.

ta (40 to 64) will increase widely. In other words, the productive age group will become more middle-aged.

The above changes are expected to take place in Japan's population in the future. The question now is what impact these will have on economic development and what new measures will be required to deal with them.

Of course, many factors besides demographic ones have an influence on economic trends. It would be extremely difficult to predict exactly how the economy will move in the future. Here, only the direct and indirect effects of future population changes on economic development will be examined:

1. The increase in the number of dependents, primarily in the over-65 group, and their increasing proportion of the total population, will bring a corresponding increase in consumption expenditure in the Gross National Expenditure (GNE). The weight of investment expenditure, including demographic investment for children, will drop.

2. Since there will be an increase in the demand for health, medical, and welfare services for the elderly, a considerable proportion of the manpower in the productive age group will have to be directed toward those sectors.

3. The comparative decline in the young, new labor force in the working population will reduce the flexibility of the industrial structure to go ahead with changes.

4. The comparative increase in the middle- and upper-age labor force will cause the wage obligations of companies operating under Japan's traditional seniority-based wage system to swell.

5. The burden of support for dependents shouldered by the middle and upper groups will become much heavier both directly and indirectly, with the lighter child support more than offset by the higher cost of elderly support.

Judging from this, the economic burden caused by the aging of the population will more than offset the benefits of the gradually reduced rate of population increase. Just as people gradually lose their energy after reaching an advanced age, a population also loses its energy as it ages. Japan will have to be satisfied with a correspondingly low economic growth. The experience of the advanced Western European nations is a precedent, and Japan is fated to follow the same course.

Structure of the Labor Force and Economic Development

Long-term trends in employment structure

The trends in Japan's working population over the last century are given in Table 4 for the primary, secondary, and tertiary industries. The following may be pointed out:

Table 4. Composition of Working Population by Industry (%)

	Primary	Secondary	Tertiary
1878–1882	82.3	5.6	12.1
1898–1902	69.6	11.8	18.3
1913–1917	59.2	16.4	24.4
1920	53.6	20.7	23.8
1930	49.4	20.4	30.0
1940	44.0	26.1	29.2
1950	48.3	21.9	29.7
1955	41.0	23.5	35.5
1960	32.6	29.2	38.2
1965	24.6	32.3	43.0
1970	19.3	34.1	46.5
1975	13.9	35.1	50.7

Source: For 1878 to 1917, Kazushi Ohkawa, ed.: *The Growth Rate of the Japanese Economy Since 1878* (Tokyo: Kinokuniya, 1956); and for 1920 to 1975, Bureau of Statistics, Prime Minister's Office: *Population Census* for each year.

1. First, roughly 100 years ago, agriculture and other primary industries accounted for 82.3 percent of persons employed. After the end of World War I, their proportion had fallen to approximately 50 percent, and the decline continued. Although a temporary rise occurred in the period of confusion following the end of World War II, the speed of decline in general accelerated rapidly, and by 1975 their weight had shrunk to 13.9 percent.

2. The secondary industries, principally manufacturing, illustrate the progress of Japan's economic industrialization. In direct opposition to the primary industries, they showed a tendency to increase in weight. The secondary industries absorbed a particularly large labor force during the rapid industrialization which followed World War II.

3. The proportion of persons engaged in both primary and secondary material production has steadily declined, while that of those employed in the tertiary industries has conversely expanded. Recently the numbers of persons employed in the material production sector and in the service industry sector have been roughly the same.

Therefore, Petty's Law has proven consistently valid in Japan: the income elasticity of demand for farm produce is less than 1 while that for other produce is greater than 1. As a result, the proportion of production value accounted for by the primary industries sharply dropped while those of the secondary and tertiary industries rose.[12]

Internationally, Japan belongs to that group of nations with fairly high proportions of tertiary industry. To reach this point, it underwent the process outlined above. Many developing countries already have had very large tertiary industrial sectors from an early stage. Even though the proportions of persons employed in the tertiary industries are similarly large, the process by which Japan reached that point differed from the process in other developing countries.

Below we will examine, according to industrial groupings, the process of economic change which Japan's employment structure underwent in reaching its present form.

Vicissitudes of primary industry

Agriculture has played an extremely important role in the development of the Japanese economy since 1868. It provided a supply of food sufficient for the population at large and higher levels of income and, through exports of raw silk and other produce, was a major source of foreign currency. In the late 19th century, over 80 percent of the labor force was engaged in primary industry. It has continued to supply the workers needed by the non-agricultural sector; even today it accounts for slightly over 10 percent. Further, the capital needed for development of the

[12] William Petty's experimental law states that labor and capital tend to shift from the primary sector to the secondary and then to the tertiary in the course of industrial development. See C. Clark: *The Conditions of Economic Progress* (New York: Macmillan, 1960), pp. 490–520.

non-agricultural sector was supplied from agriculture to the non-agricultural industries through, for example, land rents.

Japan's agricultural development from 1880 to 1965 is often classified into six major periods, as shown in Table 5. Production of rice, Japan's main crop, has increased about 2.5 times in the approximately 90-year period, while other cultivated crops have increased 3.5 times. Cultivated crops as a whole increased approximately 3 times. Sericulture reached a peak around 1930 when it increased to 10 times that of the late 19th century. During World War II, however, it sharply declined and currently stands at less than one-third the prewar level. Livestock has shown the greatest development by far, growing more than 100 times in size during the 90 years.

This sector-wise difference in growth rates means that the proportion of rice dropped from slightly under 70 percent of agricultural produce to 45 percent in the 90-year period in terms of 1934–36 prices. The percent composition of other cultivated

Table 5. Sector-wise Growth of Agricultural Production (%)

Period		Cultivated crops			Sericulture	Livestock
		Rice	Others	Total		
I	1880–1900	0.9	2.1	1.3	3.9	6.8
II	1900–1920	1.7	1.4	1.6	4.7	3.8
III	1920–1935	0.4	0.7	0.5	1.7	5.7
IV	1935–1945	−0.4	−1.6	−0.8	−10.3	−7.6
V	1945–1955	1.4	4.5	2.5	−0.5	16.3
VI	1955–1965	2.2	1.9	2.1	−0.3	11.0
Prewar period	1880–1935	1.1	1.5	1.2	3.6	5.4
Postwar period	1945–1965	1.8	3.2	2.4	−0.4	13.6
Total period	1880–1965	1.1	1.5	1.2	0.9	5.6

Source: M. Umemura *et al.*: *Estimates of Long-term Economic Statistics of Japan Since 1868*, Series No. 9, Agriculture and Forestry (Tokyo: Toyo Keizai Shimposha, 1966).

crops remained in the 30-percent range throughout the period. Sericulture peaked at over 10 percent in the 1923–37 period, but later declined to the 2 percent range. In contrast, livestock expanded widely after World War II and has now passed the 20-percent mark.

The level of agricultural production is determined by the input and quality of production factors and the sophistication of the technology which combines the two. A glance at the general way in which input factors changed during the 90-year period reveals that the labor force shrank from 15.5 million to 11 million, or by one-third.[13] Labor was the only agricultural input to shrink. The area of cultivated land increased by close to 30 percent, from 4.7 million hectares to 6 million hectares. Fixed capital, consisting of livestock, machinery, buildings, etc., nearly quadrupled in terms of 1934–36 prices. Current assets from purchases of fertilizers, feed, etc., increased 25 times. In other words, while the labor force declined, agricultural production came to be supported by a gradual increase in amount of cultivated land and a wide increase in capital assets, especially current assets.

The trends of agricultural input differed considerably at times. Labor input, however, declined continuously except during the postwar period when the economy was in confusion and large numbers of people were repatriated from overseas. This is related to the fact that agriculture has supplied the labor force for the non-agricultural industry sector during Japan's economic development. The decline in period VI (1955 to 1965), which at times reached 3 percent a year, resulted from the strong influence of the high growth of the postwar economy. Compared to the prewar average, there was an approximately two-thirds reduction in the postwar period. Of note is the fact that the male rate of decline was at times twice that of females.

Let us trace back the factors causing the change in persons employed in the primary industries. Columns (1) and (2) of Table 6 give the annual increase in persons employed in the primary, secondary, and tertiary industries. Column (3) shows the natural increase in the persons employed in the primary industries. Column (4) is the net outflow (outflow—intake) derived by subtracting the figures in column (1) from those in column (3).

According to the table, the net outflow was higher than the natural increase in all except the 1920–30 period. This resulted

[13] The decline began after 1920. Before that, the labor force remained fairly constant.

Table 6. Factors of Change in Number of Persons Employed in Primary Industries (Annual Average)

	Increase in no. of employed		Persons employed in primary industries			
	Primary (1)*	Secondary & tertiary (2)*	Natural increase (3)*	Net out-flow (4)*	Net outflow rate(%) (5)	Contribution rate(%) (6)
1906–10	164	268	64	228	1.47	85.0
1910–20	73	237	93	166	1.12	70.0
1920–30	5	233	132	127	0.88	54.5
1930–40	30	319	135	165	1.15	51.7
1950–55	219	955	321	540	3.24	56.5
1955–60	353	1.153	290	643	4.22	55.7
1960–65	523	1.371	120	643	4.92	46.9
1965–70	333	1.231	194	527	4.84	42.8

Source: R. Minami: *The Turning Point in Economic Development: Japan's Experience* (Tokyo: Sobunsha, 1973).

in a decline in the number of persons employed in primary industry. Also, the natural increase for the postwar period was higher than that for the prewar period. Since the net outflow increased widely after the war, an unprecedented drop was consequently seen in the numbers of employed. That is, the net outflow remained at from 1.3 to 2.3 million a year in the prewar period, but more than trebled in the postwar period, reaching 5.3 to 6.4 million. Column (5) shows the rate of outflow, derived by dividing the net outflow by the increase in the number of persons employed in the primary industries. This jumped from 0.9–1.5 percent in the prewar period to 3.2–4.9 percent in the postwar period. Column (6) shows the outflow from the primary industries divided by the increase in the number of persons employed in secondary and tertiary industries and attempts to show how many of the persons employed in secondary and tertiary industries can be accounted for by the outflow from the primary sector. The contribution rate was as much as 85 percent by 1906–10, but it gradually fell later, despite a sharp increase in the net outflow after the war, to 43 percent by 1965–70.

Attention must be drawn to the fact that the outflow from the primary industries shown in the table includes farmers' children who become employed in nonagricultural industries immediately after graduating from school. Because of this, the occupational trends of new graduates also become an important factor in the employment structure. Data on the prewar period are scarce, but from 1929 to 1938 there were about 900,000 new primary-school graduates annually, of whom 400,000—40 to 50 percent—became employed in the primary sector. Data for 1971 to 1975 indicate that this fell to no more than 6.3 percent for even male middle-school graduates and dropped to slightly under 3 percent for new graduates as a group. (In the 1970s 41 percent of the graduates found employment in secondary and 55 percent in tertiary industries.

The current long-term forecast of the Japan Economic Research Center indicates that the weight of the tertiary industries in the employment structure will expand still further. By 1990, primary industry will account for 6.8 percent, secondary industry for 35.7 percent, and tertiary industry for 57.2 percent. Japan will be faced with the serious problem of how to ensure a certain degree of self-supply in key agricultural products with a continually shrinking and rapidly aging pool of farm workers. More than half of all farm workers today are over 50 years old, and the situation is expected to rapidly worsen in the future.

Changes in secondary and tertiary industries

In the section above a look was taken at the primary industries, especially agriculture. In the process of Japan's economic development, these functioned primarily as a labor supply source. Now we will look at the development of the secondary and tertiary industries which absorbed this labor force, focusing on changes in the employment structure.

The dynamic force behind Japan's economic growth from the late 19th century on was manufacturing. In the 1880s, manufacturing still accounted for only slightly over 10 percent of the net national income. By 1926, however, its share had climbed to 26 percent. (The peak was 30.5 percent in 1969. It has subsequently declined.) During this same period, agriculture's share dropped from 40 percent to 6 percent; industry in the broad sense (manufacturing, mining, construction, transportation and communications, public utilities) rose from 20 to 43 percent, and service industries increased from 40 to 51 percent.

Recent studies have provided estimates of Japan's industrial production dating back to 1874. According to these estimates, production increased 29.5 times from 1874 to 1940. During most of World War II (1941 to 1945), industrial production remained almost the same, but it was sharply reduced by the destruction wrought in the last months of the war and the confusion of the postwar period. The peak was in 1944, when a level 30.7 times that of 1874 was attained. If the 1944 level is assigned a value of 100, then industrial production fell to 42.4 in the final year of the war, 1945, and 16.0 in 1946. The 1946 level was equivalent to that of 1912. The war consequently set Japan's production back 34 years.

Damage to the capital stock and labor force, however, was not as serious as the drop in production, and Japan had not lost its technological and educational reserves, the building blocks of industrialization. Japan's experience shows that so long as there is no major damage to the fundamentals, production will start to rapidly recover from any temporary slump as soon as exterior restraints are removed. Table 7 shows the growth rate of industrial production after World War II. Growth of over 30 percent a year was attained from 1946 to 1951, the period directly after cessation of hostilities, and in 1955 the prewar peak was matched. The average annual growth rate for the 20 years from 1951 to 1971 was 14.1 percent.

Table 7. Growth Rate of Industrial Production after World War II (%)

1946–51	31.2
1951–56	14.4
1956–61	16.3
1961–66	10.7
1966–71	15.2
(1951–71)	14.1

Source: Ministry of International Trade and Industry: *Indexes of Manufacturing Industries' Production,* published annually.

The growth rate of industrial production in the last century was 3.8 percent in the 31 years from 1874 to 1905, 6 percent in the 39 years from 1905 to 1944, and 8.4 percent in the 27 years from

1944 to 1971, or an increase of slightly over 2 percent in each period.

Three growth phases in industrial production can be discerned from the late 19th century to World War II: 1885 to 1895, 1905 to 1915, and 1925 to 1935. Of note here is the change in the industries leading the growth. During the first phase, food and textiles were by far the most important, while the heavy and chemical industries were still relatively insignificant. During the second phase, food and textiles and the heavy and chemical industries (chemicals, metals, and machinery) were almost equal. During the third phase, the heavy and chemical industries became the strongest.[14]

During the recovery period directly following the end of the war, the degree of slump in each industry differed. Each industry, however, subsequently achieved a growth rate of 20 to 30 percent. Later, during the high-growth period from 1955 to 1971, a marked gap appeared between the growth rates of the different sectors. This was due to the trend of heavy and chemical industrialization. The incorporation of new technology further strengthened this trend, which had already begun before the war.

We have seen that there were three phases in the rise of industrial production from the late 19th century to World War II. The annual rate of increase in number of persons employed in the secondary industries was an average 4.7 percent for 1885–95, 2.5 percent for 1905–15, and 2.5 percent for 1925–35. The growth rates in the total number of employed during the same periods were much lower: 1.2 percent, 0.4 period, and 1.0 percent. Because of this, the proportion of persons employed in the secondary industries expanded from 7.3 percent in 1885 to 19.8 percent in 1935. In numerical terms, this amounted to a fourfold rise over a 50-year period, from 1.55 million to 6.22 million.

In 1955 to 1971, the period of high growth after the war, industrial production expanded by an annual average of 14 percent; consequently a strong demand for labor from the primary industries was generated. From 1955 to 1965, there was an outflow of as many as 640,000 workers a year from the primary sector, and from 1965 to 1970 the outflow was 530,000 (see Table 6). Not

[14] Miyohei Shinohara: *Estimates of Long-term Economic Statistics of Japan Since 1868, Series No. 10, Mining and Manufacturing* (Tokyo: Toyo Keizai Shimposha, 1972).

all of this outflow was absorbed by the secondary industries, of course, but the number of persons employed in them did almost double in the 15-year period from 1955 (when it stood at 9.25 million) to 1970 (when it stood at 17.78 million). Therefore, the rate of increase during this period reached an annual average of 4.5 percent. The proportion of all employed persons who were working in the secondary industries climbed to 34 percent by 1970. Japan can thus legitimately be said to have been transformed into an industrialized nation in both name and reality during those 15 years.

The proportion of persons employed in the tertiary industries expanded extremely steadily, as shown in Table 4, from 12 percent around 1880 to 51 percent in 1975. In contrast, income produced expanded from 26 percent in 1880 to 58 percent in 1975. This implies that the productivity of the tertiary industries was higher in the past than that of the other material production sectors. Productivity gradually declined as the weight of the relatively low-productivity primary industries dropped and that of the secondary industries rose.

Meaningful study of employment in the tertiary industries can begin only with 1920, when the first population census was conducted. Table 8 shows how the composition of the tertiary labor force changed from 1920, when its proportion of the total number

Table 8. Changes in Persons Employed in Tertiary Industries (thousands)

	Wholesale and retail trade	Finance, insurance and real estate	Transportation and public utilities	Services	Government	Total
1920	828	13	65	1,074	16	1,995
	(41.5)	(0.6)	(3.3)	(53.8)	(0.8)	(100.0)
1975	11,293	1.790	3.690	8,730	1,954	27,456
	(41.1)	(6.5)	(13.4)	(31.8)	(7.1)	(100.0)

Source: *Population Census*, 1920 and 1975 (Bureau of the Census, Prime Minister's Office).

Note: Figures in parentheses are percent of total tertiary employment.

of employed was 23.8 percent, to 1975, when it was 50.7 percent. The first thing to come to one's attention is the drop in the weight of the service industries, which had accounted for the largest share in 1920. The major factor behind this drop was the almost total disappearance of live-in household help, which accounted for more than half of the service-sector employment in the 1920s. In recent years, the number of persons employed in health care, education, automotive servicing, and so on has rapidly expanded, but this has not been enough to offset the drop in household help. Further, the share of finance, insurance, real estate, transportation, and public utilities has grown since these are strongly tied to the development of the secondary industries. Japan's wholesale and retail trades were previously typically small-scale operations and were said to harbor excess labor. The percent composition of 1975 shows them still accounting for the largest share. Government jobs expanded 120 times from 1920 to 1975.

The weight of Japan's tertiary industries—primarily education, research services, and medicine-related industries—in terms of share of national income is expected to continue to expand. By 1990, it is projected to reach 57 percent. The weight of the service economy in the employment structure will probably also finally begin to become stronger.

Migration and Economic Development

Migration and economic growth

Modernization is a combination of two main factors: industrialization and urbanization. Industrialization and urbanization are made possible by the demographic pattern known as migration. Consequently, without migration there can be no successful modernization. The history of the two are closely intertwined, as exemplified by the long-term rural-to-urban regional migratory pattern.

One of the fundamental features of Japan's modernization during the last century was the continuing migration of population from the rural areas to the cities, even though the numbers of migrants fluctuated at times. Demographically, it was a movement of people from the high-fertility rural areas to low-fertility urban areas, and it may be understood as a pressure valve for the overpopulated rural areas and as part of the regional redistribution of population throughout the country. Economically, it supplied the labor force required in the urbanized and industrialized regions and contributed to both a higher GNP and a higher national standard of living. This migration continued at an abnormal rate in Japan's economic recovery period after World War II and, far from abating, has increased still more rapidly in the subsequent period of high economic growth.

Japan's manufacturing industries and heavy and chemical industries, which provided the main thrust behind its accelerated economic growth, flourished primarily in two centers of long-standing historical significance, the Tokyo and Osaka metropolitan areas. As a result, there was a massive flow of the labor force from rural villages and small cities all over Japan and a massive concentration and crowding of population in the small region known as the Pacific Industrial Belt.

The tremendous labor force required for the high economic growth commencing in the late 1950s was provided by the more than 6 million overseas repatriates living in rural areas (including military personnel and civilians) and the large numbers of soldiers demobilized after the war. The number of people supported by the primary industries, 14 million in prewar days, reached over 17 million in 1950. In 1965, however, 15 years later, this had fallen sharply to 11.7 million, illustrating indirectly the influence of the available labor supply. (Incidentally, it should be remembered that the baby boom of 1947 to 1949 became the source of supply of the large young labor force in the 1960s.)

This large-scale migration also had its detrimental aspects. Major cities became overcrowded and local rural areas under-populated, so much so as to cause serious concern in the government and among experts.

In studies on what causes migration, theories emphasizing economic factors such as regional disparities in standards of living and income have been dominant.[15] From the microeconomic view-point, people move to cities in search of job opportunities through

[15] Minoru Tachi's works may be cited as representative studies in this field: "Regional Disparity and Internal Migration of Population in Japan," *Economic Development and Cultural Change,* Vol. XII, No. 2, 1964; "Major Cities and the Economic Role of Migration," in Minoru Tachi (ed.): *Internal Migration of Populations in Japan* (Tokyo: Kokon Shoin, 1962), pp. 1–22; "The Role of Internal Migrations of Population," in Tachi (ed.): *Internal Migration of Population in Japan,* 4th ed. (Tokyo: Kokon Shoin,

which they can raise their standard of living. Cities offer a wide selection of diverse employment opportunities as well as many social and public facilities. The lure of the big city, with its ample entertainment facilities, is particularly strong for the young people in local rural areas.

Not all the people in rural areas, of course, leave their villages for the cities. There is a more or less fixed number of young people who never migrate in the first place, and some young people who return after having once left. Aside from purely economic reasons, one can imagine the strength of Japan's family system, inheritance, land system, etc., holding or bringing back these people. No general theory exists which can unravel the complicated factors determining whether or not a person will move. Migration differs in form with each country, each region, each time period, and with people's social, economic, and cultural level.

The Japanese government began to show concern over the intensified concentration of population in the cities at a fairly early stage and moved to suppress overconcentration in the major urban areas.[16] In 1962, for example, it enacted the New Industrial Cities Promotion Law. Designed to contribute to development of local areas and the national economy, this law regulated industrial land use and development and municipal facilities in an attempt to prevent overconcentration of industry and population in the major cities, correct regional disparities, and stabilize employment. The Comprehensive National Development Plan, submitted and passed the same year, also had as one of its goals the correction of urban overcrowding.

In 1969, the government adopted the New Comprehensive National Development Plan, which was directed at dispersing industrial development to local areas and at encouraging large-scale developmental projects. Its basic policy called for balanced coordinated development throughout Japan. The Third Comprehensive National Development Plan was proposed and passed in December 1977. It may be said that a typical policy of population migration dispersion has been designed to foresee the establish-

1967), pp. 146–77. See also Ryoshin Minami and Akira Ono: *Theory and Analyris of Populalion Urbanization* (Tokyo: Keiso Shobo, 1965), especially Chapter 3, "Economic Theory of Migration."

16 Bernard Berelson (ed.): *Population Policy in Developed Countries* (New York: McGraw-Hill, 1974), Chapter 23, "Japan," pp. 704–730.

ment of "human habitation zones" based on a special redistribution of population.

Changes in amount of migration and features of regional migration

The numbers of migrants, rates of increase compared with the previous year, and total migration expressed as a percentage of Japan's total population in the approximate quarter-century from 1954 to 1977 are given in Table 9.

Table 9. Trends in Numbers of Migrants in Japan

Year	Numbers (thousands)	Increase (%)	Total migration (%)	Year	Numbers (thousands)	Increase (%)	Total migration (%)
1954	5,498	—	6.27	1961	6,012	6.4	6.42
1955	5,141	−6.5	5.80	1962	6,580	9.4	6.95
1956	4,860	−5.5	5.43	1963	6,937	5.4	7.26
1957	5,268	8.4	5.83	1964	7,257	4.6	7.51
1958	5,294	0.5	5.81	1965	7,381	1.7	7.56
1959	5,358	1.2	5.82	1966	7,432	0.7	7.55
1960	5,653	5.5	6.09	1967	7,479	0.6	7.51
1968	7,775	4.0	7.72	1973	8,539	—	7.90
1969	8,126	4.5	7.97	1974	8,027	−6.0	7.34
1970	8,273	1.8	8.02	1975	7,544	−6.0	6.78
1971	8,360	1.1	8.01	1976	7,392	−2.0	6.58
1972	8,225	−1.6	7.78	1977	7,395	0.0	6.52

Source: *Annual Report on the International Migration in Japan Derived from the Basic Resident Registers,* 1977, Bureau of Statistics, Prime Minister's Office.

Note: Number of migrants refers to numbers of people moving between cities, wards, towns, or villages. Migrants to and from Okinawa are included only after 1973.

Japan is considered to have entered its era of high economic growth about 1957. A general long-term increase in the numbers of migrants began in the same year, although considerable fluctuations were seen in the actual year-by-year increase rates. The average in the late 1950s was 5.2 million a year; in the early 1960s, 6.5 million; in the late 1960s, 7.6 million; and in the 1970s, over 8 million, reaching 8.5 million in 1973. This last year was also the one in which oil prices rose drastically, touching off an economic

Table 10. Changes in Net Regional Migration in Postwar Japan (thousands)

	Region	1955 – 59	1960 – 64	1965 – 69	1970 – 74	1975 – 77
A	Hokkaido	+23	−151	−199	−217	−10
B	Kita-Tohoku	−160	−298	−250	−204	−30
C	Minami-Tohoku	−280	−361	−219	−79	−8
D	Kita-Kanto	−285	−201	−90	+95	+53
E	Minami-Kanto (Tokyo metropolitan area)	+1,442	+1,854	+1,452	+876	+169
F	Hokuriku	−245	−254	−212	−121	−30
G	Tosan	−222	−137	−87	−20	−22
H	Chukyo	−70	+311	+157	+111	−24
J	Keihanshin (Osaka metropolitan area)	+633	+929	+526	+62	−164
K	Environs of Keihanshin	−57	−37	+22	+107	+62
L	Sanin	−88	−115	−93	−46	−4
M	Sanyo	−127	−185	−53	+25	−19
N	Shikoku	−212	−289	−199	−79	−3
P	Kita-Kyushu	−177	−606	−407	−241	+25
Q	Minami-Kyushu	−293	−461	−349	−228	+9

Source: Computation based on *Annual Report on the Internal Migration in Japan Derived from the Basic Resident Registers,* Bureau of Statistics, Prime Minister's Office. Data up to November 9, 1967, are based on the Resident Registration Law, superseded by the Basic Resident Register Law enacted in November 1967.

(+) indicates an excess of in-migrants over out-migrants.

(−) indicates an excess of out-migrants over in-migrants.

Note: The prefectures contained in each of the 15 regions are as follows:

A. Hokkaido; B. Aomori, Iwate, Akita
C. Miyagi, Yamagata, Fukushima
D. Ibaraki, Tochigi, Gunma
E. Saitama, Chiba, Tokyo, Kanagawa
F. Niigata, Toyama, Ishikawa, Fukui
G. Yamanashi, Nagano, Shizuoka
H. Gifu, Aichi, Mie
J. Kyoto, Osaka, Hyogo
K. Shiga, Nara, Wakayama
L. Tottori, Shimane
M. Okayama, Hiroshima, Yamaguchi
N. Tokushima, Kagawa, Ehime, Kochi
P. Fukuoka, Saga, Nagasaki, Oita
Q. Kumamoto, Miyazaki, Kagoshima

downturn. The numbers of migrants peaked and later declined sharply, falling to 7.5 million in 1975 and 7.4 million in 1976.

Let us examine the changes in the total number of migrants from the standpoint of movement between different regions. Japan's 46 prefectures (excluding Okinawa) were classified into 15 regions and the net migration (in-migration—out-migration) calculated for each five-year period since 1955 (with a three-year period from 1975 to 1977). The results are given in Table 10.

Table 10 indicates the following: First, regions E and J, the Tokyo and Osaka metropolitan areas, absorbed a vast amount of people from almost all of the other regions. Second, this migratory trend began to change around 1965: net in-migration in the Tokyo and Osaka metropolitan areas sharply declined. An excess of out-migrants over in-migrants is already evident in the Osaka metropolitan area. Some local areas, at the same time, have been shifting in the long term from out-migration regions to in-migration regions (Kita-Kanto, Kita-Kyushu, Minami-Kyushu). Others have continued to show an excess of out-migrants over in-migrants, but on a sharply reduced scale (Kita-Tohoku, Minami-Tohoku, Tosan, Sanin, Shikoku).

These changes in migration patterns indicate that the concentrated migration to the giant urban areas has also reached a peak and new changes have begun. Migratory patterns have begun to diversify, resulting in a decline in the inflow to metropolitan areas, an increase in the outflow from metropolitan areas to local areas (U-turn), a transition from migration to the large cities to migration to medium and small cities, and an increase in migration between local neighboring areas (for example, migration between Kita-Tohoku and Minami-Tohoku or Kita-Kyushu and Minami-Kyushu). These may be thought of as the first stirrings in the movement toward population redistribution in the Japanese archipelago.

Migration in three metropolitan areas

Let us look at the changes in the net number of migrants in the three metropolitan areas where migratory changes appear most pronounced (see Table 11). Overall in-migration in the three areas was over 600,000 a year in 1961, 1962, and 1963. In-

Table 11. Changes in Net Migration of Three Metropolitan Areas

(thousands)

Year	Tokyo area	Osaka area	Chukyo area	Total
1955	235	95	23	353
1956	247	612	42	401
1957	295	165	44	507
1958	273	123	26	422
1959	300	145	45	490
1960	333	189	72	594
1961	359	221	75	655
1962	364	211	72	647
1963	354	185	80	619
1964	327	174	76	578
1965	298	131	52	481
1966	266	103	37	406
1967	255	107	42	404
1968	259	112	48	418
1969	250	121	55	426
1970	248	91	54	393
1971	206	47	37	289
1972	159	24	24	207
1973	97	△ 5	22	114
1974	53	△21	7	39
1975	45	△30	△ 4	11
1976	26	△41	△ 7	△23
1977	35	△45	3	△ 6

Source: Computation based on *Annual Report on the Internal Migration in Japan Derived from the Basic Resident Registers*, Bureau of Statistics, Prime Minister's Office.

Remarks: Included in the Tokyo metropolitan area are Saitama, Chiba, Tokyo, and Kanagawa; in the Osaka metropolitan area, Kyoto, Osaka, and Hyogo; and in the Chukyo metropolitan area, regions in Aichi, Gifu, and Mie Prefectures. (△) indicates an excess of out-migrants over in-migrants. Figures for each area area are rounded off, and the total of the three may not necessarily correspond to the figures in the Total column.

migration declined after that, totaling only 110,000 in 1973, the year of the oil embargo, and in 1976 an excess of out-migrants over in-migrants was recorded for the first time. This suggests that migration in Japan had entered a crucial stage of transition.

Attention should also be drawn to the marked change in the position held by migration in the population increases of metropolitan areas. Changes in regional populations are not, obviously, due to migration alone, but also to natural increases. The change in the relative weight of migration and natural increases in the growth of the Tokyo and Osaka metropolitan populations are given in Table 12. Up until 1965 more than 50 percent of the

Table 12. Changes in Migration and Natural Increase in Population Growth in Tokyo and Osaka Metropolitan Areas

(thousands)

Time period	Tokyo area				Osaka area			
	Population increase A	Natural increase B	Migration C	C/A %	Population increase A	Natural increase B	Migration C	C/A %
1950 ~ 55	2,346	889	1,457	62.1	1,142	533	609	53.3
1955 ~ 60	2,440	877	1,563	64.1	1,230	510	721	58.6
1960 ~ 65	3,153	1,294	1,859	59.0	1,665	758	907	54.5
1965 ~ 70	3,096	1,740	1,356	43.8	1,469	973	495	33.7
1970 ~ 75	2,926	2,039	887	30.3	1,157	1,122	35	3.0

Source: Census results and vital statistics on population movement.

Remarks: Increase caused by migration (excess of in-migrants over out-migrants) computed by subtracting five-years' natural increase from five years' population increase of each metropolis or prefecture comprising the metropolitan area. Prefectures (Tokyo) comprising the metropolitan areas correspond to those in other statistical tables.

population increase in both areas was attributable to the excess of in-migrants over out-migrants. The relative weight of migration started to decline after that year, however, and in the five-year period 1970 to 1975 had fallen to no more than 3 percent in the Osaka area. Natural increase accounted for 97 percent of the population rise. Even in the Tokyo area, the relative weight of migration had fallen to 30 percent in the 1970–75 period. In the Third Comprehensive National Development Plan, the government envisioned a population increase in the metropolitan areas no greater than the amount resulting from natural increase. The level of a so-called "closed population" has been maintainable because of this recent reversal in the relative weights of migration and natural increase.

Study of "mobility transition"[17]

The statistics given in each previous section clearly point to changes in the behavior of people in selecting places of residence.

Population redistribution is manifesting itself as a rapid increase in medium and small city populations and an increase in their share of Japan's total population, a pronounced drop in the rate of increase of big-city (over 1 million) populations, and a declining trend in the rate of population increases in areas centered around giant cities. A Hoover Index analysis was made to ascertain the degree of concentration of urban populations using data from 644 cities in Japan.[18] This analysis showed a rapid rise in the index from 0.4260 in 1955 to 0.4709 in 1965. The rapid speed of the rise slowed down somewhat after that, and the index rose to only 0.4874 in 1970 and 0.4936 in 1975. It then dropped to 0.4900 in 1976 and 0.4903 in 1977, suggesting that dispersion of urban population in the global sense had actually begun.

This mobility transition implies a trend toward redispersion and manifests itself as a change in the regions selected by migrants for residence. This change in the regions migrated to is clearly suggested in Tables 10 and 11. It is impossible, however, to determine the concrete nature of this change, so a preference index is used. An analysis of the 1955–77 period using this index[19] reveals that there has been a pronounced outflow from the metropolitan

[17] Toshio Kuroda, "The Role of Migration in Population Distribution," in *Japan's Economic Transition*, Papers of the East-West Population Institute, No. 46, July 1977.

[18] Reported in *Nihon Keizai Shimbun* (The Japan Economic Journal), July 24–30, 1978.

$$\text{Hoover Index} = \frac{1}{2}\sum_{i=1}^{n}\left|X_i - S_i\right|$$

X_i = the proportion of the population in unit *i* of the total national population.
S_i = the proportion of the space of unit *i* over the total land area.
n = the total number of the units in the country.

[19] S. Uchino, "Two Major Migration Streams in Japan," *The Journal of Population Problems*, No. 139, July 1976. Data for 1977 are from unreleased provisional calculations by Ms. Uchino. The following method was used to compute the preference index:

$$PI = \frac{Mod}{mPo\dfrac{Po}{\sum Pi - Po}} \times 100$$

Mod: Actual out-migration
m: Ratio of regional migrants to total population
Po: Population of outflow area
Pi: Population of intake area
$\sum$Pi: Total population

areas to several local areas. For example, there was an increase in selective outflow from the Tokyo metropolitan area to Kita-Kanto, Minami-Tohoku, Tosan, Kita-Tohoku, and Hokuriku (migrants returning to their regions of origin), and an increase in selective outflow from the Osaka metropolitan area to its environs (suburbs) and to the Sanin, Shikoku, and Minami-Kyushu areas. There has also been a striking outflow increase to neighboring regions. Up until 1965, for instance, the Tokyo metropolitan area was the region of strongest selective outflow for Kita-Tohoku. After 1965, however, Minami-Tohoku laid claim to this position. The Osaka metropolitan area had the highest selective index for both Sanin and Sanyo until 1960, but after 1965 this changed to Sanyo for Sanin and vice versa. The same relationship held true for Kita-Kyushu and Minami-Kyushu.

There was also a change in the ages of the migrants. The majority of migrants are known to be young people. Existing statistics do not contain information on the age composition of migrants in Japan, so a census survival ratio was used to compute the changes by sex and age in prefectural populations caused by migration. Changes in the pattern for males 20 to 24 years old after 1965 are especially noteworthy. In 1970 an excess of out-migrants over in-migrants in this group was shown in Tokyo, Osaka, Kyoto, and Fukuoka, with the net outflow exceeding 20 percent in the first two. Almost all the other prefectures showed a net inflow of this group.[20] During the 1970–75 period, the population of males 20 to 24 years old declined in the Tokyo, Osaka, and Chukyo metropolitan areas by 9.3, 7.1, and 0.2 percent, respectively.[21] The same group increased in all other regions. The rate of increase was especially high in Sanin and Shikoku: 19.1 and 17.8 percent, respectively. Even more noticeable was the decline in the three metropolitan areas by 1975 of males who were aged 25 to 29 in 1970 (and had become 30 to 34 in 1975). The other regions in Japan, except for Hokkaido, showed increases. This indicates an expansion of the age group of migrants to local areas from the 20-to-24-year-old group to the 25-to-29-year-old group.

[20] Shunsaku Nishikawa: "The Reversal of Population Migration," *Nihon Keizai Shimbun* (The Japan Economic Journal), April 27, 1973; "Regional Migration of Labor, 1970 to 1975," Chapter 7 in *Economic Analysis and Policy* (Tokyo: Nihon Keizai Shimbunsha, 1975), pp. 109–128.

[21] Based on unreleased provisional calculations by S. Uchino.

Conclusion

A study was made of the notable transitional stages in the numbers, regional selection, and age of Japan's population migration. Two basic trends were assessed: a change from concentration in metropolitan areas to dispersion in local areas, and a predominance of the young productive age group in their 20s among migrants. This "U-turn" in the young labor force was made possible by the Comprehensive National Development Plan of 1962, the New Comprehensive National Development Plan of 1969, the many measures taken to encourage local development, and the comprehensive development plans of each individual prefecture. These created more developed regional economies and greater employment opportunities. Additional factors encouraging this "U-turn" were the deterioration of living conditions in the large cities and changes in attitudes toward life in general.

The basic concept behind the Third Comprehensive National Development Plan of 1977 was a human habitation scheme.[22] Behind it may be seen the aforementioned mobility transition. The government hopes to keep future population increases in the Tokyo and Osaka metropolitan areas below those of a closed population—in other words, below natural increase levels. It is planning to establish 200 to 300 "human habitation zones" which will act as basic areas for regional development. Just how these zones will be equipped and coordinated in terms of economic activities is a topic for the future.

The massive internal migration in postwar Japan proved to be a significant contribution to the rapid economic growth and development of Japan's metropolitan areas. At the same time, however, it not only obstructed the development of those regions supplying the large young labor force but also created overcrowded conditions in the high-density industrial and population regions. A new method of development aimed at upgrading the quality of life must be studied when redirecting migration for redistribution of the population.

[22] Government of Japan, Land Agency: *Third Comprehensive National Development Plan*, November 1977.

The Experience of Economic Planning in Japan

The General Character of Economic Planning

Although the government has produced several economic plans since the end of World War II and there exists an Economic Planning Agency in the government, Japan's economic system is not a planned economy but a predominantly private-enterprise economy. There are fields, here and there, where government intervenes in the private activities, but the basic nature of the present Japanese economy is a highly competitive market economy.

Foreign visitors to Japan very often hear about "excessive competition" from business people, government officials, and economists. This may sound strange for visitors from highly industrialized countries where one of the basic problems is the trend toward less competition among private enterprises. It may sound strange also because Japan has so far been known as a country with strong government leadership.

Contrary to the prevailing image of a highly concentrated and organized economy, Japan today has very keen competition among enterprises, big and small. The market share of companies in various branches of industry is still fluid, and quite a few firms have newly sprung up since World War II, such as Sony and Matsushita. In a sense, the private sector of the economy is very dynamic, and it maintains the flexibility of a competitive market system to a large degree.

This is a revised version of a paper prepared for the Organisation for Economic Co-operation and Development (OECD) in 1963. The revised version was issued as Japan Economic Research Center (JERC) Paper No. 23 in April 1974. It is reprinted with the permission of the JERC.

There are two conflicting trends in regard to government-business relations. One is the historical role of the government in looking after the private sector. Nearly a century ago Japan started its modernization as an economically underdeveloped and industrially backward country. The government gave strong backing to the modernization and gave protection, encouragement, and inducement to new industries. This paternalistic attitude of the government toward private industry has been gradually diminishing as a result of the rapid expansion of private industries and the strengthening of their power. Direct intervention by the government in individual private enterprises is practiced to a very small extent in present-day Japan. Postwar reforms disbanding the *zaibatsu* (big family concerns) and discouraging direct government intervention in the private sector have greatly stimulated the free competition among enterprises, however.

Another trend in business-government relations is the increasing responsibility of the government in preventing unemployment and serious business fluctuations, in improving social overhead capital, in expanding educational and training facilities, in maintaining rules for fair competition, in promoting social security measures, and in preventing pollution.

The character of economic planning reflects basic features of the government-business relation of the specific country. In Japan, economic planners have avoided introducing strong planning elements into the private sector and have stated explicitly in the plans that figures for the private sector are only estimates and that the direct responsibility for making plans and implementing them rests with the private enterprises themselves. Government plans also provide guideposts for the decisions to be made by private enterprises and the broad lines of policy which will influence industries in indirect ways.

On the other hand, planners are trying to introduce stronger planning elements into the public sector, for which government has both direct responsibility and means for implementation. There are practical administrative problems, however, concerning the planning of the public sector. When the old established departments of the government, such as the Ministry of Finance, have strong independence from the planning agency, and when the political climate is not necessarily understanding of the merits of planning, there are natural limitations on effective planning for the public sector. In Japan, there is growing recognition of the usefulness of planning in a free-enterprise economy, and the preparation of the economic plans itself has had an educational effect upon the various ministries, on business, and on the general public.

Another factor which has embarrassed government planners is the unpredictability of the future growth potential of the Japanese economy. When the 1958–62 plan was being prepared in 1957 nobody predicted the possibility of a 13 percent annual growth of GNP in real terms, an average which actually was reached during 1959, 1960, and 1961. When the National Income Doubling Plan of 1961–70 was being processed in early 1960, no economist ever expected the ratio of gross capital formation to GNP to rise from the level of 30 percent (actual data for 1956–58), to the much higher level of 35–40 percent of GNP reached in 1961–63. Repeatedly the future estimates made by the economic planners have proven to be too conservative, and the revision of each economic plan became necessary long before the expiration of the plan period.

Both the dynamic nature of the private sector and the uncertainty about the future growth potential have put limitations on the use of economic plans for determining the level of investment in individual sectors of the economy, unlike the plans of the French government. Some economists feel it may be advisable to prepare a revolving type of four- or five-year plan every year or every other year. In fact, in the past, the government plans were revised rather frequently. The 1956–60 plan, the first official plan, was prepared in 1955, the second one (1958–62 plan) in 1957 and the third one (1961–70 plan) in 1960. The third plan (1961–70 plan) was formulated in 1963, and the fourth plan (1964–68 plan) was prepared in early 1965. The fifth plan (1967–71 plan) was prepared in 1967, the sixth one (1970–75 plan) in 1970; and the seventh one, which is the current plan (1973–77 plan), was made in 1973.

In view of the above-mentioned experience, economic planners in Japan emphasized the importance of the use of the economic plan as a guidepost for making current decisions with long-term perspective. It is especially important for Japan because it is undergoing a far-reaching and rapid structural transformation from a labor surplus to a labor shortage economy and from an economy with a low income level and large pre-modern elements to one with a high income level and a modernized economic structure. It is useful to predict in a government plan the direction of major changes in agriculture, industry, foreign trade, and people's daily life which are likely to occur in the future; to indicate possible bottlenecks and imbalances which may arise in the course of future growth; and to determine the long-term policies necessary to meet these changes and problems. It helps if people have reasonable insight about possible future changes and receive some explanation of the current trends, many of which are quite new to their experience.

The plan also helps individual persons or enterprises to evaluate their positions in the setting of the entire national economy and long-range movement. Thus the plan has contributed to introducing macro-economic concepts in the way of thinking of the people and has worked to reduce sharp political differences among various groups.

As a whole, economic planning in Japan has not been designed for stimulating rapid growth but rather for attaining balanced growth and indicating beforehand lines of long-term economic policy to be pursued.

Review of Postwar Growth of the Japanese Economy

The postwar recovery and expansion of the Japanese economy was very rapid and remarkable. As early as in 1953, per-capita real national income reached the prewar level of 1934–36, and the rapid economic growth still continued. In 1972, the per-capita national income was estimated to have reached $2300, as high as that of the U.K. and about half that of the U.S., but much higher than those of other Asian countries.

The growth rate of Japan's economy during the 1950s and 1960s was remarkably high when compared with the Western countries (see Table 1).

The rates of economic growth of the countries severely damaged by the war, that is, Germany, Austria and Italy, were high especially during the first half of the 1950s, but they declined in the

Table 1. Rate of Growth of GNP in Selected Countries at Constant Prices

Countries	1950–55	1950–60	1960–65	1965–70
Austria	7.0	5.2	4.4	5.1
France	4.5	4.2	5.9	5.8
West Germany	9.0	6.0	4.9	4.8
Italy	6.0	5.9	5.1	5.9
Sweden	3.1	3.3	5.4	3.9
U.K.	2.6	2.4	3.3	2.4
U.S.A.	4.3	2.3	4.9	3.3
(Japan)	(9.1)	(10.0)	(10.0)	(12.1)

Source: Bank for International Settlements: *Annual Report* 1962. Figures for 1960–65 and 1965–70 are derived from OECD statistical bulletins.

latter half of the decade. On the contrary, Japan showed a higher rate of growth in the latter half of the decade, and maintained much higher rate of growth in the following decade of the 1960s. This fact shows that Japan's high rate of growth depends not only on postwar recovery factors but also on some other factors peculiar to Japan.

The growth rate of the Japanese economy is also higher than those reached by Eastern European countries (although there are some statistical problems in comparing national income figures of communist countries with those of non-communist countries). The People's Republic of China also claims a very high rate of growth of national income. However, no statistics are available after 1959, and it is likely that the average growth rate of Japan's economy during the last twenty years was somewhat higher than that of the People's Republic of China.

The postwar growth rate of Japan's economy is also remarkably higher as compared with the prewar records. The average annual growth rate of 9.6 percent for the 1950s and 11.0 percent for the 1960s was more than double the prewar rate of 4.6 percent for the period 1926–39.

Table 2 and Figure 1 show the annual rate of growth of GNP in Japan in terms of current and constant prices. As seen from the table, the rate of growth shows fluctuations from a high rate of about 20 percent to a low rate of about 3 percent. It seems that the changes in the rate of growth correspond with the approximate

Table 2. Annual Rate of Growth of Japan's GNP at Current and Constant Prices, 1951–72

Fiscal year beginning in April	At current prices	At 1965 constant prices
1951	38.8%	—%
1952	16.3	13.C
1953	18.1	7.9
1954	4.0	2.3
1955	13.3	11.4
1956	12.3	6.8
1957	13.0	8.3
1958	4.8	5.7
1959	15.5	11.7
1960	19.1	13.3
1961	22.5	14.4
1962	9.1	5.7
1963	18.1	12.8
1964	15.9	10.8
1965	10.6	5.4
1966	17.2	11.8
1967	17.9	13.4
1968	17.8	13.6
1969	18.0	12.4
1970	16.3	9.3
1971	10.7	5.7
1972	17.6	12.0

Source: Economic Planning Agency.

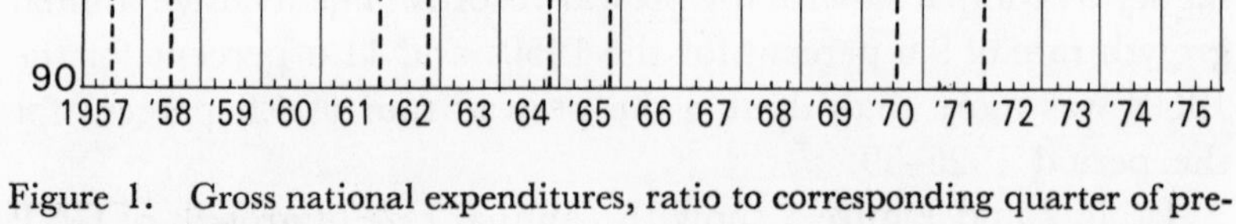

Figure 1. Gross national expenditures, ratio to corresponding quarter of previous year (%).

——at current prices
——at constant prices

Source: Economic Planning Agency.

four- to five-year business cycle. It is noteworthy that even at the bottom of the cycle, a 2 percent growth rate was maintained.

The leading factor in Japan's recent economic growth has been the rapid expansion of manufacturing industry. The industrial production index (1934–36 = 100) rose from 160 in 1955 to 1345 in 1970. Although primary industry (agriculture, forestry, and fishery) is also growing rather rapidly, its relative share in the national income continued to decline from 22.8 percent in 1955 to 6.0 percent in 1970. The reduction of the labor force in agriculture and forestry has also been remarkable: it came down from 16.0 million in 1955 to 8.4 million in 1970, and its share in the total labor force declined from 38.3 percent to 17.4 percent during the same period.

Among various branches of secondary industry, the expansion of heavy and chemical industries (machinery, metals, and chemicals) was most conspicuous, as shown in Table 3. The expansion of the machinery industry was most remarkable as its index (1965 = 100) rose from 14.6 for 1955 to 291.6 for 1970, more than twenty times in fifteen years. On the other hand, the index for the textile industry has registered a relatively small expansion: from 42.2 for 1955 to 154.0 for 1970.

Table 3. Industrial Production Index by Major Branches (1965 = 100)

Branch	1955	1960	1965	1970
Textiles	42.2	68.2	100	154.0
Paper and pulp	34.1	63.9	100	175.9
Chemicals	25.2	51.0	100	204.0
Petroleum & coal products	18.7	47.2	100	216.7
Ceramics	32.0	62.5	100	175.8
Iron & steel	24.6	56.3	100	230.9
Non-ferrous metal	25.9	61.6	100	211.4
Machinery	14.6	51.2	100	291.6
Total (manufacturing industry)	26.0	56.9	100	218.5

Source: Ministry of International Trade and Industry.

As a result of the above-mentioned development, the share of the heavy and chemical industries in the total output of the manufacturing industry reached 57 percent in 1970, higher than the corresponding share in West Germany or the United States.

Table 4. Gross National Expenditure and Its Components (at current prices)

Fiscal years	GNE = GNP (1,000 million yen)	Gross capital formation		Consumption	
		Total (%)	of which private equipment investment (%)	Total (%)	of which personal consumption (%)
1955	8,864.6	24.7	(10.3)	74.5	(64.1) 10.4
1956	9,950.9	28.8	(14.1)	71.4	(61.8) 9.6
1957	11,248.9	33.3	(16.8)	68.6	(59.5) 7.1
1958	11,785.0	27.7	(14.9)	70.8	(61.2) 9.6
1959	13,608.9	29.8	(15.6)	69.1	(59.7) 7.4
1960	16,207.0	33.8	(18.8)	65.8	(56.9) 8.9
1961	19,852.8	40.5	(21.4)	61.2	(52.8) 8.4
1962	21,659.5	35.8	(20.0)	64.2	(55.4) 8.8
1963	25,575.9	35.8	(18.2)	65.3	(56.3) 9.0
1964	29,661.9	36.2	(18.6)	65.8	(56.6) 9.2
1965	32,812.5	33.0	(15.9)	65.9	(56.7) 9.2
1966	38,449.5	33.6	(15.8)	63.7	(55.2) 8.7
1967	45,322.1	37.3	(17.4)	61.9	(53.8) 8.1
1968	53,368.0	38.1	(18.7)	59.5	(51.9) 7.6
1969	62,997.2	38.4	(19.9)	57.6	(50.4)
1970	73,248.1	39.5	(20.2)	56.6	(49.6)
1971	81,093.2	36.4	(18.7)	57.4	(50.2)

Source: Economic Planning Agency.

With regard to the expenditure side of GNP, as shown in Table 4, the most conspicuous fact is the remarkable expansion of private equipment investment since 1956. In six years from 1955 through 1961 it expanded over five times. As a result, private equipment investment as percentage of GNP reached 21.4 in 1961, which is extremely high when compared with both Japan's own records and that of other industrialized countries. The high ratio of gross capital formation to GNP was maintained at the level of 35 to 40 percent during the 1960s, except during recessions in 1965 and 1966. On the other hand, the ratio of personal consumption expenditure to GNP declined from 62.1 percent in 1955 to 52.8 percent in 1961 and 49.6 percent in 1970.

These figures are somewhat abnormal since the period 1959–61 was a period of an unusual investment boom, and the share of investment came down to a lower level in the following years as can be seen in Table 4. In 1962, the economy suffered a slight recession or adjustment, a reaction to the investment boom of 1959–61. The rate of expansion of the economy slowed down, and the level of private equipment investment declined. Capital goods industries which expanded most during the boom years suffered most from the surplus capacity, while the supply of consumer goods, including agricultural products, lagged behind the increasing demand, causing a rather rapid rise in the consumer price index. After a year of adjustment, the level of economic activitiy turned upward in early 1963, with somewhat delayed recovery in private equipment investment. Japan's economy suffered a recession in 1965, and the level of private equipment investment declined considerably. However, the level of economic activity again turned upward in 1966, and the investment boom continued during 1967–70. Japan's economy is still likely to continue at a relatively high rate of growth, although it may not be as high as that of the past decade.

Factors contributing to the high rate of growth of the Japanese postwar economy can be briefly enumerated as follows[1]:

a) Postwar recovery.

b) Substantial reduction in military expenditures as compared with the prewar period.

c) Increase in the rate of savings and investment in the postwar years.

d) Abundant supply of labor as compared to other highly industrialized countries.

e) Increase in the supply of capital goods from domestic industry.

f) Technological innovations and absorption of foreign advanced techniques.

g) Postwar institutional reforms encouraging competition and stimulating business activity.

h) Expanded domestic market due partly to postwar land reform and labor movement.

i) Favorable climate for exports of manufactured products due to liberalization of trade and expansionary policy for inter-

[1] The author has published elsewhere more detailed accounts of this subject. See, e.g., "Japan's Economic Prospect" (*Foreign Affairs*, October 1960); "The Economic Growth of Postwar Japan" (*The Developing Economies*, September-December 1962).

national trade adopted by international organizations and by major countries.

Economic Plans and Their Impact on the Economy

Since the end of World War II, several economic plans have been prepared in Japan with a variety of objectives. Although their primary objectives were commonly to secure a continuous increase in per-capita income, to raise the standard of living, and to achieve a full-employment economy, they put emphasis on different objectives in accordance with the stages of the recovery and development of the economy (see Table 6).

For convenience's sake, various plans prepared by the Japanese government so far can be classified into three groups in accordance with their historical background: (a) plans in the "rehabilitation" stage, (b) plans for the "self-supporting" economy, and (c) plans in the "development" stage.

The first group of economic plans put emphasis on the reconstruction of the war-damaged economy and the effort to combat the rising chronic inflation. World War II brought about serious damage to the Japanese economy, isolating it from external markets, cutting its imports from the traditional sources of supplies, destroying the greater part of its transportation and communication facilities, and creating a high level of unemployment. Economic activities fell sharply below the level prevailing during the 1930s.

Under this condition, three studies[2] were published by the Foreign Ministry, with the purpose of explaining Japan's need to maintain an economy of peace and defending Japan's position against possible demands for severe reparations payments.

In 1946, the Economic Stabilization Board, which was later reorganized as the Economic Deliberation Board (1952) and subsequently changed to the present Economic Planning Agency (1954), was established on the recommendation of the Allied Occupation Forces in order to stabilize and reconstruct the economy. To this board, a special committee charged with the task of

[2] These were (1) *Basic Problems of the Japan's Economic Reconstruction* (1946), (2) *A Study on Japan's Ability to Make Reparations Payments* (1945), and (3) *Living Standards and the Japanese Economy in 1950* (1946).

preparing a reconstruction plan was attached, and this committee prepared a draft, "Economic Rehabilitation Plan, 1949–53," in 1948. This draft was never officially adopted by the government because of political changes in the Cabinet. The draft, however, served the purpose of providing background information for the government in requesting economic aid from the United States.[3] This coincided with the beginning of the Marshall Plan in Europe, where the United States government requested the aid-receiving countries to prepare a joint four-year program for reconstruction and, on the basis of that program, an estimate of necessary aid from the United States.

This period of recovery from the war lasted nearly five years until, after a short recession in 1949, economic activities were suddenly stimulated by the impact of the Korean War.

Nearly two billion dollars in economic aid was received by Japan during the five years following the defeat. However, Japan had a windfall dollar revenue from the U.S. Army special procurements of commodities and services. This source of foreign exchange made up the gap between normal exports and import requirements. In 1953, for example, this source of dollar revenue amounted to 800 million dollars and financed nearly half of the 1.6 billion dollar imports. Under these circumstances, the idea gradually developed that the Japanese economy could not, and should not, be dependent upon windfall sources or on foreign aid for its exchange needs but should stand on a "self-supporting" basis. Thus, economic plans such as the "Three-year Economic Plan" of 1952 and the "Five-year Plan for Economic Self-support" of 1955 were prepared with the goal of attaining a "self-supporting" economy instead of emphasizing "rehabilitation" from war damage.

The plan which was prepared in December 1955 was the first one officially adopted by the government as an important means for coordinating government economic policy and activity. The plan was called the "Five-year Plan for Economic Self-support." Its target was to attain an average 5 percent growth in the GNP during the period of 1956–60. Industrial policies outlined in the

[3] Besides this draft, there were a few other plans which basically had the purpose of estimating the demand for foreign aid from the United States or for loans from the World Bank.

plan centered on the modernization of export industries and the promotion of industries which would reduce import dependency. Thus, for example, machinery, chemical products, and synthetic textiles were designated "promising" industries, to which long-term loans with a preferentially low rate of interest were to be provided.

In the meantime, the employment problem arising from the presence of heavy underemployment and the steep rise in the population of the age groups 14 to 60 called for urgent attention. The solution of this problem constituted the basic objective of government policy. Shortly after the preparation of the plan, however, the economy experienced a boom with a growth rate of nearly double the target of the plan, and many of the five-year plan targets were attained in only two years.

In 1957, the industrial level recovered to the prewar (1934–36 average) level, and the economy passed from the recovery stage into the new stage of development. In December of the same year, the "New Long-range Economic Plan" was prepared with the objective of "providing for a steady increase in the standard of living and providing for full employment by accomplishing persistently the maximum rate of economic growth consistent with economic stability."

As regards the measures for implementing the plan, it stated:

> Based on the character of the plan, it is necessary to restrict to the minimum direct control measures by the government and give free rein to private enterprises as much as possible, recognizing that it is the motive power for the development of the economy. The government also must establish measures from a long-range point of view, in order to accomplish the plan, by undertaking projects which are difficult for private enterprise to carry out. That is, the government must reinforce social overhead capital such as roads, railways, and port facilities.

The plan set the growth rate of 6.5 percent per annum as the most feasible rate and for the first time gave estimates of gross investment in basic public facilities in some detail.

The actual course of the growth, however, revealed that the

planned rate was again underestimated. The annual rate of growth of GNP from 1958 through 1960 was about 10 percent, far exceeding the plan target of 6.5 percent. The following points are noted as the causes of this underestimation:

(a) The terms of trade turned favorable to Japan by over 10 percent owing to the unexpected drop of about 15 percent in the import price index in the course of three years, and this fact facilitated larger imports with a given amount of exports.

(b) The rate of growth of gross capital formation rose to over 35 percent of GNP both in 1959 and 1960, as compared with the planned 28.5 percent for the year 1962, and this made a larger supply of capital necessary for supporting the higher rate of growth.

(c) Industrial production, particularly in the machinery industry, expanded much faster than expected.

In compliance with the following statement in the above-mentioned plan, a Long-range Prospect Committee was established in the Economic Deliberation Council in 1959: "It is desirable to make a long-range projection covering a period longer than five years on population, employment, agriculture and forestry, energy, transportation, and basic raw materials such as iron ore. Such a long-range projection can be useful background information for an economic plan of shorter duration."

In 1960, the Committee published a report on "Prospects for Japan's Economy in 1980" which was composed of more than fifty individual reports on specific fields. This study was used in an extensive way in the preparation of the "National Income Doubling Plan."

The "National Income Doubling Plan" and Its Impact on the Current Economy

The "National Income Doubling Plan" (plan period: 1961–70) originally developed from the dream of Hayato Ikeda (former Prime Minister), made public in early 1959, of doubling people's incomes in about ten years' time. In November 1959, then Prime Minister Nobusuke Kishi officially requested the Economic Deliberation Council, the advisory body attached to the Economic

Planning Agency, to draft a new plan for doubling national income.

The Economic Deliberation Council, in compliance with the Prime Minister's request, worked out the draft and presented it to the government (Ikeda Cabinet) in late 1960, after an extensive study in detail under its seventeen subcommittees which were grouped into four committees: The Over-all Policy Committee, the Public Sector Committee, the Private Sector Committee, and the Calculation Committee. Based on this draft, the government officially adopted the new long-range plan, called the "Plan for Doubling National Income," on 27 December of the same year.

This plan aimed to double the national income within the next decade, setting a 7 to 8 percent annual growth rate as a feasible and realistic target, the ultimate goal being "to advance toward the outstanding improvement of the people's living standard and the attainment of full employment." The plan emphasized the following five points as major long-term policy to be implemented:

(a) *Strengthening of social overhead capital.* With a rapid expansion of the private sector, lack of basic public facilities such as roads, harbors, water supply, etc., becomes a serious hindrance to further growth of the economy. It was considered necessary to restore balance between the private and public sectors by accelerating social overhead investment. Also, from the welfare point of view, improvement of public facilities including city planning, sewage systems, low-rent housing, etc., was strongly emphasized. It was planned that the ratio of investment in basic public facilities to enterprise investment be raised from the current level of 1:3 to 1:2 by 1970.

(b) *Inducement to realize a highly industrialized structure for the economy.* The plan considered secondary industry the leading sector for growth. It also emphasized the growth of heavy and chemical industry—in particular, machinery industry—as a strategic sector. Although the attainment of these objectives mainly rests with the initiative of private business, government can provide various inducements by means of tax provisions, supplementary investment through government financial institutions, and various legislative measures.

(c) *Promotion of exports and strengthening of economic cooperation with less developed countries.* The plan assumed a 10 percent average annual increase in exports. The reason for a higher rate of growth for exports than for GNP was the expected decline in special procurement dollar receipts from the United States and the rise in import dependency due to import liberalization policy. The plan assumed that the share of machinery products (including vehicles) in total exports would rise from 24 percent in 1959 to 37 percent in 1970. It also emphasized the importance of expanding economic and technical assistance to less developed countries.

(d) *Development of human ability and advancement of science and technology*. The plan emphasized the importance of human factors in economic growth. It assumed an increase in public and private research expenditures from 0.9 percent to 2.0 percent of GNP. The plan also set targets for the number of university graduates in science and technology, college graduates in engineering, and vocational trainees.

(e) *Mitigation of the dual structure and securing of social stability*. Dual economic and social structure is one of Japan's peculiar characteristics, which allows for the coexistence of modern and pre-modern sectors. There have been wide differentials in wages and income among various sectors of the economy. This structure has, in part, supported the competitive strength of Japan's export products and has also contributed to a high rate of savings and, accordingly, a high rate of growth. At the same time, however, this structure was a source of inequality and backwardness for Japan's social structure. Moreover, as the economy modernizes, it has become a hindrance to higher efficiency and technological progress. Therefore the plan emphasized the importance of mitigating the dual structure and of expanding social security measures.

The plan had several features, some of which were found already in the earlier plans but not as distinctly as in this plan. The first is that the plan emphasized the long-range viewpoint with regard to structural changes in the economy. The plan covered the ten years from 1961 to 1970 and described the long-range prospects of the national economy in order to facilitate the preparation of individual plans by various government agencies. In this connection, the long-range investment program, especially in the public sector, was seen as a useful means for attaining the objectives of the plan. In 1954, when the government had no long-range economic plan and faced a balance-of-payments crisis, it curtailed public investment without giving due consideration to long-term implications. Later, the introduction of planning, especially in the public sector, prevented sharp fluctuations in government expenditures when the economy experienced similar balance-of-payments problems.

The second feature is that the plan divided the whole economy into two sectors: the public sector, for which the government is directly responsible, and the private sector, in which private enterprises have their responsibility and initiatives. The plan for the former sector included an allocation of funds for the major types of public works which link the long-term economic plan with fiscal budgeting.

The third feature of the plan is the emphasis on long-run policy issues. Since planning in Japan aims principally at providing guidelines for economic activities to be conducted in a system of basically free enterprise, it does not aim at fixing detailed targets for every sector of the economy but, instead, emphasizes long-term policy measures. In this connection, the income-doubling plan included various policy recommendations related to institutional and organizational reforms.

The fourth feature is that, for the first time in postwar planning, problems related to "differentials" were taken up: the "imbalances" or "differentials" in income among different groups of people, the "differential" between large and small enterprises in productivity and wages, and the regional "difference" in income levels. Following this over-all national plan, the government worked out a new regional development plan in October 1962, one of its major purposes being to overcome the excessive differentials in income among the various regions of the country.

The fifth feature is the emphasis upon the importance of the human factor in economic development. In view of the fact that the human factor is the basis for economic growth in the age of transformation, a Committee for Education and Training was set up in 1960 as one of the 17 subcommittees working for the preparation of the National Income Doubling Plan. Later, in April 1961, a Committee for Development of Human Resources was set up in accordance with the recommendation, included in the National Income Doubling Plan, to undertake further studies in this field. In January 1963, the Committee submitted its report to the government and recommended a manpower policy for economic development.

The Medium-term Economic Plan (1964-68)

After the implementation of the National Income Doubling Plan, it was again found that the projected rate of economic growth was substantially underestimated. The average annual rate of growth for 1961–63, the first three years of the plan period, amounted to 11 percent as against 7 to 8 percent projected in the plan. Particularly striking was the fact that private equipment investment increased so much that the level projected for 1970 was almost attained in the very first year of the plan, 1961.

In view of these developments, the Economic Deliberation Council made extensive follow-up studies of the Income Doubling Plan in 1963 and issued a report late that year. In this report, the Council emphasized the need to formulate a new economic plan covering a period of four or five years, not only because the projected figures in the Income Doubling Plan had been considerably over-attained, but also because the environment of the Japanese economy had changed substantially, requiring new policy measures. Outstanding among these changes were the shift to an open-door economy through the liberalization of foreign trade and the change from surplus to shortage in the labor market.

In accordance with this recommendation, the government asked the Economic Deliberation Council to prepare a new five-year plan in early 1964. Accordingly, the Council worked out a draft plan covering the period from 1964 to 1968, and presented it to the government in late 1964. Based on this, the government officially adopted the "Medium-term Economic Plan" on January 22, 1965.

The major aims of this plan were, first, to cope with the new situation created by a labor shortage and the shift to an open-door economy; second, to remedy various imbalances that had emerged during the period of rapid economic growth, such as sharp rises in consumer prices and widening income differentials; and third, to promote "social development" in order to recover a proper balance between the economic and social progress of this country.

To achieve these aims, the plan emphasized the following five policy objectives:

(a) Expansion of foreign trade and modernization of industrial structure.

(b) Development of manpower and promotion of science and technology.

(c) Modernization of the low-productivity sectors, *i.e.*, agriculture, small business, and distribution.

(d) Better utilization of the labor force.

(e) Improvement of the quality of people's living, through improvement of housing, expansion of physical environment facilities, and strengthening of social security programs.

In pursuing these objectives, the plan stressed that certain boundary conditions should be observed. As for the balance of international payments, an equilibrium in the current account was projected for 1968, the target year of the plan, though in preceding years current transactions had recorded substantial deficits. The plan attempted to keep wholesale prices stable while minimizing the increase in consumer prices, which rose nearly 6 percent yearly in the previous three years. The rate of economic growth compatible with these conditions was estimated to be around 8 percent per annum during the plan period, somewhat lower than the average of 10 percent for the preceding ten years.

The salient features of the plan are as follows: The first is the strong emphasis on changing the pattern of resource allocation. Previously, a large part of available resources had been channeled into those sectors which could most effectively expand production. This had brought about a remarkable growth of modern and big enterprises accompanying the rapid growth of the economy and, consequently, a considerable rise in the income level of the nation as a whole. On the other hand, however, this pattern of economic development had resulted in a lag in modernizing agriculture and small businesses and delay in building up housing and social overhead capital, especially public facilities closely related with people's daily life. Hence differentials of income, increases in consumer prices, housing shortages, traffic congestion, air and water pollution, etc., have emerged. Now that the production capacity has reached a fairly high level, the plan points out, more resources should be diverted to improve directly the quality of people's life, including the promotion of housing construction, expansion of the sewage system, modernization of low-productivity sectors, and prevention of public nuisances.

Second, planners were very careful about the announcement effects of the plan. The announcement of the National Income Doubling Plan stimulated the already bullish business circles to take a still more aggressive attitude towards new investment, thus bringing about an investment boom and a foreign exchange crisis in 1961. To avoid a repetition, the new plan refrained from giving detailed estimates of production in the private sector.

Third, the method used in drawing up the plan was much different from previous plans. For the first time in Japan, econometric models were extensively utilized. Major features of the economy in 1968 were derived from a medium-term macro model with 43 equations including wage and price functions. Projections for various sectors were derived from an input-output model of 60 sectors for 1968. The major objective in taking full recourse to econometric method was, of course, to secure consistency among various projected variables.

The Economic and Social Development Plan (1967-71)

After the implementation of the Medium-term Economic Plan, the rate of economic growth was slowed down by the depression in 1965, but the recovery was remarkable in 1966; consequently, the Japanese economy expanded approximately along the lines projected in the plan. However, the increase in consumer prices was ominous; it amounted to 5 percent in 1964 and to 7.2 percent in 1965, exceeding dramatically the 2.5 percent rate projected in the plan.

In view of these development, the Medium-term Economic Plan was scrapped in January 1966, and in May the government asked the Economic Council to prepare a new long-term economic plan. Accordingly, the Council worked out a draft plan covering the period from 1967 to 1971 in February 1967, and presented it to the government. Based on this, the government officially adopted the Economic and Social Development Plan on 13 March 1967.

The major aims of this plan were, first, to remedy various imbalances which had emerged during the preceding ten years of rapid economic growth, such as sharp rises in consumer prices, delay in improvement of the living environment, including housing, and the increase of pollution; second, to cope with external and internal changes such as the shift to an overall open-door economy through the liberalization of capital, labor shortages, and the advance of urbanization; and third, to promote a balanced development of economy and society by solving these problems.

To achieve these aims, the plan emphasized the following three important policy objectives:

(a) compatibility of economic growth with price stability;
(b) reorganization of economy to more efficient system;
(c) promotion of social development.

In pursuing these objectives, the plan stressed that certain boundary conditions should be observed. As for consumer prices, economic growth should be compatible with price stability through promoting structural policies and assuring the conditions of competition. By the implementation of these policies, the rate of consumer price increases was to be decreased to 3 percent per annum by the end of this plan period. As for the promotion of social development, first, the efficient use of national land was to be promoted by construction of nationwide transportation and communication networks, to enable closer links between metropolitan and local regions. It was also stressed that improvement of the living environment, decreases in pollution, and improvement of social securities are prerequisites to social development. The rate of economic growth compatible with these conditions was estimated to be 8.2 percent per annum during the period of the plan, somewhat lower than the average of 10.3 percent for the preceding ten years.

The New Economic and Social Development Plan (1970-75)

After the implementation of the Economic and Social Development Plan, the rate of economic growth, the consumer prices, and the balance of international payments projected in the plan moved gradually away from the reality. The rate of economic growth was projected to be 8.2 percent, but in 1967 it had already exceeded 13 percent. As for prices, the rate of consumer prices was expected to be slowed down to 3 percent annually by the end of the plan period, but in reality, it continued rising. Wholesale prices were projected to be stable during the period of the plan; however, in reality, the symptoms of rising soon appeared. As for the balance of international payments, the surplus enlarged over the level estimated in the plan.

In view of these developments, the Economic Council started to revise the Economic and Social Development Plan in January 1969, and the government asked the Council to prepare a new plan covering the period of 1970–75 in September of the same year. After seven months' deliberation, the Council presented the new draft to the government in April 1970, and the government officially adopted it as the New Economic and Social Development Plan on the first of May in the same year.

The major aims of this plan were, first, to improve economic efficiency in order to cope with international competition stimulated by the liberalization of trade and capital; second, to attain simultaneously economic growth and price stability; and third, to achieve social development on a long-term basis, rather than short-term adjustment of the imbalances caused by the past development.

To achieve these aims, the plan emphasized the following six important policy objectives:

(a) price stability;
(b) development of new foreign policies;
(c) innovation of industrial structure;
(d) promotion of social development;
(e) cultivation of a stable foundation for development.

The most outstanding feature of the plan was its recognition of the high potential growth capacity of Japan's economy and its attempt at attaining simultaneously high economic growth, price stability, and social development. The plan attempted to make a preferential allocation of the abundant resources obtained through high economic growth to the areas which are closely related to promotion of social development and stabilization of prices. This new outlook was clearly reflected in the selection of the high rate of 10.6 percent for economic growth and 3 percent for consumer price rises, in comparison with the modest rate of 8.2 percent for growth and 3 percent for price rises in the previous plan.

The Basic Economic and Social Plan (1973-77)

The New Economic and Social Development Plan provided that the plan should be revised, if necessary, in its third year. However, rapid change in the domestic and international situation since the plan was made has required a fundamental policy shift, and has made it necessary not merely to revise but to produce an entirely new plan.

The basic background which requires a policy shift, and therefore a new plan, consists of three major changes. The first is a change in the international socioeconomic system. In particular, a change in the international economic balance resulting from the rapid expanding economic strength of the EEC and Japan on the one hand, and the growing shakiness of the position of the U.S. on the other, is accompanied by an incipient instability in the postwar world economic order, which was primarily based on the IMF–GATT system, and consequent movement toward formation of a new world economic order. Another aspect of this change is relaxation of East-West tensions—as witnessed by China's admission to the United Nations, reestablishment of Sino-Japanese diplomatic relations, realization of a Vietnam peace agreement, progress in peace diplomacy in Europe, and other developments—and continuing failure to reduce the gap between the so-called countries of the North and countries of the South, which, if left unresolved, could very well stand in the way of the harmonious development of human society as a whole.

The second is domestic socioeconomic structural change, which can be classified into the following three elements:

(1) Maldistribution of wealth

Inequality in income distribution has increased in spite of the increase in average income level. There is an inadequate stock of social overhead capital, as attested by a lagging behind of improvement in the living environment, including housing, in comparison to an abundance of productive capital accumulation.

(2) Expansion of externalities

With the increase in interaction among socioeconomic activities, various kind of externalities, such as the problem of environmental disruption and that of overcongestion in some places and oversparseness in others, have been expanding.

(3) Emergence of limits

As the scale of production and consumption has increased, the problem of the limits of natural resources, energy, environment capacity, etc, has arisen.

The third major change is in national consciousness, which has become diversified and sophisticated as the level of income has risen. Another change has been the emergence of the desire for greater social justice and a rise in the desire for safety. (A survey of national consciousness was undertaken in conjunction with the drafting of this plan.)

It was necessary for an overall policy shift to respond to the above-mentioned structural change in both the domestic and the international situation. Prime Minister Kakuei Tanaka officially requested the Economic Council to draft a new plan in August 1972, and the Council worked out the draft and presented it to the government in early 1973. Based on this draft, the government officially adopted the new plan, called the Basic Economic and Social Plan, on the 13 February 1973.

The Basic Economic and Social Plan aims at shifting policy from an orientation toward high economic growth to an orientation toward national welfare. For this purpose, it is necessary to remodel the Japanese socioeconomic structure into one more compatible with the new era at hand after reconsidering the whole range of systems and rules presently embodied therein. The plan outlines the following four principles, on the basis of which the policy shift should be carried out:

(1) To change the nature of economic activity from the pursuit of economic efficiency in the narrow sense of the term to a compatibility with pollution control, preservation of the natural environment, and prevention of disorderly urban concentration.

(2) To secure social justice through making income distribution more equitable and proceeding with equalization of educational, employment, and other opportunities.
(3) To promote decentralization of decision making in order that welfare policy may be implemented on the basis of selection by regional or community residents.
(4) To take the road of international collaboration for the purpose of contributing to the harmony and progress of mankind, as is fitting in view of the international standing of Japan as the second-ranking economic power in the Free World.

This plan, aiming at the simultaneous promotion of national welfare and international collaboration, indicates the basic guidelines for policy implementation in the first five years (F Y 1973–77) of the long-term process of building a vigorous welfare society.

This plan has several features which are not found in the earlier plans. The first feature is that the plan gives targets to be attained within the period of the plan in detail and in quantitative terms as much as possible (see Table 5). Since the government's role will become much more important and cover a much wider field, the targets are given as a detailed commitment to the people by the government.

The second feature is that the plan indicates policy measures to be given particular emphasis in the first half of the planning period. These are as follows:

(a) Pollution control;
(b) Prevention of soaring of land prices;
(c) Improvement of social security;
(d) Achievement of external equilibrium.

This is an attempt to set priorities among various targets with a time schedule.

The third feature of this plan is to make explicit the desirable direction of long-term development of Japan's economic and social structure with the goal of achieving a of vigorous welfare society by 1990. The plan which covers the next five years (1978–82) holds a very important position in setting in motion this long-term process. In line with this goal, the Economic Planning Agency has developed a long-term planning model called COSMO (Comprehensive System Model) in order to foresee the direction of long-term development.

Table 5. Targets to Be Reached during the Period of the Plan

Area	Item	Standard
(Creation of a rich environment)		
Preservation of the environment	Air pollution due to sulfur oxides	(1) Environmental quality standards more stringent than those presently in force shall be established to avoid adverse effects on human health.
		(2) In the Big Three Bay Areas, the amount of discharge shall be reduced to about half the FY 1970 level.
	Water pollution	(1) At least the present water quality standards or the provisional targets shall be met during the period of the plan, with a view to restoration of a situation of no adverse effects on the health or living environment by 1985.
		(2) In the Big Three City Areas, BOD[3] discharge load will be reduced to about one-half of the 1970 level.
Living environment facilities	City parks	4.7 sq. m per capita (estimated figure for FY 1972, 3 sq. m; goal for FY 1985, 9 sq. m)
	Sewerage systems	Service to 42% of the population (estimated figure for FY 1972, 19%)
	Disposal of refuse Human wastes	Within areas covered by plans: 100% sanitary disposal (FY 1975; estimated figure for FY 1972, 87%)
	Combustible refuse	100% disposal (FY 1980; estimated figure for FY 1972, 81%)
Nationwide transportation and communications network	Super express railways (*Shinkansen*)	Extension to attain the total length of approx. 1,900 km in operation (construction target by FY 1985, about 7,000 km)
	National	Extension to attain the total

Area	Item	Standard
	expressways	length of approx. 3,100 km in operation (construction target by FY 1985, about 10,000 km)
	Telephone subscription	Catching up with backlog demand on a nationwide scale
Improvement of the agricultural and forest environment	Agricultural land	Doubling of hectarage which supports highly efficient farming (approx. 1.2 million ha. in FY 1972)
	Reserve forests	Designation of 10% more reserve forest area (6.9 million ha. in FY 1972)
(Ensuring a comfortable, stable life)	Ratio of transfer income to national income	8.8% (estimated figure for FY 1972, 6.0%)
Social security	Pensions	
	Employee's pension insurance	From FY 1973, a standard monthly pension of ¥50,000, with further improvements thereafter
	National pension insurance	Setting of a level commensurate with that of the employee's pension insurance
	Non-contributory old age pension	¥5,000 a month in FY 1973, ¥10,000 a month in FY 1975, and further generous improvements thereafter
	Social welfare facilities	Setting such facilities on a footing that will make it possible to accommodate elderly bed-ridden people, the seriously mentally or physically handicapped, and others who need care
Housing	Publicly funded housing	Construction of 4 million new units
	Housing developments	Early completion of large-scale "new town" housing developments and other smaller projects already under way in the Tokyo and Osaka metropolitan areas covering approx. 30,000 ha. (to accommodate a total population

Area	Item	Standard
		of about 4 million) and commencement of new projects
Employment environment	5-day workweek	General adoption
	Raising of compulsory retirement age	General adoption of compulsory retirement at age 60 (presently 55)
Education, sport	Educational facilities	Improvement of facilities for kindergarten, primary, and secondary compulsory education, and higher education, as well as extension of medical colleges and university departments of medicine to cover all prefectures
	Community sports	Provision over a period of about 10 years of readily accessible sports facilities such as athletic grounds, gymnasiums, swimming pools, playgrounds, etc.
Price stability	Consumer prices	An average annual rise of not more than 5%
	Wholesale prices	Stable, unaccelerated rise
Promotion of international collaboration	Balance of international payments	A balanced basic account within 2–3 years
	Economic aid (flow of financial resources)	Early realization within the period of the plan of a level of the flow corresponding to 1% of gross national product
	Official development assistance	Raising of its ratio to GNP to the international level by an early date, attainment of the international goal of 0.7% over a longer period, and improvement of the terms and conditions of assistance

Notes: 1. The Big Three Bay Areas—areas along Tokyo Bay, Osaka Bay, and the northern part of Ise Bay.
2. The Big Three City Areas—the part of the Kanto Area along the coast, the Tokai coastline, and the Osaka-Kobe area.
3. BOD—biochemical oxygen demand, widely used as an index of water pollution.

Table 6. Selected Features of Economic Plans in Japan

Name of plan		Five-year Plan for Economic Self-support	New Long-range Economic Plan	Doubling National Income Plan	Medium-term Economic Plan	Economic and Social Development Plan	New Economic and Social Development Plan	Basic Economic and Social Plan
Date published		December, 1955	December, 1957	December, 1960	January, 1965	March, 1967	April, 1970	February, 1973
Cabinet at the time plan approved		Hatoyama	Kishi	Ikeda	Sato	Sato	Sato	Tanaka
Plan period (fiscal years)		1956–60	1958–62	1961–70	1964–68	1967–71	1970–75	1973–77
Economic growth rate	Performance prior to the plan	F. 1952–55 8.6%	F. 1953–57 7.3%	F. 1956–60 9.1%	F. 1960–64 11.3%	F. 1962–66 10.0%	F. 1965–69 12.7%	
	Projection in the plan	F. 1956–60 5.0%	F. 1956–60 5.0%	F. 1961–70 7.2%	F. 1964–68 8.1%	F. 1967–71 8.2%	F. 1970–75 10.6%	F. 1973–77 9.4%
	Actual performance during the plan period	F. 1956–60 9.1%	F. 1956–60 10.0%	F. 1961–70 10.9%	F. 1964–68 10.8%	F. 1967–71 9.9%	F. 1970–72 7.5% (est.)	
Method for projection		Colm method (labor × productivity)	Desirable balance chosen from 3 cases with different growth rates	Growth rate previously decided	Econometric model	Econometric model	Econometric model	Econometric model

	Self-support of the economy, full employment	Maximization of growth, improvement of standard of living, full employment	Maximization of growth, improvement of standard of living, full employment	Rectifying imbalances	Balance and steady economic development	Construction of admirable society through balanced economic growth	Promotion of national welfare and international collaboration
Major policy objectives	Modernization of production facilities, promotion of international trade, reduction of dependence on import, discouraging consumption	Improvement of infrastructure, heavy industrialization; promotion of exports, encouraging savings	Improvement of social overhead capital, improvement of industrial structure, rectifying the dual structure of the economy and improvement of social stability	modernization of low productivity sectors, efficient use of labor force, qualitative improvement of standard of living	Stabilization of prices, improvement of economic efficiency, promotion of social development	Improvement of economic efficiency from an international viewpoint, securing price stability, promotion of social development, maintaining adequate economic growth and cultivating development foundations	Creation of a rich environment, ensuring a stable and comfortable life, stabilization of prices, promotion of international collaboration

The fourth feature of the plan is to indicate various constraints on the desirable development of Japan's economy and society. Difficulties in making desirable shifts in the industrial structure, the trade-off relationship between expansion of production capacity and preservation of the environment, constraints of supply of natural resources, especially energy and water, against economic development and some other items are shown explicitly in order to forecast long-term development.

The fifth feature is that the plan declares that it should be followed up by a system for steady implementation of the policy goals it outlined. For this purpose, the plan provides that the Economic Council should conduct each year a follow-up study of progress being made and publish its findings in the form of an annual report. Arrangements will also be made to reflect the findings of these reports in the actual management of the economy.

Conclusion

Economic planning in Japan is still in the experimental stage. Economists are groping for an appropriate type of planning to meet the requirements both of free enterprise and and of the basic features of Japan's economy.

Among the general public the work of economic planning has aroused interest in and hope for the future economy and has helped to introduce long-range considerations in the decision-making process of government departments, private enterprises, and individuals.

The government plans gave confidence to private entrepreneurs and, combined with the keen competition for the market share among enterprises, have often led to overexpansion of the economy and resulting adjustments. In many cases, government plans acted as a brake on economic activity rather than as a stimulant for growth, and thus the main objectives of the plans were to attain balanced growth. The plans have also opened up consideration of the economic implications of education and social security and have had an important influence upon the thinking and policy-making in these fields.

There are some shortcomings in the economic planning of Japan. The most vital one is the lack of a quantitative link between the targets of the plan and policy measures. In order to eliminate this shortcoming, the following studies are indispensable:

(1) Analysis of the effects of implementation of policy and changes in the institutional system.

(2) Study of the consistency and trade-off relationship between targets and policy measures.

(3) Appraisal of alternative targets–measures systems.

In spite of the above shortcomings, however, economic planning in Japan has gradually rooted deep in the soil of the nation and has become an indispensable element of economic life in present-day Japan.

PART III
Japan's Relations with the Developing World

North-South Dialogue, 1979

From the viewpoint of the world economy of the 1970s, the economic order which was established after World War II began to collapse, and the decade became the transitional period in the search for a new order.

First of all, the Bretton Woods System, the world monetary system which was supported by a strong dollar and placed emphasis on the International Monetary Fund, was no longer working effectively. Accordingly, as of March 1973, the fixed exchange rate system based on the Bretton Woods System was replaced by a floating system which is now affecting the world economy. At present, there is no clear-cut outline of the sort of new stable monetary system that will be established in the future. In Europe, a European Monetary System has now been established. In Asia, however, there still remains the problem of how the monetary system will change in the future.

Secondly, the GATT system, the free-trade system which had been the core of the world economy after World War II, started to face jolts in the 1970s. Improvement in the form of world trade is being negotiated by the countries concerned at the current Tokyo Round. One of the great concerns, in this connection, is to what extent the free trade which we have been enjoying so far can be maintained. Of particular concern is the protectionism now gaining currency in the developed countries. The trade friction vis-à-vis Japan and the U.S.A. and Europe presented another problem in the 1970s.

The chapter is the text of the keynote address delivered to the International Symposium on North-South Relations in the Pacific Asian Region, held in Tokyo in March 1979 under the sponsorship of the Japan Committee on North-South Relations.

Thirdly, the problem of resources should also be mentioned. The oil crisis in the fall of 1973 created consciousness of the problem of resource supplies—above all, of energy resource supplies. Before the oil crisis, the world had taken it for granted that these resources were infinite and that supply would always meet demand. Economic theories had also been based on this premise. Today, severe restraints have been imposed, particularly on oil supplies. While we cannot say that the limitation of material resources supplies will necessarily restrict economic growth when technological progress and the exploitation of resources other than oil are taken into account, oil restraint is apparently a new and important phenomenon in the world economy of the 1970s.

Fourthly, I would like to refer to developments in North-South relations. It is noteworthy that the Declaration of an Action Program on the New International Economic Order was adopted at the 6th Special Session of the United Nations in 1974, and that the Charter for Economic Rights and Duties of Nations was adopted at the General Assembly of the United Nations at the end of the same year. The North-South problem has been approached by the South with unified opinions since the time of the First UNCTAD in Geneva in 1964, and we should pay attention to the fact that the New International Economic Order was proposed on the initiative of the South. Active discussion is expected to take place at UNCTAD V which will be held this coming May in Manila.

In Asia, political developments were even more important than economic ones, although these certainly existed in the 1970s.

First, there was an end to the prolonged Vietnam War involving the U.S.A. The unification of South and North Vietnam was a significant political event, which had a far-reaching impact on Southeast Asia as well as the whole region.

Second, the ASEAN, which was set up in 1967 through the efforts of five Southeast Asian countries, has strengthened its unity in order to cope with the situation in Vietnam. The ASEAN, in the future, will be an important force in the political and economic arena of Asia and the world.

Third, the policies of the People's Republic of China were greatly altered after the Cultural Revolution. While modernization policies in agriculture, industry, scientific technology, and military affairs were set forth, official conclusion of the Japan-China Peace and Amity Treaty was followed by the normalization of U.S.-China diplomatic relations. These also were significant events affecting the political climate in Asia.

Fourth, friction or confrontation among communist countries in Asia, particularly in Northeast and Southeast Asia, developed in ways which had been unforeseen. The China-Vietnam war and the Vietnam-Cambodia conflict in the 1970s are very large events influencing the political situation in Asia. Another major influential factor in this region is the China-Soviet confrontation.

So far, I have mentioned macroscopic trends in the world economy and the Asian political picture. In spite of the fact that the world was faced with various problems, the world political situation as a whole was stable. In Asia, economic development and the several large political changes I have mentioned took place simultaneously. Taking these events into consideration, I would like to examine a few important problems and the outlook for the 1980s.

First, it is anticipated that the economic growth rate of the industrialized countries will continue to be relatively slow. The perspective for the 1980s is that the major industrialized countries—the U.S., Japan, and the West European countries—will continue to experience slower rates of economic growth, as they have since the oil crisis.

Second, the importance of Northeast Asia and Southeast Asia in the world economy is expected to increase. This tendency has already been observed during the 1970s. These two regions are undergoing more dynamic development than other regions. Australia and New Zealand might be included in this group.

For example, U.S. trade with the Asia-Pacific region (total amount of export and import) in 1977 reached $66 billion, exceeding that with Europe ($64 billion the same year) for the first time. This is a very symbolic phenomenon in the sense that the U.S., lying between the Pacific Ocean and the Atlantic Ocean, has conducted more trade with the Pacific countries than with Europe. Furthermore, taking into account the difference in regional growth rates, the gap between U.S. trade with Europe and that with the Asia-Pacific region, though it is slight now, is expected to widen in the future. In other words, the importance of the Asia-Pacific countries to the U.S.A. will probably be enhanced.

Third, various new developments in North-South relations are anticipated for the 1980s. One of them might be called "the dynamic international division of labor." There are some countries in Northeast Asia and Southeast Asia which are developing into exporting countries of manufactured goods after successfully achieving rapid industrialization. This rapid industrialization and rapid increase in exports of manufactured goods are changing the existing international economic order to a considerable extent. These rapidly industrializing countries are gaining competitive economic strength. How the existing developed countries will cope with this trend by industrial adjustment will be a great concern in the 1980s.

Next comes the problem of stabilizing the prices of primary goods, which is also an important problem for North-South relations. A common fund or commodity agreement is one of the important items on the agenda of the upcoming UNCTAD V to be held in Manila. As a large number of countries in Southeast Asia still depend largely on exports of primary goods to support their economies, ways and means of coping with the commodity issue are of great concern to these countries.

Debt must be mentioned as the third problem. Developed countries are giving financial assistance or loans to developing countries in order to supplement their capital. It is necessary for the semi-developed countries now in the process of industrialization to acquire capital through commercial deals in the capital market.

It is also necessary that assistance on soft and concessional terms should be expanded for the poor countries. In this connection, the problem of raising development funds will be an important issue in North-South relations in the 1980s. In particular, we should look for the means to connect large-scale unemployment and underutilization of facilities, which vex the developed countries, with the problem of raising funds needed by the developing countries.

In connection with the North-South relations, the "basic human needs approach" has been discussed by international organizations in the latter half of the 1970s. This approach is a sort of philosophy stressing that the international community should help the poor people in the poor countries, and it has gradually gained momentum. The U.S.A. has placed particular emphasis on this philosophy in government aid since President Carter assumed office.

On the other hand, the developing countries are skeptical of this approach on the ground that the problem of basic needs is a sophisticated political problem that should be dealt with within each country, and thus that it is not appropriate for an international organization or any foreign government to prescribe redistribution of income within another country (although it is necessary for developing countries to do so internally). In conjunction with assistance to the poor countries, the question of the type of assistance to be extended and how the developing countries in the South should improve their distribution of income is an important issue for the 1980s.

What type of assistance should be extended to the developing countries?

Japan has been giving assistance in the field of what is called the infrastructure: the development of hydroelectric facilities, transportation, and communication (roads, railways, ports, airports, telecommunications, etc.) or concentrating on fundamental facilities such as irrigation, which can increase production of not only rice but also other food staples. These are productive tasks which will bring about a better standard of living for the poor farmers in almost all of the Asian countries. I might mention in passing that I myself have participated in the preparation of a so-called "plan for doubling rice production in Asia."*

In any case, the task of determining the best basic approach to development aid remains an important problem to be solved in the 1980s. Under these circumstances, I would like to predict some overall trends in Asia in the 1980s.

First of all, the independence of Asia will probably be enhanced gradually in the areas of politics, diplomacy, and security. Asia will no longer be vulnerable to foreign powers and be the arena of conflicts among the superpowers. Instead, we will probably be witnessing an era in which Asian problems will be tackled by the Asian countries themselves, and the conditions for solutions will gradually evolve.

In this sense, the formation and development of the ASEAN is a great step towards the goal of Asian countries dealing with their own problems. This trend is expected to prevail not only among

* See pp. 23–45 in this volume.

the ASEAN countries but also among other Asian countries, including the Indochina states and the Northeast Asian countries. This is a major current, which started in the latter half of the 1970s and which is seen today and will continue in the future.

Now, let us move from the aspect of politics, diplomacy, and security to that of economy. The economic trend is expected to be one of open regionalism. With worldwide economic exchange being enhanced, solutions to economic problems cannot be reached within the concept of closed regional cooperation in closed regional blocs. A cooperative organization in the Asia-Pacific region has been called for recently, and is being discussed in various forums. However, if the organization is to be based on closed regionalism, desirable results should not be expected. A move towards open regionalism will bring about a more effective strengthening of the economic welfare of the respective countries.

An OPTAD (Organization for Pacific Trade and Development) proposal has been discussed at the Pacific Trade and Development Conference, which is a conference participated in mainly by economists in the Asia-Pacific region, the first meeting of which was convened in Tokyo ten years ago and the tenth meeting of which will be held at the end of this March in Canberra. This proposal is worth consideration. OPTAD is an organization similar to OECD having loose ties, not emphasizing regional discriminatory measures such as preferential trade arrangements, but promoting frequent mutual consultation among its members.

The question remains as to whether there is scope for loose regional cooperation among the industrialized countries in the Asia-Pacific region (Japan, the U.S.A., Canada, Australia, New Zealand) and the developing countries (ASEAN and the South Pacific islands). Various ideas are still being examined at this stage; nothing has been determined and no discussion has yet been carried out by the governments concerned. However, some kind of regional cooperative organization in the Asia-Pacific region will be required in the future if, for example, the EC countries strengthen their inward ties and outward discrimination.

I have heard that Prime Minister Ohira has a vision for establishing a Pacific community, but that no concrete plan has yet been made. Since this concept will primarily be based on what the countries of the Pacific region think, I would like to invite the views of the participants on this matter, particularly those of the attendants from abroad; these will be very helpful to Japan in future policy formulation.

Another big question in Asia is how China will emerge in the 1980s after the shifts in its policy toward modernization. I believe that it is of great importance for the Asian countries to consider how the Chinese economy will develop and what implications it will have on other Asian countries: will it be inconsistent with the development policies of other Asian countries and consequently induce frictions, or will it contribute to enhancing mutual interests?

Lastly, I would like to discuss the role Japan should play in view of the basic trends in the world economy and the Asian situation.

Japan has become a highly industrialized country; its GNP (*i.e.*, economic output), based on the present exchange rate, has become exactly half that of the U.S.A. As the Japanese population is also half that of the U.S.A., per-capita GNP is almost the same. However, most Japanese feel that they are much poorer than Americans, and some feel that this parity results from recent changes in the exchange rate which does not reflect the real purchase power of the yen and the dollar.

A majority of Japanese economists project that the Japanese annual growth rate, which reached 10 percent at one time, will go down to approximately 6 percent. On the other hand, the savings rate is has remained very high despite the lowered growth rate: 22 percent of personal disposable income is saved in Japan, while in the U.S.A. less than 6 percent is saved. This saving has been an important financial resource in supporting Japan's high growth rate. Should the Japanese economy become slow-growing, there should be a sizable surplus of savings over domestic investment. It is apparent that Japan, which has been a capital-importing country until recently, will basically transform itself into a large capital-exporting country in the 1980s. In that case, the surplus capital should be used productively to promote the economic development of the developing countries as much as possible.

Japan has so far been an exporter of manufactured goods, with 95 percent of its exports accounted for by manufactured goods; among its imports, 70–80 percent are raw materials, food, and energy resources. Japan must gradually expand its imports of manufactured goods. Aside from the fact that we are being strongly urged by the U.S.A. and European countries to open our domestic market, we need to do so in view of the industrialization being promoted in other Asian countries. In this context, imports of manufactured goods into Japan will probably increase rapidly in the 1980s. Some domestic industrial adjustment will be necessary in order to facilitate smooth expansion of imports of manufactured goods, involving shifts of labor among industries.

But liberalization of the Japanese market for imports will greatly contribute to the economic development of other Asian countries; and in turn, Japan will be able to find ways to develop its own economy as well.

Technology transfer is another issue. Japan developed its industries and technologies in the past by introducing and digesting technologies from other industrialized countries. Now it is Japan's turn to offer its own technology and know-how to other developing countries. In other words, Japan will become a technology-exporting country.

When Japan offers its technology to others, its own experience in introducing and digesting technologies from other countries will be helpful. The conventional western-style technology transfer was made in the form of a "big-enterprise" package (for example, a petrochemical plant or aluminum refinery), including technology, management, and capital. However, Japan's method was to "depackage," importing only technology and furnishing management and capital in Japan. We must review our experience and examine how our experience can contribute to the future industrialization of developing countries.

Medium and small enterprises play an important role where the working population is large and income is low. They have always played an important role in Japan as well. But a large number of medium and small enterprises have become uncompetitive as a result of rising wages in Japan and the appreciation of the yen. Many fields in which these medium and small enterprises were concentrated have potential in the developing countries. Methods of transferring the technology and experience of these enterprises to developing countries effectively becomes a matter of great importance. Unlike large enterprises, it is very difficult for medium and small enterprises to expand their business overseas themselves. Accordingly, we need to devise an effective way to transfer technology by combining government technical assistance with the experience and know-how of the medium and small enterprise.

In agriculture Japan should also play an important role in the 1980s in effectively applying various Japanese experiences in such areas as rice production to the developing countries, especially in Asia, in cooperation with the recipient countries.

Furthermore, in helping to teach the fundamental technology in agriculture, industry, health and sanitation, etc., Japan, which has been busy absorbing the technology of the advanced countries so far, has an international commitment to offer that fruit in the most convenient form to the developing countries.

One of the participants in this symposium, Professor Yujiro Hayami of Tokyo Metropolitan University, has proposed the establishment of a graduate course in Japan in which all the lectures would be given in English and the context of the lecture would be on agricultural and industrial production, with a focus on technology. We may have the opportunity to get more detailed information from Professor Hayami during this symposium.

In conclusion, the ASEAN countries are calling for peace, security and economic growth. Japan's role in maintaining peace and stability and promoting the economic growth of this region to the best of its ability will in turn lead to our own security and prosperity in the broadest sense.

Economic Relations between Japan and Latin America

I first visited Latin America in 1958. The purpose of the visit was to study the economic situation and development plans of Mexico, Peru, Chile, Argentina, and Brazil. Since then, I have returned to Latin America more than a dozen times.

Through these visits, which brought me varying experiences, my interest in the economic development of the Latin American countries as well as the economic relations between Japan and Latin America has been strengthened.

Latin America and the World Economy

As we all know, many of the Latin American countries are blessed with oil, hydroelectricity, uranium, and other energy resources. They also abound in forestry resources. They furthermore have a great potential to expand their agricultural production by utilizing their vast land. Latin America, along with North America, is likely to become a major food-supplying base of the world. Industrialization, at the same time, is proceeding rapidly in some of the Latin American countries, and exports of manufactured goods are expanding. The income level is rising in the Latin American countries. Their positions in the world economy are expected to greatly improve during the 1980s.

Some of you may recall that at the UNIDO (UN Industrial Development Organization) Annual Meeting held in Lima in

This chaptr is the text of an address the Latin America-Japan Business Cooperation Symposium, held in Tokyo in April 1979 under the sponsorship of the Inter-American Development Bank and the Export-Import Bank of Japan.

1975, a declaration was adopted calling for an increase in the share of industrial production by the developing countries from the 7 percent of the early 1970s to 25 percent by the year 2000. The Arusha Conference of the Group of 77 nations held in Tanzania in February this year in preparation for UNCTAD V in Manila adopted a resolution to raise the share of the trade in manufactures of developing countries from the current level of 8 percent to 30 percent by 2000. By the year 2000 many of the Latin American countries will join the industrial world. Attainment of the target of the Lima Declaration should not be impossible in view of the high rate of industrial growth of newly industrializing countries and the possibility of other developing countries joining such a process of industrialization. To facilitate attainment of this objective, industrial adjustment and prevention of protectionism in the industrial countries will become one of the major issues; at the same time, expansion of the domestic market in the developing countries as well as enlarging trade among the developing countries will become important. A new international economic order which will cover both the developing and industrial countries will become necessary for that purpose.

The Industrialization of Asia

Let me make a few comments on East Asia as a potential partner to Latin America. The East Asia region, along with Latin America, maintains a very high economic growth rate and has made dynamic progress. Japan's GNP in relation to that of the U.S. was 1:13 in 1960 but grew to 1:2.7 in 1977; by 1978, helped by the yen appreciation, it is estimated to have reached about half of the U.S. GNP. In recent years, the growth rates of Korea, Taiwan, Hong Kong, and the ASEAN nations (Thailand, Malaysia, the Philippines, Singapore, and Indonesia) have been also high. Their combined GNP in 1976 was about one-fourth of Japan's GNP. China, too, has maintained a relatively high growth rate—the average annual GNP growth rate in 1960–75 is estimated at 5.3 percent. And the new Ten-year Plan (1976–85) of China targets an average annual growth rate of 8 percent (4 percent in agriculture and 10 percent in industry). Even Japan, which can no longer attain the double-digit growth rate of the past, should be able to maintain a somewhat higher growth rate than that of the U.S. and Europe, at around 6 percent, for some years to come.

East Asia is relatively poor in natural resources for the size of its population and is not self-sufficient in food. The Latin American countries in the future should consider not only Japan but also the East Asian region as a whole, including China, as their market for exports. Recently Brazil began to sell iron ore to China, and China's food imports may reach 10 million tons in the near future.

Japan and Latin America

Japan's trade with Latin America has increased remarkably since 1960. Exports increased by 20-fold, from $300 million in 1960 to $6.29 billion (7.8 percent of total Japanese exports) in 1977. Imports increased by 10-fold from $310 million to $3.06 billion, which is 4.3 percent of total imports. From the Latin American side, trade with Japan during the first half of the 1970s accounted for 5 percent of total exports and 7.2 percent of total imports. Since the corresponding figures in the first half of the 1960s were 3.2 percent and 3.5 percent, respectively, it is clear that Japan is gaining importance as Latin America's trading partner.

The cumulative amount of Japan's direct investment in Latin America totaled $3.5 billion as of September 1977, which amount accounted for 16.9 percent of the aggregate amount of Japan's external investments. As you can see, it is substantially higher than the trade shares.

Since Japan has had large surpluses in its international balance of payments in recent years, increasing imports, particularly of manufactured products, is being urged from abroad. Moreover, although the economic growth rate has decelerated to the 5–6 percent level from the double-digit rate of the pre-oil crisis years, the household savings ratio has stayed high, accounting for 22 percent of disposable income (compared to 5 percent in the U.S. and 15 percent in West Germany). The economic structure of Japan has been transformed into that of a capital exporter which invests its saving surplus abroad. On the other hand, domestic wage increases, combined with the yen appreciation, are expanding imports of manufactured products and making some of Japan's exports less competitive in the world market. We are aware that transformation of Japan's industrial structure to a more sophisticated level has become our impending task.

Some of Japan's experience in the modernization of the economy may have relevance to the economic development of Latin America. Here I might mention our experience with a minimum wage system. Japan introduced a minimum wage system at a late stage, some twenty years ago. Recently I visited Mexico and was told that unemployment was 8 percent and underemployed about 40 percent of the labor force in Mexico. Level of employment is a function of wages. In Japan we have a relatively flexible wage system, with graduation according to the size of the enterprise. The average wage in smaller enterprises is about half of that in larger enterprises. This system gives greater job opportunities and more competitiveness.

Conclusion

Let me conclude by stressing the complementarity of Latin America and Japan, which are both dynamic regions in the world economy. Although the Pacific Ocean and the long distance have stood as an obstacle to more active interchange in the past, technological progress in air travel, container cargo ships, and telecommunications facilities are making it possible for us to overcome the obstacle of distance. It is, of course, most desirable to increase benefits to the two regions by strengthening economic and cultural interchanges.

Comparison of Two High-growth Economies: Brazil and Japan

The Brazilian economy started rapid expansion during the latter half of the 1960s, and its GNP reached $50 billion in 1972, ranking number eight in the non-communist world. Per-capita GNP has exceeded $500. This was roughly equal to the Japanese GNP in 1960 when Japan ranked fifth in the non-communist world, following the United States, Federal Republic of Germany, United Kingdom, and France.

A good reason to compare the Brazilian and Japanese economies is that although both countries are not of the West—that is, North America and Western Europe—which shares a common cultural background, they are rapidly catching up to the advanced West in the level of economic activities and in technology. So far, Japan has been the only country which has achieved a highly industrialized economy outside of the West and the Soviet bloc. The record of Japan's catching-up process is phenomenal. For example, the ratio of the GNP of Japan to that of the United States was 1:12 in 1960 and 1:5 in 1970, and then, partly because of the revaluations of the yen, the ratio became 1:4 in 1972.

This accomplishment of Japan may present a useful example for developing countries, including Brazil, which are trying to narrow the gap of economic activities with the advanced West. As both Japan and Brazil are attaining high rates of economic growth which are of similar magnitude, comparison of the two economies may serve to clarify the mechanism of rapid growth. Moreover, as both the population and GNP of today's Brazil are about equal to those of Japan 10 to 15 years ago, Japan's recent experiences

This chapter is based on a lecture given at Banco Nacional Do Desenvolvimento Economico (BNDE), Rio de Janeiro, Brazil, in August 1973.

may indicate some of the possible problems Brazil is likely to face in the course of future economic growth.

Similarities

There are many similarities between the two economies. Let us first look at macro indicators. The Brazilian economy after the 1964 Revolution (that is, taking the 1966–70 average) was similar to the Japanese economy of 1953–57, the period when Japan was attaining a self-supporting economy (see Table 1). Population was just about the same for both countries: 89 million. The GNP of Brazil for 1966–70 averaged $30.5 billion, while that of Japan for 1953–57 averaged $24.6 billion. If the depreciation of the value of the dollar is taken into account, the corresponding GNP of Brazil was about $23.0 billion, which was almost equal to the Japanese figure. This means that the per-capita GNP was also at about the same level. Moreover, the average annual rate of economic growth was 7.4% for Japan for 1953–57 while it was 7.5% for Brazil for 1966–70. Rates of growth of per-capita GNP, however, differed, being 4.3% for Brazil and 6.1% for Japan, as the rate of population increase was much higher in Brazil. Since 1971, the Brazilian economy has been growing at an average annual rate of more than 10% and this will correspond to Japan's 1958–64 period, when the annual average rate of growth was 10.7%.

Much the same situation is indicated by micro or sector figures (see Table 2). Production of crude steel in 1972 in Brazil was 6.5 million tons, which equals the Japanese production in 1951. Production of such items as iron and ferro-alloys, aluminum, and cement in 1971 was nearly equal to the production of Japan in the 1951–55 period. Chemical industries in Brazil, however, seem to be lagging far behind those of Japan; for instance, caustic soda production in 1972 was less than half that of Japan in 1951.

Compared with the basic industries I have enumerated, consumer durable goods industries are relatively more advanced in Brazil. For example, passenger car production in 1971 Brazil was about the level of 1963 Japan, which means a difference of only eight years between the two countries. Production of commercial vehicles in Brazil, however, is lagging relatively behind that of

Table 1. Comparison of Economic Scale and Growth Rate

	Brazil		Japan			
	1961–1965	1966–1970	1947–1952	1953–1957	1958–1964	1965–1970
Stage			Reconstruction	Achievement of economic independence	High growth; transfer to open economy	Open economy; growing foreign reserves
Population (million)	76.50	84.49	88.23	89.12	94.38	100.89
GNP (million US $)	17,947	30,456 (22,723)[a]	9,332	24,620	3,038	136,684
GNP per capita (US $)	235	340	106	276	562	1,355
Average real growth rate	4.5%[b]	7.5%[b]	11.6%[c]	7.4%	10.7%	10.8%
Average real growth rate per capita	1.2%[b]	4.3%[b]	9.7%[c]	6.1%	9.6%	9.6%

Source: UN *Statistical Yearbook.*

Notes: [a]At constant U.S. dollar prices in 1953; [b]GDP; [c]1948–52 average

Table 2. Comparison of Production of Major Manufacturing Products

	Brazil	Japan		
	1971	1951	1955	1971
Crude steel (1,000 m/t)	6,012	6,502	9,408	88,560
Iron & ferro-alloys (1,000 m/t)	4,740	3,227	5,426	74,640
Aluminum (1,000 m/t)	48.7	36.9	57.5	892.8
Cement (1,000 m/t)	9,660	6,548	10,563	59,460
Caustic soda (1,000 m/t)	135.6	325	502	2,892
Synthetic rubber (1,000 m/t)	78.2	—	—	759.6
Passenger vehicles (1,000 m/t)	363.0	3.4	13.4	3,715.2
Commercial vehicles (1,000 m/t)	152.4	35.1	46.9	2,104.8
Auto tires (1,000 m/t)	9,420	—	—	64,956
Power generation (1,000 kwh)	48,264	47,729	65,193	379,116

Source: UN *Statistical Yearbook.*

Japan: the 1971 production in Brazil about equals that of Japan in 1958. The total registered number of cars, including both passenger and commercial vehicles, per thousand of population, was 37 in 1970 Brazil, which equals exactly the figure for 1962 Japan. Production of electric refrigerators in 1972 Brazil was about 700,000, which was about the level of Japan in 1960.

In short, for macro-economic indicators there exists a gap of 12 to 15 years between Brazil and Japan, and for individual branches of industry, particularly for basic industries, the gap is roughly 12 to 20 years. Relative lag in industrial production as compared to macro indicators is probably due to the higher proportion of agricultural production in Brazil than in Japan.

From the institutional point of view, also, there are some similarities between the two countries. These include the mixed economy system of private and governmental initiatives, the importance of the role of the government, political stability, continuity in the government's policy, a "growth-first" orientation in economic policy, and so on. The two countries base their economies on the free competitive market system. In Japan, government has continued to exercise strong leadership over the private sector of the economy since the beginning of modernization, and in Brazil the government leads the process of economic development by various policy measures including state ownership of basic industries such as iron and steel and petroleum. Since 1964 in Brazil, under the strong leadership of the technocrat government, continuity of policies has been maintained. In Japan, the continuation of the Conservative government for more than 20 years has contributed to the stability of policies. Both governments have relatively efficient bureaucracies.

The Brazilian government and the Japanese government, at least until recent years, have followed a production-first policy and have given priority to growth rather than distribution. There seem to be various similarities between the National Income Doubling Plan of 1961–70 in Japan and the Brazilian economic model adopted after the 1964 Revolution. Both governments are following basically a pro-West policy, and the share of foreign trade with the United States accounts for about 30% of total trade in the case of both countries.

Differences

The total land area of Brazil is 23 times that of Japan. While Japan lacks natural resources, Brazil is endowed with rich mineral and agricultural resources. The beginning of modernization of the economy was around 1900 in the case of Japan; in Brazil it was around 1950. Such differences in the natural conditions and the stage of development are reflected in the industrial structure of the two countries. The share of primary industry in the net domestic product of Brazil and Japan was 17 percent (1969) and 23 percent (1955) respectively, while the share of the labor force was 44 percent (1970) in Brazil and 41 percent (1955) in Japan. Another feature of the Brazilian economy is a higher proportion of tertiary industry as compared with the Japanese economy of similar per-capita GNP. This is partially due to the relative lag in the growth of secondary industry and the absorption of labor into the services sector.

The commodity structure of foreign trade is also different in the two economies. While more than 70 percent of exports from Brazil are agricultural products, as much as 96 percent of Japan's exports are manufactured goods and 75 percent are products of heavy industry (1971 data). Japan's imports are mostly agricultural products, raw materials, and fuel, although in recent years imports of textiles and other manufactures have been sharply increasing. Brazilian imports are mostly manufactured items, including capital goods. Thus, the structure of foreign trade is different and complementary between the two countries. Such complementarity is likely to continue into the future when Brazil exports more manufactured and processed goods and Japan imports an increasing amount of industrial products.

Policy toward foreign capital inflow has also been different. While Japan was strictly regulating foreign capital imports, and only since around 1967 has begun overall liberalization of foreign capital inflow, Brazil has followed a relatively liberal policy toward foreign capital inflow. This difference may partly be due to the following factors. First, abundant natural resources existing in Brazil have attracted foreign capital from, for example, Canada and Australia, while Japan had a very different situation in this respect. Second, a higher rate of savings enabled Japan to finance its domestic capital requirements while in Brazil foreign capital inflow has been an important element supplementing domestic savings as well as satisfying the foreign exchange requirement.

The total fixed capital formation in Brazil in 1969 was estimated to be about 17 percent of the GNE (= GNP) while the corresponding figure in Japan was 20 percent for 1955, 30 percent for 1960, and 35 percent for 1970. There may be some statistical underestimation for the Brazilian case, and there may have also been a substantial increase in the rate of capital formation in very recent years. The capital output ratio of Brazil may be substantially lower than Japan. Also, the transfer of foreign savings accounts for about 2 percent of GNE in the case of Brazil. However, there will have to be a serious effort to step up the rate of domestic savings in order to finance economic growth of similar magnitude to that of Japan.

As alternative channels of obtaining financial resources Brazil has heavily depended on direct or indirect governmental sources; Japan has been mainly dependent on borrowings from private banking institutions and on the reinvestment of corporate savings.

A more important difference between the two countries is regional disparity in income and in the level of economic activities, which is greater in Brazil than in Japan. This is mainly due to the combination of the underdeveloped North and the highly developed South within one national boundary. Partly due to this regional difference, income disparities in Brazil are much larger than in Japan. In a study by the International Development Center of Japan, when the average income of the richest 10 percent and poorest 10 percent of the population are compared, the former is found to receive 32 times as much as the latter in the case of Brazil (1970) and 10 times as much in the case of Japan (1956).[1]

Causes of Rapid Economic Growth

Next, I would like to compare the causes of rapid economic growth in the two countries. The major causes of Japan's rapid economic growth may here be summarized as the following four factors:

1. Postwar recovery and reforms;
2. Semi-backwardness of economic structure;
3. Policies and attitudes; and
4. The international environment.

With the combination of the above factors, the Japanese economy has achieved a high rate of growth for more than two decades. It is of great interest that there are possibly several factors here in common with the Brazilian economy. The International Development Center of Japan in its report cited the following factors as the causes of Brazil's rapid economic growth:

1. Reforms introduced after the 1964 Revolution
   a. Reduction of distortions in the economy caused by inflation
   b. Use of "monetary corrections" to neutralize inflation and use of a crawling peg exchange rate
   c. Reforms in taxation, banking, export policy, etc.
   d. Spread of education
   e. Political and social stability
2. Policies for promoting growth
   a. Introduction of the "economy-first" principle
   b. Production-centered economic policy
   c. Parallel growth of agriculture and industry
   d. Export promotion
   e. Inducement of foreign investment

[1] International Development Center of Japan: *Comparative Study of Economic Development of Brazil and Japan*, 1974.

3. International environment
   a. Strong prices and demand for agricultural and mineral products in recent years
   b. Expanding world economy and trade

Some of the above factors are common to Japan's case. Both economies have benefited by an intermediate stage of development combining the features of an economically poor society with its work-oriented social climate and the advantages of the highly developed technology in the modern sectors.

Conclusion

It is evident, from the foregoing analysis, that the two economies are basically complementary. Brazil is endowed with rich natural resources and abundant labor, but has a shortage of capital and technology. On the other hand, Japan now possesses a large reserve of foreign exchange and a high level of technology, while she is badly in need of raw materials and agricultural products. The huge ocean-going vessels now in use have greatly reduced the disadvantage of the distance separating the two countries. Trade between the two countries is increasing rapidly.[2] Investment from Japan to Brazil is also expanding very rapidly both in number of cases and in value. Under these circumstances, Japan should cooperate in the fields where the long-range development of the Brazilian economy is directed. It is desirable to promote cooperation in the expansion and establishment of new basic industries, small- and medium-scale industries, and infrastructure, by supplying know-how and capital. Cooperation in the development of natural resources and the establishment of industries should take into account the possible contribution which may be made to reducing regional income gaps in Brazil.

It is also likely that future exports from Brazil will gradually shift to industrial manufactures and processed goods, and the rapid expansion of Japanese imports will provide a promising market for Brazil's manufactured products in the future. It should also be

[2] Exports from Japan to Brazil increased from $54.5 to $395 million during 1967–72, and imports from Brazil to Japan increased from $85.6 to $294 million during the same period.

mentioned that we recognize the importance of cooperating with the economic development of other Latin American countries and not confining our efforts too narrowly on Brazil alone.

We are now facing many new problems in Japan. Some of these, such as environmental problems, could have been avoided, at least to a certain degree, if we had introduced countermeasures earlier. We are also facing a very serious problem in the form of over-concentration of the population and economic activities in metropolitan areas, and this too could have been avoided somewhat if the government had introduced, well in advance, a much stronger policy for balanced regional development and for the regulation of land use. Both for success and for failure, Japan's experience of the past 15 years, during which period the per-capita GNP rose from $300 to $3,000, should provide useful lessons for Brazil, which is likely to follow a process of rapid economic expansion in the future.

The ASEAN-Japan Relationship: Conflict and Interdependence

The decade of the 1970s, now nearly at its close, has been an important one in many respects both for Japan and for the Association of Southeast Asian Nations (ASEAN). During the 1970s, some of the global systems instituted since the end of World War II became ineffective, making it necessary to find alternative and better systems, and to formulate new philosophies and principles with which to manage the global community. It has been a decade of challenge, in which our task has been to set a firm course for the 1980s and on into the 21st century.

There has been considerable turmoil and difficulty as the world sought a new international order to replace the old. The Bretton Woods international monetary system collapsed. The GATT system became ineffective as a framework for international trade, which changed radically both in volume and in quality. The "trade war" among the advanced countries became a sensitive and crucial issue. The conflict between North and South further intensified. The South, in particular, made many explorative efforts in pursuit of a "new international economic order." In 1973, OPEC declared a unilateral hike in oil prices which oil-consuming countries, both advanced and less advanced, had no choice but to accept. The effects of the confusion and dislocation unleashed by the oil shock are still reverberating in many parts of the world.

During the 1970s the United States withdrew from Vietnam and began its "disengagement from Asia." At the same time, the

This paper was delivered at the Second Odawara Symposium, "Asian Dialogue," in March 1979. The author acknowledges with thanks the assistance provided by Tsukasa Kimoto of the Japan Center for International Exchange in its preparation.

United States and China took a dramatic step toward normalization of relations, and the basic structure of power politics among the United States, the Soviet Union, and China began to change. The normalization of U.S.-China relations as well as profound changes in China's economic policy suggest that a new economic sphere in the Pacific is now emerging.

The decade has not been easy for Japan. Its huge surplus in the balance of international payments has drawn severe criticism from all over the world. The yen exchange rate rose as far as 180 yen to the U.S. dollar in October 1978, a 50 percent increase over the Bretton Woods rate of 360 yen to the dollar. In Southeast Asia a series of anti-Japanese movements occurred, forcing modifications in Japan's trade and investment policies.

ASEAN nations' power and importance have grown throughout the 1970s, and they now possess considerable bargaining power in the international arena. The age when Japan and ASEAN could be concerned only with themselves is over. Now the ASEAN-Japan relationship must be defined in a global context, particularly in view of the emerging international order in the Asian and Pacific area. This relationship is in part one of strong interdependence based on mutual understanding, but it contains inherent conflict as well. We can only hope that the ASEAN-Japan relationship will be not only strengthened and improved, but also restructured. In fact, a new ASEAN-Japan relationship has begun to form in the course of the turmoil of the 1970s.

Japan in the World Community

Japan has been called a "superpower" for a long time, but just when did it first earn this appellation? Japan's economy has maintained an extraordinary growth rate since 1960 when a National Income Doubling Plan was launched. As head of the Planning Bureau of the Economic Planning Agency at that time, I was deeply involved with its implementation. But by 1967 the target of doubling the national income had already been achieved. Even after that it continued to rise until, in 1975, it was about 9.2 times as large as the 1960 economy in nominal terms, or 3.6 times in real terms. The gross national product (GNP) of Japan in 1960 was less than one-tenth that of the U.S., but in 1975 it was about 490 billion dollars, or approximately one-third that of the U.S.

If at the beginning of the 1960s the Japanese economy was still an insignificant force in the world economy, its strength and trade volume increased rapidly; Japan can be said to have joined the ranks of the advanced countries in 1964 when it accepted IMF Article 8 and became a member of IMF and OECD. It was not until sometime around the beginning of the 1970s, however, when Japan's GNP became the second largest in the free world, that Japan came to be called an economic "superpower." For a long time Japan did not recognize its own economic power and position in the world economy and was somewhat taken aback to be called a "superpower." The rapid growth of the economy occurred before either the Japanese people or the rest of the world could properly adjust to its new importance. This has created a perception gap between Japan and the rest of the world concerning Japan's international status. Japan does not consider itself a particularly powerful nation, while the rest of the world considers it a major economic force. This perceptual gap underlies many of the conflicts between Japan and other nations and, it would seem, is actually growing more intense.

After the oil shock of 1974, Japan's rate of economic growth declined. Yet because of the appreciation of the yen vis-à-vis the dollar, in a sense the economy maintained its high growth rate even after the oil crisis, especially if production is calculated in terms of dollars. The Japanese government estimates Japan's GNP for fiscal 1978 at about 212 trillion yen (US $1,116 billion at the November 1978 exchange rate: 190 yen to the dollar). The United States's GNP for the same year is estimated at about $2,100 billion or approximately twice that of Japan. Since the U.S. population is also twice the Japanese population, Japan's per-capita income is thus almost the same as that of the United States (at the 190 yen/dollar exchange rate). Comparing balances in current accounts for the 1978 calendar year, Japan's surplus is estimated at approximately $17.7 billion, while the OPEC surplus is $11 billion. The U.S. has an estimated deficit of $17 billion.

These figures indicate that the Japanese economy is now an eminently significant part of the world economy. Understandably, as the Japanese economy continues to expand, expectation from abroad that Japan should take greater responsibility and a more active role in the world community will rise. At the same time, there is not enough understanding among Japan's general public of problems such as the rapid appreciation of the yen, trade practices and the trade surplus, and the need for adjustment in industrial structures and policies. In other words, the Japanese economy has not fully adapted to the changing international environment. Conflict often arises because of the persistence of the feeling in Japan that it is a small, powerless country and the failure to recognize that, viewed from abroad, Japan looms very large economically.

Japan's relations with the United States also changed during the 1970s. As the Japanese economy grew, Japanese industries became more serious competitors with their U.S. counterparts, and trade friction between the two countries emerged early in the decade. Friction occurred first in the textile sector, and the problem worsened as the trade imbalance between the U.S. and Japan enlarged. Japan's trade balance with the United States, which showed a deficit throughout the 1960s, became a surplus in the 1970s and has continued to increase ever since. By contrast, U.S. deficits in international payments worsened. This deepened anti-Japanese feeling in the U.S. It was widely believed that at the rate of 360 yen to the dollar the yen was undervalued, accelerating a Japanese export rush to the United States. The nadir in U.S.-Japanese relations occurred in the form of President Nixon's new economic policy announcement of August 1971. Known as the "Nixon economic shock," this policy change had a profound and serious effect on the Japanese people. In fact, however, it was not aimed at Japan alone, but at the entire world. It was meant to precipitate the abandonment of the Bretton Woods fixed dollar/gold exchange rate system. This policy suspended the conversion of dollars into gold, and world monetary relations were greatly disturbed. In December of the same year, an alternative monetary framework was set up under the Smithsonian Agreement, but it did not last even one year. By the spring of 1973, major currencies, including the yen, adopted floating regimes, still in use at the present.

After the Nixon shock, Japan experienced double-digit inflation, exacerbated by excess liquidity and the rapid expansion of investments in the private sector which had been stimulated by Prime Minister Tanaka's "Plan for Remodeling the Japanese Archipelago." The oil crisis also cut deep, and Japan's current accounts showed a large deficit in 1973. Current accounts vis-à-vis the United States were balanced for a few years after 1973, and few disputes arose between the two countries. Japan succeeded in appeasing inflation and stabilizing wages, quickly restoring its international competitiveness. In turn Japan's balance of payments position vis-à-vis the United States has improved, although there has been renewed friction over trade.

Relations between Japan and the EC were fairly smooth in the early 1970s. However, in the latter half of the decade, difficulties arose between Japan and both the EC and the United States. One reason for the friction is that Japan was quicker and more successful in adjusting domestically to the oil crisis than were the EC or the U.S. Compared with other advanced countries, Japan possessed, and still possesses, the characteristics of a semi-advanced economy and therefore was more flexible than other advanced countries in adjusting to changes in the environment such as the oil crisis. This flexibility in fact contributes to the acceleration of Japan's surplus.

As for the United States, although it did not feel the direct effects of the oil crisis, its balance of payments deteriorated rapidly. This was due partly to the policies of domestic demand and acceleration of employment, and partly to inflation and increases in oil imports.

Economic relations were particularly affected by the rising tide of protectionism in the United States and Europe. Although the Tokyo Round multilateral trade negotiations support the principle of free trade, a protectionist trend in the U.S. Congress and in most of the European countries is quite clear in such forms as quantitative restrictions on imports. The drift toward protectionism among advanced countries runs counter to trade liberalization, and is one of the most pressing problems of the world economy.

Besides protectionism, Japan is also experiencing growing expectations and pressure from other advanced countries to liberalize its import market. As shown in Table 1, liberalization of Japan's imports has much improved, though the number of

Table 1. The Number of Unliberalized Items of Major Advanced Countries, February 1978

	Total	Agricultural items	Industrial items	Japanese items discriminated against
U. S. A.	7	1	6	—
Canada	5	4	1	—
U. K.	3	1	2	—
France	46	19	27	28
W. Germany	15	4	11	3
Italy	8	3	5	35
Benelux	7	4	3	9
Japan	23	22	6	—
Average	14.8	7.3	7.6	

Source: *1978-nen Tsusho Hakusho* (White Paper on International Trade, 1978), p. 251.

restricted items, particularly agricultural products, is still greater in Japan than in most of the advanced countries. By stimulating domestic demand, Japan hopes to increase imports of finished products. But it may be some time before the effect of these efforts will show. The appreciation of the value of the yen will also reduce the import cost of raw materials, contributing to the strengthened competitiveness of Japanese finished-product exports.

The larger the Japanese economy has grown, the louder are the accusations that Japan is not taking responsibility commensurate with its economic power. The U.S. Congress's criticism that Japan is getting a free ride in security arrangements was first heard some time ago; the appeal that Japan should take a larger responsibility and role in security concerns is often voiced. As Table 2 shows, Japan's present defense expenditure (0.9 percent of GNP) is actually quite large in absolute terms. Meanwhile, neither the United States nor neighboring Asian countries agree totally that Japan should become a strong military power. Much more frequent is the call by both advanced and less developed countries that Japan should expand its efforts and activities in economic and technological assistance and cooperation to less developed countries.

The time has come when Japan, supported by its economic power, should play a larger role in the world community. Japan should seek an international role not as a military power but in

Table 2. A Comparison of Defense Expenditures

	Defense expenditures (in million dollars)		Per-capita expenditures (in $)		GNP ratio (%)	
	1975	1977	1975	1977	1975	1977
U.S.S.R.	124,000	133,000	490	508	11–13	
U.S.	88,983	104,250	417	480	5.9	6.0
China	n.a.	29,750	n.a.	32	n.a.	8.5
W. Germany	16,142	17,130	259	271	3.7	3.4
France	13,984	13,666	264	254	3.9	3.6
U.K.	11,118	12,103	198	214	4.9	5.0
Iran	8,800	7,894	268	224	17.4	10.9
Saudi Arabia	6,771	6,539	1,153	1,005	18.0	13.6
Egypt	6,103	n.a.	163	112	22.8*	n.a.
Japan	4,620	6,135	42	54	0.9	0.9

Source: *The Military Balance, 1979* (Tokyo: Jiji Tsushinsha, 1978).
*Data as of 1974

economic affairs and recognize that as a nation entirely dependent on international trade for the supply of vital resources, playing a greater international role and taking a larger responsibility in the world community is essential for its national security.

In this regard, it is urgent that Japan establish comprehensive strategies for national security conceived in an international framework. Such strategies have been suggested by experts like Kiichi Saeki, who has introduced the idea that national security expenditures should include not only the cost of reserves and stockpiles of energy and food, but also expenditures for scientific and technological research and development, as well as direct military defense expenditures. I myself have proposed a similar idea, that Japan should devote 5 percent of its GNP to a comprehensive national security budget, allocating 1 percent to defense, 1 percent to international development assistance, and 3 percent to scientific and technological research and development.[1]

The North-South Conflict and ASEAN-Japan Relations

As stated before, the structure of the cold war, the East-West relationship, has changed; in its place, the North-South conflict is

[1] *Nihon Keizai Shimbun* (Japan Economic Journal), Jan. 4, 1978.

becoming a crucial issue all over the world. This trend has been particularly marked since the mid-1970s. As the 1980s progress, the issues over which the advanced countries of the North and the less developed countries of the South diverge will have to be carefully dealt with. Although Japan joined the OECD fifteen years ago and became an economic "superpower," its economic structure and foundation are still, in many respects, fragile and retain some characteristics associated with an underdeveloped economy. Nevertheless, Japan should take an active role as an economic power and accept greater international responsibilities.

Japan's economic assistance has gradually increased; as Table 3 shows, official development assistance (ODA) surpassed that of West Germany in 1977 and became the third largest after the United States and France among member countries of the OECD Development Assistance Committee (DAC). Japan's total assistance for the same year, including other types of economic cooperation, was $5,520 million, the fourth largest amount among DAC countries. When former Prime Minister Takeo Fukuda attended the ASEAN summit in Kuala Lumpur in 1977, he expressed Japan's intention to double its ODA within five years. He then made an "international promise" at the Bonn summit meeting of advanced industrial leaders in 1978 that Japan would double its ODA over a three-year period, based on 1977 figures. It is expected that this promise will be kept in 1979. Obviously, Japan's aid performance is progressively improving, although the quality and quantity of its aid activities are still relatively poor compared with other advanced countries.

As shown in Table 3, 0.21 percent of Japan's GNP was devoted to ODA in 1977, a figure not only far below the international target of 0.7 percent but also as low as fourteenth among seventeen DAC countries, a further decline from Japan's standing as thirteenth for the previous year. The total aid amount, although the third largest, was 0.81 percent of the GNP, still below the international target of 1 percent and the 1.02 percent average for DAC member countries. The grant element of Japanese aid was 70.2 percent. This improved Japan's rank from lowest to sixteenth among DAC countries, but it was lower than the 74.9 percent for the previous year. These figures reveal that Japan's economic

Table 3. Overseas Development Assistance (ODA) and Economic Aid of DAC Countries (1977)

	ODA ($million) (1)	% of ODA in GNP (2)	Total of economic cooperation ($million) (3)	% of (3) in GNP (4)
U.S.A.	4,160	0.22	11,010	0.63
U.K.	910	0.38	5,930	2.44
W. Germany	1,390	0.27	5,750	1.12
Japan	1,420	0.21	5,530	0.81
France	2,280	0.60	5,210	1.37
Canada	990	0.51	2,420	1.24
Italy	190	0.10	1,990	1.02

Source: *1978 Keizai Kyoryoku Hakusho* (White Paper on Economic Cooperation, 1978).

assistance has improved in general, but still leaves much to be desired in terms of quality.

North-South tensions are not limited only to the question of economic aid, but also include such problems as development strategies, the claim of permanent sovereignty over resources, the economic disparity and inequitable distribution of wealth between the North and the South, the international trade and monetary systems, investment in and transfer of technology, international debt problems, nationalism, and so on. The North-South problem grows increasingly complicated and encompasses ever more diversified problems. There are now more than 150 independent nations, most of which are categorized as "less developed countries (LDCs)." The number of LDCs is so large that they have a decisive influence on decision-making at international meetings. For example, the Declaration of the Establishment for a New International Economic Order and its Action Plan as well as the Charter for Economic Rights and Obligations of Nation States were adopted at the United Nations' Sixth Special Meeting in May 1974 and at the Twenty-ninth General Meeting in late 1974, respectively, though without the full consent of the advanced countries. These instances clearly show the changing structure of decision-making in international forums, where LDCs have increased their influence by uniting in a single force. Such activities initiated by the South are based on changes in these countries' basic philosophies and strategies of development. Where they once depended on unilateral aid from the North, they now seek to influence and alter the world economic structure by promoting international trade arrangements. In other words, LDCs are casting off their passive posture in favor of a more active role. This change, however, adds political elements to what was basically an economic problem.

The close relationship between ASEAN and Japan is often pointed out. For example, as shown in Table 4, Japan's economic aid to the five countries of ASEAN in 1977 was 29.9 percent of its

Table 4. Japan's Economic Assistance to ASEAN (million dollars, percentage share in parentheses)

	ODA			Other official and private assistance			Grand total	Cumulative total 1960–1976
	Grant element	Official credit	Total	Direct investm't	Export credit	Total		
Indonesia	2,420 (10.2)	12,415 (18.7)	14,835 (16.5)	24,336 (14.3)	△4,319	20,017 (5.5)	34,852 (7.7)	444,018 (15.5)
Malaysia	534 (2.3)	2,411 (3.6)	2,945 (3.3)	738 (0.5)	918	1,656 (0.5)	4,601 (1.0)	68,033 (2.4)
Philippines	1,378 (5.8)	1,683 (2.5)	3,061 (3.4)	4,154 (2.5)	4,996	9,150 (2.5)	12,211 (2.7)	166,571 (5.8)
Singapore	209 (0.9)	674 (1.0)	883 (0.98)	10,217 (6.2)	△1,278	8,939 (2.5)	9,822 (2.2)	51,858 (1.8)
Thailand	1,533 (6.5)	3,650 (5.5)	5,183 (5.8)	2,713 (1.7)	△693	2,020 (0.6)	7,203 (1.9)	55,764 (1.9)
ASEAN total	6,075 (25.7)	20,833 (31.4)	26,907 (29.9)	42,158 (25.7)	△376	41,782 (11.5)	68,689 (15.1)	786,244 (27.4)
World total	23,668 (100)	66,257 (100)	89,925 (100)	164,097 (100)	199,543	363,640 (100)	453,565 (100)	2,871,983 (100)

Source: Ministry of Foreign Affairs: *1978 Waga Gaiko no Kinkyo* (The Recent Conditions of Japan's Foreign Policy) (△ shows minus)

total ODA and 15.1 percent of total economic cooperation (combined ODA and other private and official economic flows). Of the total amount of economic cooperation from 1960 to 1977, 27.4 percent was allocated to ASEAN. This shows that Japan has been gradually giving greater emphasis to economic assistance to ASEAN. The ASEAN-Japan relationship is also close in terms of

Japan's investment in ASEAN. As shown in Table 5, Japan's investment in ASEAN increased so rapidly that it provoked fears of overpresence and sparked anti-Japanese sentiment in Southeast Asia, especially between 1972 and 1974. The problem of investment overpresence is a universal North-South problem, not one confined only to ASEAN and Japan.

It is pointed out that Japan has been expanding its economic activities into Southeast Asia without enough consideration and care. Japanese tend to overlook differences because of shared cultural and geographical factors, and this has meant that Japanese economic activities tend to ignore the environments of host countries and to forget the need to explain themselves to the people of the host country. The absence of such efforts naturally results in arousing anti-Japanese sentiment among the people of the people of the host country. Careful attention should be given to three factors in making overseas investments: speed, share, and balance. It seems that Japanese business expansion into Southeast Asia did not give adequate attention to these factors. For example, as Table 5 shows, Japanese investments in ASEAN countries accelerated so rapidly that they were viewed as a threat by local

Table 5. Japan's Investments in ASEAN (thousand dollars)

	1970	1972	1974	1976	Cumulative total (1960–1976)
Indonesia	44,570	124,800	231,250	784,770	2,113,464
Malaysia	12,690	21,050	68,720	45,160	303,092
Philippines	28,770	12,920	71,640	56,290	323,445
Singapore	na	na	59,120	55,570	312,966
Thailand	13,790	25,060	40,550	7,710	190,499

Source: Ministry of Foreign Affairs: *Nanboku Mondai to Keizai Enjo* (The North-South Problem and Economic Assistance), 1978.

indigenous businesses. Japan's share in overseas direct investment in ASEAN countries increased; as we will see later, trade imbalances also expanded in such countries as Thailand and Singapore.

Anti-Japanese movements which became widespread in many parts of Southeast Asia between 1972 and 1974 were epoch-making in the sense that they forced Japan to seriously review its attitudes and policies toward business in Southeast Asia. For example, the move to boycott Japanese goods in Thailand in 1972 was taken seriously by the Japanese business world. As a result, the Federation of Economic Organizations (Keidanren) and four other leading economic associations, as well as the Japan External Trade Organization (JETRO), issued "Guidelines for Investment in Developing Countries" and "Overseas Investment Standards" as guidelines for Japanese businesses expanding abroad.

A major aspect of the ASEAN-Japan relationship is the problem of trade imbalance. Trade imbalances are particularly conspicuous between Thailand and Japan, and the Thai government has strongly expressed its dissatisfaction even though there is little sign that matters will improve. Among the more notable characteristics of ASEAN-Japan trade relations, the most prominent is an asymmetry in trade between ASEAN and Japan, a problem which arises basically from differences in GNP. As Tables 6 and 7 show, in 1977 Japan's share of ASEAN's total trade was about 25 percent of both exports and imports, while ASEAN's share of Japan's trade was 8 percent in exports and 12 percent in imports. Japan has trading partners all over the world, and in terms of trade share, Japan is not as dependent on ASEAN as vice versa. This is why the interdependent structure of ASEAN-Japan trade is characterized as asymmetrical.

Indonesia, in particular, has the most extremely asymmetrical trade relationship with Japan. In 1977, Japan imported 40.2 per-

Table 6. Export Share Matrix between ASEAN, U.S.A., and Japan (percentage)

Export from		Export to				
		ASEAN	U.S.A.	Japan	Others	Total
ASEAN	1972	20	18	23	40	100
	1977	15	22	25	39	100
U.S.A.	1972	3	—	10	87	100
	1977	3	—	9	88	100
Japan	1972	9	31	—	60	100
	1977	8	25	—	67	100
Others	1972	2	15	6	77	100
	1977	3	27	11	59	100

Source: International Monetary Fund: *Direction of Trade Annual*, 1972, 1977.

Table 7. Import Share Matrix between ASEAN, U.S.A., and Japan (percentage)

Import by		Import from ASEAN	U.S.A.	Japan	Others	Total
ASEAN	1972	13	12	22	53	100
	1977	17	14	24	45	100
U.S.A.	1972	3	—	17	81	100
	1977	5	—	14	82	100
Japan	1972	8	22	—	70	100
	1977	12	16	—	73	100
Others	1972	1	15	6	78	100
	1977	3	24	12	60	100

Source: International Monetary Fund: *Direction of Trade Annual*, 1972, 1977.

cent of Indonesia's total exports, but Indonesia's share in Japan's imports was 7 percent.[2] Indonesia imported only 2.2 percent of Japan's total exports, but that accounted for 27.1 percent of Indonesia's total imports. Similarly, exports from the Philippines to Japan accounted for 23.2 percent of its total exports but only 1.3 percent of Japan's total imports. Japan sent to the Philippines 1.4 percent of its total exports, but this made up 25.1 percent of total imports into the Philippines. Japan's share in Thailand's exports was 19.7 percent, while the latter's share in the Japan's imports was 1.1 percent; 32.4 percent of Thailand's total imports were from Japan, while only 1.7 percent of Japan's total exports were to Thailand. Malaysia sent 20.5 percent of its total exports to Japan, accounting for 2.2 percent of Japan's total imports. On the other side of the ledger, Malaysia received 23.4 percent of its total imports from Japan while Japan's share of total exports to Malaysia was 1.1 percent. For Singapore, where the extent of trade asymmetry with Japan is least of all ASEAN countries, 9.5 percent of total exports went to Japan, and Japan imported 1 percent of its total imports from Singapore. Singapore imported 17.5 percent of total imports from Japan, an amount accounting for 2.1 percent of Japan's total exports.

A similar asymmetry is clearly observable in many trade items, particularly primary products, upon which ASEAN economies

[2] IMF, *Direction of Trade Annual*, 1971–1977.

depend heavily. For example, Indonesia sends 100 percent of the nickel ore it exports to Japan, although this accounts for only 22 percent of Japan's total imports of nickel ore. Other similar examples are bauxite from Indonesia (100 percent of exports and 18.1 percent of imports) and from Malaysia (100 percent and 12 percent), nickel from the Philippines (100 percent and 12 percent), and copper ore from the Philippines (93 percent and 27.9 percent).

There are both advantages and obvious risks for a country in a commodity which depends on only one market. This point has been dealt with by the dependent theory and the dislinkage theory within the framework of North-South relations. It also involves quite sensitive political questions. Due to the extreme asymmetry of the interdependent structure of trade, the ASEAN economies are vulnerable to and easily affected by any alteration in the Japanese economy. It was once said that if the U.S. sneezed, Japan would catch a cold; now a similar relationship exists between ASEAN and Japan.

The STABEX (Stabilization of Export Earnings) scheme between ASEAN and Japan is a measure to ameliorate the interdependent relationship between ASEAN and Japan and to diffuse the effects of the asymmetrical trade structure, thus stabilizing shifts in export earnings of primary products. The ASEAN STABEX (ASEBEX) scheme, which aims at securing and stabilizing steady export earnings, is in accordance with the basic change in development strategies. The LDCs are emphasizing industrialization based on the expansion of foreign trade, but, needless to say, they will be unable to implement economic development plans if their export earnings are unstable and easily affected by business fluctuations in the advanced countries.

In 1978, the International Development Center of Japan, under the sponsorship of the National Institute for Research Advancement (NIRA), carried out an econometric study and simulation of the ASEBEX scheme with the participation of a group of experts from Southeast Asia and Japan. This simulation study examined the basic model and its twenty-one variants for the period between 1966 and 1975, evaluating such items as costs and benefits, profit distribution among products and among ASEAN countries, and efforts to stabilize export earnings within the framework of the proposed ASEBEX scheme.[3] The simulation showed, among other things, the ASEBEX requires about $100 million annually, that the average outstanding fund is about $160 million, and that the so-called basket method which aims at stabilizing exports of primary products as a whole requires only two-thirds of the funds required by the individual-item method. As noted before, Japan's economic aid to ASEAN in 1976 exceeded $1,500 million, suggesting that the ASEBEX scheme, which requires $100 million funding annually, will not be an intolerable burden on Japan.

The STABEX scheme, however, is not desired or welcomed by the LDCs as a whole. The Group of 77 of the UNCTAD strongly desires the establishment of a Common Fund rather than the STABEX scheme. Even among ASEAN scholars there has been the feeling that ASEBEX would increase ASEAN's dependency on Japan too much. There has also been the alternative opinion that international commodity agreements rather than STABEX should be sought, or that global arrangements, rather than regional ones, should be made. Some of these points are valid and should not be totally ignored. However, STABEX would not exclude international commodity agreement arrangements, while implementing a global arrangement from the beginning would require too much time and unnecessarily strenuous effort. Therefore, it is suggested that STABEX be applied to a more comprehensive Asian and Pacific area so as to include the United States, Canada, Australia, New Zealand, and other developing countries in the region rather than ASEAN alone. Japan might take a leadership role in establishing such an expanded ASEBEX scheme.

In any event, the ASEBEX scheme is one effort to improve relations within the North-South framework between ASEAN and Japan. In a sense, it is natural that ASEAN peoples should exhibit anti-Japanese sentiments. However, real efforts have been made, though perhaps not yet sufficient efforts, to search for a more viable, stable, and mutually beneficial relationship between ASEAN and Japan.

[3] National Institute for Research Advancement and International Development Center: *The Relationship of ASEAN and Japan*, 1978.

ASEAN and Japan in the Asian-Pacific Region

The year 1979 started with the epoch-making normalization of relations between the United States and China. A relationship between the United States, with the world's greatest wealth, and China, with the largest population, is expected to bring about the opening of a "Pacific Age." One of the basic postures advocated by the Ohira Cabinet, which came to power at the end of 1978, is pan-Pacific diplomacy. Whether or not the "Pacific Age" is the proper term, it is true that international relations in Asia and the Pacific area are drastically changing. The ASEAN-Japan relationship is one of the most important aspects of international relations in the Asian and Pacific area. It sets the stage for the whole international environment of Asia and the Pacific area, and it is in turn directly or indirectly influenced by changes in Asian-Pacific international relations. An accurate analysis of the international environment in the Asian-Pacific region is therefore indispensible in creating and maintaining a viably interdependent relationship between ASEAN and Japan.

Normalization of relations between the U.S. and China has totally changed (and perhaps even basically destroyed) the cold war structure among the three superpowers. It has also resulted in the emergence of a new conflict structure between the Soviet Union and a group consisting of the United States, China, and Japan. However, since Japan does not have a military force comparable to that of the U.S. and China, the common activities of this alliance will be limited to the economic domain. In that case, however, it is also quite possible that the U.S. and Japan will intensify their competition in the Chinese market. In fact, it is said that one of the reasons why the U.S. hastened normalization with China was the growing anxiety among Americans that Japan might monopolize the vast Chinese market if the U.S. delayed much longer in establishing economic ties.

On the other hand, Japan as an economic superpower has been increasingly involved in the games of power politics being played in Asia by the U.S., the U.S.S.R., and China. Accordingly, Japan is experiencing growing pressure to play a larger role not only economically, but also politically. This is only natural since

Japan's economic activities are indeed global, and Japan must give serious consideration to maintaining and improving relations not only with ASEAN but with all other countries as well. In other words, it is not enough for Japan to consider her relations with ASEAN alone. Although it is best not to judge the importance of countries to one another only on the basis of trade volume, there is an obvious asymmetry in Japan-ASEAN economic relations. In a similar manner, there is asymmetry on another level, for ASEAN is devoted to basically regional interests, and Japan must pursue its interests on a global scale. Bridging the gap between ASEAN's regionalism and Japan's globalism harmoniously will become a concern of the greatest importance.

Assisted by the shift in China's economic policy as well as its geographical propinquity, Japan has rapidly improved and accelerated economic relations with China since the normalization of diplomatic relations in 1972. Japan has promoted economic relations with China within a global framework, but ASEAN seems to be worried by Japan's rapid approach to China. The concern has been expressed that Japan might become too involved in China and less engaged with ASEAN. There is also concern in ASEAN that Japan's ASEAN investment might decrease as its economic relations with China grow. The asymmetrical trade relationship between ASEAN and Japan means that even a slight change in Japanese policy would profoundly affect the ASEAN economies. In that sense, it is only natural that Japan's activities vis-à-vis China are a source of anxiety to ASEAN. Another concern of ASEAN is that Japanese economic and technological cooperation with China may so stimulate the Chinese economy that it will grow rapidly and become an international market competitor, thus threatening ASEAN products. However, it seems to me that it will be many years before such fears could become reality.

The Chinese economy tends to be overestimated. For example, China's estimated production of crude steel in 1977 was 24 million tons, which was less than a quarter of the Japanese production of 107 million tons in the same year. Its steel production target for 1985 is only 60 million tons, although it is one of the main targets proclaimed in the ten-year Economic Development Plan accompanying the Four Modernizations. Even if China succeeds in the annual production of 60 million tons of steel by 1985, per-capita consumption of steel in China will still be about 0.06 kilograms. This is much smaller than the Japanese per-capita steel consumption in 1976, which was 0.58 kilograms (Japan exported 42 million tons out of its production of 107 million tons). Since domestic demand is expected to increase along with rising standards of living, these figures suggest that China's steel production will be absorbed domestically.

However, it cannot be denied that economic relations between China and Japan will further intensify in the near future. Japan now faces such problems as a persistent surplus in the balance of payments, the appreciation of the yen, strong criticism and protectionism in the United States and Europe, the overpresence of Japanese business in Southeast Asia, and the imbalance of trade in that region, all of which slow down Japan's exports. Some sectors of Japanese business have already experienced serious recession as a result of these problems. Under these conditions, Japan is more than happy to develop a market in China.

China-Japan economic relations also tend to be overestimated. In 1977, China's share in Japan's total imports was only 2.2 percent, and Japan sent 2.4 percent of its total exports to China. At the same time, Japan's share in China's total exports was 20.1 percent, and China imported 33.9 percent of its total imports from Japan in the same year. That is to say, Japan's trade relationship with China is just as asymmetric as that with the ASEAN countries. We should also note that China is not strengthening economic ties with Japan alone, but striving to diversify its economic partnerships and increase trade with the U.S. and European countries as well.

It seems quite certain that the Chinese economy as a whole will grow. But China, whose population the CIA estimated at 950 million in 1976 (UN statistics estimated 850 million), may have to pursue a domestically-oriented policy in order to respond to the demands of its large population. In a sense, whether or not China becomes a threat to the ASEAN economies depends on how fast they themselves grow and develop. Economic development in Asia, including China, can increase the purchasing power of all the countries in the region and achieve a horizontal division of labor. Therefore, economic development and increased purchasing power in China should bring some benefits for ASEAN. Meanwhile, Japan will not, and should not, reduce or sacrifice its economic activities in the ASEAN region while it strengthens relations with China.

Japan's relations with the Asian newly industrialized countries (NICs)—Korea, Taiwan, Hong Kong, and Singapore—are also very important. In August 1972 Japan adopted a Generalized System of Preference (GSP) aiming at accommodating the exports of and promoting the industrialization of less developed countries. Apparently the Japanese GSP was effective for Asian NICs, and the United States adopted the system in 1976, further assisting Asian NICs in expanding their business in the U.S. market. In fact, exports from the Asian NICs have been increasing so rapidly that they are facetiously called the "Gang of Four." As shown in Table 8, the exports of these four Asian countries to Japan have increased so rapidly that Japanese are beginning to talk about the "catching-up" phenomenon in the NICs. A rapid increase in exports from the NICs to Japan is potentially threatening to the small and medium-sized businesses which are such an important sector of the Japanese economy. How Japan can and should accommodate the economic expansion of the NICs will become a more and more important issue.

Table 8. Exports from NICs and ASEAN to U.S. and Japan (million dollars)

	Japan			United States		
	1971	1974	1977	1971	1974	1977
Korea	273	1,567	2,160	491	1,561	3,175
Taiwan	288	954	1,297	867	2,257	4,052
Hong Kong	98	273	352	1,051	1,751	3,157
Singapore	115	619	693	144	590	916
Indonesia	855	4,569	5,033	220	1,813	3,756
Malaysia	374	979	1,579	286	826	1,393
Philippines	516	1,104	904	526	1,169	1,230
Thailand	231	685	754	103	198	384

Source: IMF: *Direction of Trade Annual* 1971–77.

The other four ASEAN countries are also gaining industrial capability, though more gradually than the NICs, and some ASEAN industries have gained competitiveness with Japan. Sooner or later Japanese will find themselves fretting over the fact that the ASEAN economies have caught up.

Needless to say, Japan cannot gain and maintain international competitiveness in all industries. Japan will have to cope with the catching-up of Asian NICs and ASEAN not by competing with or destroying emerging industries in these countries, but by promoting industrial adjustment within Japan. Changes in the industrial structure and adjustment of Japanese domestic industries will further the development of NICs and ASEAN economies as well as improve the so-called dual economy in Japan.

In short, the "Pacific Age" opens above all with a call to coordinate adjustments among all the countries of Asia and the Pacific. It is true, however, that dynamic change is occurring within ASEAN, in the NICs, and in China-Japan and China-U.S. relations. The Asian-Pacific region, particularly Southeast Asia, is one of the most economically dynamic regions in the world. The fact that the trade volume of the U.S. with Asia and the Pacific region in 1976 exceeded that with Europe illustrates this point. The Asian-Pacific region is equipped with abundant natural and human resources, capital and advanced technology, as well as vast markets, all of which are necessary for rapid economic growth. Whether or not the Asian-Pacific region can continue this dynamism depends on how smoothly and harmoniously internal adjustments and cooperative arrangements within the region can be made.

Japan's Role in the International Community

I noted previously that Japan depends heavily on supplies of resources and food from overseas. Elsewhere I have described this dependence on overseas supply as "defenselessness on all sides."[4] In order to avoid this dependence on overseas supply and to increase self-sufficiency, Japan may be forced to reduce the size of the economy as a whole and to lower living standards. Needless to say, the Japanese people are not likely to tolerate such a move; it is, in fact, unrealistic for Japan to change its dependent economic structure. In short, it is necessary for Japan to produce goods with a large value-added for export in order to build its foreign re-

[4] Saburo Okita: *Happo Yabure no Keizai Senryaku* (Tokyo: Toyo Keizai Shimposha, 1978).

serves, which are in turn needed to pay for overseas supplies of resources and food together with the imports of manufactures for which Japan has lost competitiveness.

It will be noted, however, that Japan's overseas dependence is global. The United States has an exceptionally large share in both Japan's imports and exports (17.5 percent and 24.7 percent, respectively). The second largest share of Japan's imports, 12 percent, comes from Saudi Arabia, and the second largest demand for Japan's exports comes from Korea (5.1 percent). Japan's existence fundamentally depends on maintaining interdependent relations with many countries all over the world. This may be a good example of international interdependence, but Japan's current attitudes and policies toward the rest of the world are not completely satisfying, as ever-growing international criticism of Japan suggests. It is one of Japan's most pressing tasks to deal with this criticism fairly and wisely, and provide a reasonable and positive example of international interdependence.

"Interdependence" is a current catch-word with political implications in the arena of international relations. It may suggest the way one country or group of countries establishes international relationships where more is gained by one party. Such interdependence as this may be harmful and dangerous in the present system of international relations. It seems essential that a network of truly fair interdependent relations be created all over the world in order for mankind to survive longer with the limited resources at its disposal. Perhaps Japan can take the lead in creating, along with other countries, interdependent relations of mutual benefit and firm trust.

However, without being better understood by the rest of the world, it will be very difficult for Japan to assume such leadership. Better understanding of Japan abroad requires much deeper international interest and concern among the Japanese people. It also requires an environment within Japan which will promote greater and more active international cooperation.

In other words, Japan can contribute to the solution of the problems of mankind by starting within its own borders to create and develop interdependent international relations. For example, reform of the educational system and the bureaucracy, the development of private-sector international cooperation through philanthropic organizations, and revision of the tax system are essential steps in initiating this effort. Obviously these reforms will not be easy to carry out, but persistent and sincere efforts should be made to see them through. Needless to say, Japan should also extend its efforts outside Japan. Below, I would like to suggest some of the roles Japan should play in the 1980s.

First of all, Japan should participate more actively and constructively in the problems of the international community. Since the end of World War II, Japan has been passive and has avoided active participation or commitments in the international community. Today this provokes severe criticism that Japan is shirking its responsibility. Japan now contributes a large amount to both the United Nations and the World Bank; naturally, it should undertake greater initiative in proposing solutions to international problems at international meetings and organizations. In particular, Japan should actively pursue solutions to such international problems as trade, currency, and North-South relations.

Second, to support and promote the above efforts, policy research organizations of high standards—private, public, or some combination of the two—should be developed to promote international policy studies. Some "think-tanks" or governmental research institutes fill this role, but their capability and scale of activity in international policy research and formulation of concrete policy proposals are not yet satisfactory. Although it rarely criticizes other nations, Japan is the constant butt of criticism from abroad concerning such problems as international balance of payments and trade imbalances. Criticisms such as these are often based on wrong information and understanding. It is important that Japan explain the specific problems behind international conflicts in order to seek more practical solutions and more viable international relations.

Third, Japan should play a greater role in North-South relations. I have mentioned that the quality of Japan's foreign aid still lags behind the international standard. It is part of Japan's international responsibility to improve the standard and quality of its economic cooperation. The conflict between the North and the South is actually intensifying, and Japan should actively initiate dialogue that will further understanding of the issues in North-South relations. In addition, these efforts must be accompanied by concrete improvements in economic cooperation. Economic aid will only be effective if it is supported by appropriate sacrifices and efforts toward development in the countries receiving assistance. Japan should emphasize economic cooperation in areas and sectors where aid will stimulate indigenous efforts at development. Perhaps Japan can play a role in seeking new ways and philosophies of economic cooperation and in leading North-South relations in a more constructive direction.

Fourth, and another aspect of North-South relations, Japan should extend cooperation to the development of Southeast Asian, particularly ASEAN, countries. In this regard, I would like to make two proposals. The first is that an ASEAN Economic Development Center be established, and that Japan underwrite most of the cost of its establishment and operation. ASEAN urgently needs to adopt well-balanced, healthy economic policies, develop manpower resources, and raise technological and managerial standards in order to accelerate dynamic economic development. It also needs to educate or employ a large number of competent technocrats who can guide the developing ASEAN countries toward mature economic integration. The ASEAN Economic Development Center should satisfy part of such needs. It may be argued that Japan lacks sufficient institutional know-how or experience to manage such an international facility. But the required know-how and managerial resources can be sought internationally, and actual management and operation of the Center can be conducted by ASEAN itself. The basic activities of the Center should be focused in three areas: (1) large-scale managerial and technical manpower training, as well as further training opportunities for ASEAN technocrats; (2) advanced policy studies of ASEAN economic integration and development strategies; and (3) compilation of statistics on ASEAN as a whole.

My second proposal is to establish a "Center of Economic Development and Cooperation for Asia and the Pacific" (CEDCAP). Already there are similar organizations such as the United Nations Development Institute for Asia and the Pacific, the Pacific Basin Business and Economic Study Center of the University of California, and the Institute of Developing Economies. Yet these do not satisfy the need to educate and prepare as many Japanese experts as possible who can deal competently with the task of international economic cooperation. There are still very few scholars and experts who study the ASEAN region. There must be many more Japanese in the field of ASEAN economics as well as in study of the broader Asian-Pacific economic region. The proposed CEDCAP is one way to respond to this urgent educational demand. However, the Center of Economic Development and Cooperation for Asia and the Pacific should be international; it should invite and involve people not only from Japan, but also from other Pacific advanced countries, the Asian NICs, and ASEAN. CEDCAP should concentrate on three core activities: (1) graduate education in Asian-Pacific studies, perhaps with the cooperation of a leading university; (2) studies of comprehensive development policy strategies for the Asian-Pacific region; and (3) compilation of statistics on the region. In the past such ideas as the Pacific Free Trade Area (PAFTA) and the Organization for Pacific Trade and Development (OPTAD) have been proposed. CEDCAP could investigate the possibility of further examining or following up such proposals.

Another idea I would like to introduce here briefly in relation to CEDCAP is that of an International Development University (IDU), as proposed by Yujiro Hayami of Tokyo Metropolitan University. The IDU would be a graduate school established in Japan to provide education and training in English in the specific subjects related to developing economies such as agriculture, industry, health and hygiene, and so forth. The IDU would accept students from all ASEAN and other developing countries (60%), Japan (30%) and other industrialized countries (10%) and offer training which would prepare them to work in the field of economic development. Although the purposes and goals of IDU and CEDCAP may overlap somewhat, both are ideas worthy of serious consideration.

Last, but certainly most important, Japan should play a leading role in pursuit of a stable international economic order. Obviously, Japan cannot solve all the problems alone, but it should be actively seeking solutions to the international problems it is deeply caught up in, such as imbalances of international payments and trade and fluctuations in the exchange rate. Japan should pursue a free trade policy and further open the Japanese market to all the items which are not yet liberalized. It should also cooperate with other advanced countries in accelerating industrial adjustment and seeking industrial policies feasible to all concerned. As far as the NICs and other semi-advanced countries are concerned, Japan should help their further growth not only by opening the Japanese domestic market, but also by helping their exports to reach markets in other countries. Regarding the international monetary problem, it should reform its restrictive monetary regulations and take positive measures to allow the internationalization of the yen and to facilitate the development of an international money market in Tokyo.

In conclusion, let me emphasize that Japan is now faced with the need for comprehensive strategies which will make it possible for Japan not only to survive economically but to play a responsible international role in the 1980s. Since the end of World War II, Japan has been regarded as a "closed country" in the international community. In the 1980s I believe there will be many opportunities for Japan to become a truly open country, playing a much larger international role.

Former Prime Minister Fukuda advocated a deeper "heart-to-heart" relationship between ASEAN and Japan. This "heart-to-heart" relationship must be created through firm trust and understanding among our peoples. It behooves Japan not only to make itself fully understood by other countries, but also to do its best to increase its own understanding of international affairs. The number of Japanese who went abroad in 1978 alone exceeded 3.5 million. However, it is dubious how much these Japanese tourists who go abroad for short periods in large groups contribute to international understanding between Japan and the rest of the world. What we need now is massive, but carefully planned, international exchange of people, in particular intellectual exchange. Such international exchange will build a much-needed intellectual infrastructure in Japan for the nurturing of deeper international understanding.

If Japan develops such strategies and programs, it can greatly contribute to international efforts to form a solid and stable network of interdependent relationships. It is within such a global context that ASEAN and Japan can and should coordinate their conflicts and interests and seek a mutually beneficial, interdependent relationship.

Index

agriculture: in Japan, 100–1, 113, 177–78; increasing output of, 9; modernization of, 212; outflow of labor from, 181–82; role of in development, 101–3; role of in labor absorption, 8–9
aid: basic human needs approach to, 6–7, 11–12, 49, 54, 232; efficiency approach to, 6–7, 19–20, 48–49, 56; technical, 237; terms of, 75–79; to Japan from the U.S., 139, 205
Allen, G. C. 115
Ando, Hirofumi, 150
Angat-Magat irrigation project (Philippines), 39
Argentina, 239; debt service ratio in, 80
ASEAN (Association of South East Asian Nations), 240, 253, 266; anti-Japanese sentiment in, 263–64, 267; development of, 233–34; Japanese investment in, 263; relations with Japan, 229–37, 253–77
Asian Development Bank, 31, 39, 74; increase in agricultural financing by, 24
Asia-Pacific region, 231, 234, 272
Association of South East Asian Nations. *See* ASEAN
Australia, as part of Asia-Pacific region, 231, 267
automobile industry: in Japan, 96, 131, 244; in Brazil, 244

balance of payments, 65, 112, 130, 136, 209, 274
Bangladesh, rice production in, 29, 32–33
birth control, 16, 153, 155, 171; in early postwar Japan, 169
birth rate, decline of, 17, 21, 25; in China, 17–18; in Japan, 120–21, 155–56, 158–59, 161–62; in Latin America, 17, 155
Brazil, 5, 48, 239, 241; as exporter of agricultural products, 247; automobile industry in, 244; chemical industry in, 244; debt service ratio in, 80; policy of toward foreign capital, 248; regional income gaps in, 250; steel industry in, 244; tertiary industry in, 247
Bretton Woods system, breakdown of, 229, 253, 254, 256
Brown, Lester, 23
buffer stocks, 69. *See also* commodities
Burki, S. J., 11
Burma, 122; rice production in, 29, 32–33

Cambodia, rice production in, 29, 32–33
Canada, 267
capital: access to, 6; foreign, 214, 248; transfer of, 75, 88, 89
chemical industry: in Brazil, 244; in Japan, 109, 128, 181, 201, 206
Chile, 239
China, 235, 240, 241; decline of birth rate in, 17–18; economic growth in, 199, 230; relations with Japan, 269–70; relations with the U.S., 254, 268
colonial economies, 121–22
colonies, Japan's loss of, 114, 138, 169
Committee for Development Planning (UN), 5, 72
Committee on International Development (Pearson Commission), 6. *See also* aid; Pearson Report

commodities, prices of, 68–69, 70, 71, 77. *See also* STABEX

death rate, decline in, 21; in postwar Japan, 120–21, 155–56, 158, 161–62
debt service ratio, 78, 80, 232
Development Assistance Committee (DAC) of OECD, 43, 62, 78, 79, 103, 260
diet, improvement of in Japan, 16, 151
division of labor, international, 51, 232
double-cropping, 9, 40
Doubling Rice Production in Asia program, 24, 36, 41, 43, 45, 55–56, 60, 102–3, 233
dualistic structure, role of in Japan's economic growth, 121, 123, 146, 168, 209

Economic Planning Agency (Japan), 204, 218, 254
education: effect of on population patterns, 154; role of in economic development, 153–54; role of in Japan's development, 94–95
electronics industry, establishment of in Japan, 100
Euro-dollar market, 65, 74, 80, 81, 229
European Economic Community (EEC), 70, 216
experimental farms, 36
export trade: development of in Japan, 129, 140–41; planning for, 206
exports, 147, 203; expansion of in postwar Japan, 111–12; of manufactured goods, 235; of primary commodities, 67; promotion of, 127, 128–29, 208; quotas on, 69; stabilization of, 266–67

family enterprise, role of in industrialization, 98
farmers' cooperatives in Japan (*nokyo*), 37, 101–2
Federation of Economic Organizations (*Keidanren*), 264
fertilizer, increasing production of, 40, 60
food: self-sufficiency in production of, 15; shortages of, 13–14, 22, 23, 55, 150–53
Food and Agriculture Organization (FAO), 13, 18, 21, 152
free trade, principle of, 50, 51
free trade zones, 82
Fukuda, Takeo, 260, 277
full employment, concept of, 11, 101

Galbraith, J. K., 8
Ganges irrigation project, 39
GATT (General Agreement on Tariffs and Trade), 20, 216, 229, 253
government, relations with business in postwar Japan, 196–97
government policy, 30–31, 61, 126–27; fiscal, 147; monetary, 136; on foreign capital, 83, 248
Greece, 6
Group of 77, 5, 51, 240, 267
growth, high rate of in postwar Japan, 105–7, 171

Hatoyama, Ichiro, 130
Hayami, Yujiro, 237, 276
heavy industry, expansion of in prewar Japan, 127–28
Hisamune, T., 21
Hong Kong, 5, 48, 49, 240, 271; decline of birth rate in, 25

Ichimura, Shunichi, 113
Ikeda, Hayato, 107, 208
imports: liberalization of in Japan, 130–31, 236; restriction of, 10; role of in Japan's economy, 111–12, 128, 236; substitution for, 82
income, internal distribution of, 7, 218
indexation of commodity prices, 70–71
India: export expansion in, 129; rice production in, 29, 32–33
Indian Education Commission, 95
Indian Planning Commission, 93, 99
Indonesia, 6, 122, 240, 264, 266; as oil exporter, 47; rice production in, 29, 32–33

Indus irrigation project, 39
industrialization: Japan's history of, 180–81; Japan's policy of, 96–97; role of in absorbing surplus labor, 10
infant mortality, 17; in Japan, 102
infrastructure investment, 233
International Bank for Reconstruction and Development (IBRD), 67, 68
International Development Center of Japan, 94, 249, 266
International Development University, 276
International Finance Corporation, 84
International Labor Organization (ILO), 7
International Monetary Fund (IMF), 62, 65, 68, 69, 70, 74, 79, 216, 229, 255
International Rice Research Institute, 27, 101
International Service Center, 40–41
Iran, 62
irrigation: development of, 9, 25, 27, 36–37, 39, 55–56, 60, 103; relation of to rice production, 28–31
Ishikawa, Shigeru, 9

Japan: absorption of labor in, 8; agriculture in, 100–1, 113, 177–78; aid to ASEAN, 260; as exporter, 111–12, 129, 140–41, 206, 208, 235, 236; as importer of manufactured goods, 236; as importer of raw materials, 102, 141–42; as importer of technology, 147, 203; changes in diet in, 16, 151; chemical industry in, 109, 128, 181, 201, 206; consumer prices in, 211, 214, 215; course of industrialization in, 180–81; decline of birth rate in, 120–21, 155–56, 158–59, 161–62; deline of death rate in, 120–21, 155–56, 158, 161–62; demilitarization of, 138–39, 203; dual structure of economy in, 121, 123, 146, 168, 209; government-business relations in, 196–97; international role of, 126–27, 255–56, 258, 272–77; investment in ASEAN, 263; investment in Brazil, 250; investment in Latin America, 241; irrigation in, 9, 25; labor force in, 101, 119–20, 143, 159, 160, 174–75, 177–78, 181–82, 203, 211, 214; land reform in, 203; life expectancy in, 16, 102, 151, 160–61; loss of colonies, 114, 138, 169; planning in, 105, 195–225, 254; population trends in, 172–73, 188–91; postwar economic growth in, 105, 112–15, 198–203, 235; protection of fledgling industries in, 130–31, 196; rate of savings in, 118, 132–33, 203, 235, 241; recession of 1965 in, 137, 146, 202; regional development in, 210, 251; relations with ASEAN, 229–37, 253–77; relations with China, 269–70; relations with Europe, 257; relations with Latin America, 239–42; relations with NICs, 271; relations with the U.S., 256–57; rice production in, 14, 29, 32–33, 55, 176; rural-urban migration in, 154, 159, 163–64, 183–85; social security in, 133, 145, 196, 209, 214, 218; textile industry in, 96, 109, 181, 206; trade with Latin America, 241–42; trade with Southeast Asia, 264–66, 274; trade with the U.S., 273; urbanization in, 154–55, 159, 163, 183–85, 214
Japan Economic Research Center, 179
Japan External Trade Organization (JETRO), 264
Jolly, Richard, 7

Kalimantan irrigation project (Indonesia), 39
Korea. *See* South Korea
Korean War, effect of on Japan's economy, 130, 138, 139, 140, 159, 205
Kothari, D. S., 95
Kuwait, 62

labor: mobility of, 143, 191–92; outflow of from primary sector, 177–78, 181–82; shortage of in Japan,

120, 159, 211, 214; supply of and demand for in postwar Japan, 119–20, 203; surplus of, 8, 51, 101, 160; underutilization of, 120, 123
labor absorption, 7–9, 11; in agricultural sector, 55; in industry, 10
labor force (Japan): age structure of, 120, 143; in agriculture, 177; patterns in, 143, 174–75
labor union movement, 114, 203
land reclamation, 31–32
land reform, 203
Laos, rice production in, 29, 32–33
Latin America: as food supplier, 239; relations with Japan, 239–42; trade with Asia, 240–41; trade with Japan, 241–42
life expectancy (Japan): 16, 102, 151, 160–61
lifetime employment, 125, 145
Lima Declaration (1975), 50, 51, 240
loans, 6, 48; terms of, 77–78
local governments: in India, 99; in Japan, 99; subsidies to, 20
Lomé Convention, 54, 68, 70

Malaysia, 6, 53, 240, 265; rice production in, 29, 32–33
malnutrition, 55, 152; effect of on economic development, 17; elimination of, 19
management, transfer of, 75, 88
manufacturing, expansion of in postwar Japan, 109
Mekong irrigation project, 39
Mexico, 5, 48, 239; debt service ratio in, 80; unemployment in, 242
migration, 8; inter-regional in Japan, 186–88, 192; rural-urban in Japan, 154, 159, 163–64, 183–85
monetary policy, 136
multinational corporations, 73; reinvestment of profits by, 82; role of in transfer of capital, 79–83

National Income Doubling Plan (Japan), 105, 197, 207–10, 211, 213, 254
National Institute for Research Advancement (NIRA), 266
Nepal, rice production in, 29, 32–33
New Zealand, as part of Asia-Pacific region, 231, 267
newly industrializing countries (NICs), 5, 48, 49, 52, 271, 272, 276, 277
Nigeria, as oil exporter, 47
non-tariff barriers, reduction of, 50, 77–78
North-South relations, 47, 53, 54, 56, 60, 66, 87–88, 230, 232, 253, 259–63; Japan's role in, 275

ocean resources, development of, 84–85
occupation of Japan, reforms during, 114, 138, 204
OECD. *See* Organisation for Economic Co-operation and Development.
Official Development Assistance (ODA), 43, 260
Ohira, Masayoshi, 234, 268
Ohiso, Toshio, 15–16, 102
Ohkawa, Kazushi, 94, 121
oil crisis (1974), 59, 64–65, 230, 231, 253, 255, 257
OPEC. *See* Organization of Petroleum Exporting Countries
Organisation for Economic Co-operation and Development (OECD), 5, 62, 68, 103, 255, 260; regulation of multinational corporations by, 81
Organization of Petroleum Exporting Countries (OPEC), 5, 47, 61, 76, 79, 84, 253, 255; aid to developing countries by, 64, 66; investment in developing countries by, 57, 61, 74
Overseas Economic Cooperation Fund, 24

Pearson Report (of Committee on International Development), 6–7, 19, 48–49, 56
Peru, 239
Petty's Law, 175
Philippines, 6, 53, 240, 265, 266; rice production in, 29, 32–33
planning: in Japan, 195–225; role of in economic growth, 131–32; targets of, 218

population: future trends in Japan's, 172–73; in Edo-period Japan, 164–65; in Europe, 163; in Meiji-era Japan, 167; in postwar Japan, 158–60, 162–63; in prewar Japan, 151, 157–58, 168–69, 171; regional variations in Japan's, 188–91; relation of to economic development, 7–8, 161, 167–68
Portugal, 6
price mechanism, 130–31
prices: increases in, 146, 211; stability of, 212, 214, 215
primary sector, 109–11; as source of labor, 179; employment in, 174. *See also* agriculture
productivity: concept of, 11; in postwar Japan, 118; relationship of with wages, 118–19
profits, role of in economic growth, 131
protection: of agriculture, 130; of fledgling industries, 130–31, 196; role of in industrialization, 96–97
protectionism in developed countries, 10, 50, 229, 240, 257

recession of 1965, 137, 146, 202
regional development, 218; in Brazil, 251; in Japan, 210, 251
resources: development of, 73; transfer of, 53, 59–89
rice: high-yielding varieties of, 8–9, 27, 56, 101; increases in production of, 26–27, 31, 55; irrigation and, 28–31; production of in Japan, 14, 29, 32–33, 55, 176; program for doubling production of, 23–45, 55–56, 60, 102–3, 233; shortage of, 103
RIO (Reshaping the International Order) Report, 50
Rosovsky, Henry, 121

Saeki, Kiichi, 259
Salas, Rafael M., 150
Saudi Arabia, 62, 273
savings: in Japan, 118, 132–35, 203, 235, 241; in the U.S., 241; in West Germany, 241
secondary industries: employment in, 168, 174; growth of, 179–81
Shinohara, Miyohei, 132
silk, as export crop, 175–76
Singapore, 5, 48, 49, 240, 263, 265, 271; decline of birth rate in, 25
Sino-Japanese War, 167
small-scale enterprises, role of in industrialization, 98–99, 123, 236
Smithsonian Agreement, 256
social overhead investment, 144–45, 147, 154, 196, 208, 212; in Japan, 144–45, 147, 154, 196, 208, 212
social security, 133, 145, 196, 209, 214, 218
South Asia: irrigation in, 9, 37; rice production in, 37–39, 55
South Korea, 5, 48, 49, 240, 271, 273; debt service ratio in, 80; decline of birth rate in, 25; irrigation in, 9
Sri Lanka, rice production in, 29, 32–33, 55
Southeast Asia: industrialization in, 232; irrigation in, 9, 37; relations with Japan, 229–37, 253–77; rice production in, 37–39, 55; trade imbalance in, 264–66, 274. *See also* ASEAN
soybeans: embargo on U.S. exports of, 21; production of in Japan, 15
Spain, 6
STABEX (Stabilization of Export Earnings), 6, 54, 266, 267
steel production, 6, 142, 244
Streeton, Paul, 11
subcontracting, 123
Sussex Group, 7

Taiwan, 5, 48, 49, 240, 271; decline of birth rate in, 25; irrigation in, 9; rice production in, 29, 32–33, 55
Takase, Kunio, 103
Tanaka, Kakuei, 217, 257
tariffs, reduction of, 72, 77–78, 117
Tauber, Irene B., 149
technocrats, development of in ASEAN, 275
technology: importation of in Japan, 116, 117, 143, 147, 203; transfer of, 75, 88, 99–100, 236, 261
tertiary sector, 175, 182–83
textile industry, 6, 10, 61; in Japan,

96, 109, 181, 206
Thailand, 6, 53, 240, 263, 264; rice production in, 29, 32–33
Thompson, Warren S., 169
Tohata, Seiichi, 11
Tokyo Round, 229, 257
trade, imbalance of in Southeast Asia, 264–66, 274
trading companies (Japan), 83
traditional sector, 121, 122, 168
Trilateral Commission, 55, 66
Turkey, 6

underutilized labor, 120, 123
United Nations, 18, 61, 68, 72, 230, 261, 274; and ocean resource development, 85–86; regulation of multinationals by, 81
United Nations Committee for Development Planning, 5
United Nations Conference on the Law of the Sea, 86
United Nations Conference on Trade and Development (UNCTAD), 5, 52, 68, 69, 87, 129, 230, 232, 240, 267
United Nations Fund for Population Activities (UNFPA), 149–50
United Nations Industrial Development Organization (UNIDO), 58, 239
United States: aid to Japan from, 139, 205; as food supplier, 19, 24; as Japan's trading partner, 273; as part of Asia-Pacific region, 267; relations with China, 268; relations with Japan, 256–57; savings in, 241
urbanization, 154–55, 159, 163, 183–85, 214

Vernon, Raymond, 80
Vietnam, rice production in, 29, 32–33

wages, dualistic structure of in Japan, 123–25
welfare society, 218. *See also* social security
West Germany, savings in, 241
World Bank, 6, 57, 62, 66, 74, 274; increase in agricultural financing by, 24
World Food Conference, 24–25
World Food Council, 55, 103
World Population Conference, 18
World Welfare Fund, 57
Worldwatch Institute, 23

Yasukawa, Masaaki, 166
Yoshida, Shigeru, 130
Yugoslavia, 6

zaibatsu, dissolution of, 114, 196